Sounding the Gallery

THE OXFORD MUSIC / MEDIA SERIES

Daniel Goldmark, Series Editor

oxford
music/media series

Tuning In: American Narrative Television Music
Ron Rodman

Special Sound: The Creation and Legacy of the BBC Radiophonic Workshop
Louis Niebur

Seeing Through Music: Gender and Modernism in Classic Hollywood Film Scores
Peter Franklin

An Eye for Music: Popular Music and the Audiovisual Surreal
John Richardson

Playing Along: Digital Games, YouTube, and Virtual Performance
Kiri Miller

Sounding the Gallery: Video and the Rise of Art-Music
Holly Rogers

Sounding the Gallery

VIDEO AND THE RISE OF ART-MUSIC

HOLLY ROGERS

OXFORD
UNIVERSITY PRESS

OXFORD
UNIVERSITY PRESS

Oxford University Press is a department of the University of Oxford.
It furthers the University's objective of excellence in research, scholarship,
and education by publishing worldwide.

Oxford   New York
Auckland   Cape Town   Dar es Salaam   Hong Kong   Karachi
Kuala Lumpur   Madrid   Melbourne   Mexico City   Nairobi
New Delhi   Shanghai   Taipei   Toronto

With offices in
Argentina   Austria   Brazil   Chile   Czech Republic   France   Greece
Guatemala   Hungary   Italy   Japan   Poland   Portugal   Singapore
South Korea   Switzerland   Thailand   Turkey   Ukraine   Vietnam

Oxford is a registered trademark of Oxford University Press
in the UK and certain other countries.

Published in the United States of America by
Oxford University Press
198 Madison Avenue, New York, NY 10016

© Oxford University Press 2013

Library of Congress Cataloging-in-Publication Data
Rogers, Holly.
Sounding the gallery : video and the rise of art-music / Holly Rogers.
p. cm.—(Oxford music/media series)
Includes bibliographical references and index.
ISBN 978-0-19-986140-8—ISBN 978-0-19-986142-2
1. Music—20th century—History and criticism.   2. Video art.   I. Title.
ML197.R57 2013
780.9'04 – dc23
2012031270

1 3 5 7 9 8 6 4 2
Printed in the United States of America
on acid-free paper

For John, Polly and Jigs

Contents

Preface ix
About the Companion Website xi

Introduction 1

1 Composing with Technology: The Artist-Composer 11

2 Silent Music and Static Motion: The Audiovisual
  History of Video 46

3 Towards the Spatial: Music, Art, and the
  Audiovisual Environment 82

4 The Rise of Video Art-Music: 1963–1970 118

5 Interactivity, Mirrored Spaces, and the Closed-Circuit Feed:
  Performing Video 152

Epilogue: Towards the Twenty-First Century 178

Notes 187
Bibliography 205
Index 217

Preface

This project was undertaken in three countries and I would like to thank everyone I met on my travels. It is an overwhelming and humbling task to acknowledge all those responsible for the moments of inspiration and large amounts of support that have enabled the completion of this work, but I'll have a good go. The first ideas for a book on audiovisual video emerged during my time at Cambridge and I would like to thank Roger Parker for reading several chunks of early research with such good humour despite its teething problems. Work began in earnest thanks to an Irish Research Council for the Humanities and Social Sciences Post-Doctoral Fellowship at the School of Music, University College Dublin and the Humanities Institute of Ireland. The inspiration I received from my Dublin-based colleagues is hard to express and I would like to thank Harry White, Wolfgang Marx, Julian Horton, Hwee-San Tan, Thérèse Smith, and Ciarán Crilly for a truly exciting (and utterly exhausting!) three years. The project continued to evolve when I joined the University of Liverpool's unique audiovisual environment, created by my colleagues and excellent friends at the School of Music: Anahid Kassabian, Freya Jarman, and Hae-Kyung Um. Our energising, thoughtful, and inspiring students have had a positive impact on various aspects of this book and I promise not to make them watch so many experimental films in the future.

Two recent fellowships have given me the space to push this project to completion. A Fulbright Scholarship allowed me to spend several months at San Francisco State University to finish the final bits of on-site research; and a visiting fellowship at the Long Room Hub, Trinity College Dublin provided a great circularity by enabling me to finish writing the book in the city where I had begun it. I would like to thank the US-UK Fulbright Commission and TCD for supporting this work and allowing me to spend time in two wonderful cities.

I have been constantly amazed by the patience and support of my Commissioning Editor at Oxford University Press, Norm Hirschy; I owe large parts of my sanity to his quick and calming replies to emails. I am also grateful to Daniel Goldmark, the series editor, who first drew my attention to the Music and Media Series at a film music conference in London several years ago. The five (yes five!) anonymous readers who commented on various stages of this work in great detail have had a significant impact on the theoretical trajectories of this project and their suggestions have been gratefully incorporated into many of the following pages. An earlier version of chapter 1, entitled "The Unification of the Senses: Intermediality in Video Art-Music" appeared in the *Journal of the Royal Musical Association*: 136:2 (2011), 399–428. I extend my thanks to Rachel Cowgill and the anonymous JRMA reviewers for their helpful contributions at this early stage.

An award from the Donna Cardamone Jackson Endowment of the American Musicological Society and the kindness of many of the artists discussed have enabled this book to include lots of useful photos of video performances and events. In particular, I would like to thank Vito Acconci, Ira Schneider, Steina Vasulka, the Nam June Paik Estate, Christo and Jeanne-Claude, Pipilotti Rist, Bill Viola, Jocelyn Pook, Cindy Keefer and the Center for Visual Music, and Julie Martin and Experiments in Art and Technology for their permission to print illustrations of their work. Several galleries kindly granted permission to include pictures of work from their collections, including New York City's Guggenheim Museum, the San Francisco Museum of Modern Art, Museum Moderner Kunst Stiftung Ludwig Wien, and the Sprengel Museum, Hannover. The iconic shots you will see in the following pages were created by photographers Manfred Montwé, Linda Nylind, John Lloyd Davies, and Lawrence N. Shustak, and I am grateful to them for allowing me to share their work with you.

Holding things together during these numerous relocations have been several constants, and I would like to dedicate this book to them. To my parents John and Polly who, as art and music enthusiasts, are largely responsible for my audiovisual interests: I wish I knew as much as they do. To Jigs, my fellow traveller and guitar player in Ireland, England, America, and beyond: here's to our next adventure; sláinte! To the rest of my family and to all of the McGraths. And to our creatures: Monty the incorrigible Scottie; and our four noisy oiseaux tropicaux.

About the Companion Website

www.oup.com/us/soundingthegallery

Oxford has created a password-protected website to accompany *Sounding the Gallery*. In light of the intermedial subject of this book, each chapter is accompanied by a range of moving image and audiovisual clips that bring to life the works discussed. As video art-music comes from, and forms, such an eclectic and interdisciplinary culture, I have included as wide a variety of examples as possible, including single-channelled video, video performance, experimental and mainstream film, performance art, sound art, and 3D video mapping. These clips are found throughout the text and are signalled with Oxford's symbol [see video ⏵].

Access with username Music1 and password Book5983.

Sounding the Gallery

Introduction

One way to write music: study Duchamp
(John Cage)[1]

Video art is often considered a visual genre. And yet when analogue video became commercially available in 1965, it was welcomed not only as a visual technology, but also as a creative medium able to record and play back sound and moving images at the same time. While musicians and artists have long sought conceptual interaction, the materials available have restricted practical realisation and few examples of such communication exist. Previous audiovisual practices, such as lantern shows, music theatre, opera, synaesthetic experimentation, early direct film, and so on, were intermedial primarily at the level of reception. The electromagnetic basis of early video technology, on the other hand, gave rise to sound and image that shared a linked material channel. This channel enabled audio and visual elements to be recorded and transmitted simultaneously, allowing a level of synergy rarely before possible.

Such synergy was particularly alluring to those interested in the ways in which art and music could fragment and recombine to produce new intermedial spaces. With the new medium, artists were able to include sound in their work in order to push the boundaries of current creative concerns. But video also presented composers with the opportunity to visualise their music. In fact, many of the earliest video artists began their careers as musicians: Nam June Paik was an experimental composer, Steina Vasulka, a classical violinist, Robert Cahen trained in electro-acoustic composition, and Tony Conrad was a member of the *Theatre of Eternal Music*. These influential musicians ensured that early video developed into a highly *musical* genre.

The musicality of video was not simply due to the specificities of its hardware, however. When placed within the broader cultural and artistic climate of experimentation and inclusivity of the '60s, the technological simultaneity of video encouraged expansive and interactive performance situations that challenged conventional methods of art and music consumption. Paik, Vasulka, Conrad, and others used their knowledge of noise making and noise collecting to broaden visual art into process-driven image-and-soundscapes via the live manipulation, processing, feedback, delay, and mirroring of the video signal. The improvisatory, interactive, and often performative result gradually coalesced into a genre that not only expanded the boundaries of visual art and its exhibition, but also those of music composition and performance. When video's synergy was presented live via a closed-circuit feed, everything within the performance space could fold into a manipulated audiovisual environment that engendered a new mode of active spectatorship. Using the early technology, artists and composers could invite visitors into the heart of their work, allowing them to dictate the structure, audiovisuality, and trajectory of the video environment. With this in mind, it becomes clear that to locate the rise of video within the visual arts is extremely reductive: at a material level, the technology was able simultaneously to digest and project music and image; when received, this interactive duality produced an intermedial performance space that drew together music, sculpture, architecture, drama, and film. By challenging the configuration of art and music venues and expanding the possibilities for audience engagement, early video performance, alive with interdisciplinary potential, vibrated in the space between artists, composers, performers, and visitors.

Video's rare ability to fuse music and image at an intermedial level led many to consider the medium as a new art form, one that had no easily identifiable lineage and thus appeared to be free from historical baggage. But this was a false assumption. Examination of creative practice during the twentieth century reveals that many composers were experimenting with spatialising their sounds, while the inclusion of time into the static arts was becoming a prevalent form of experimentation. Rather than creating a new art form without a history, video's intermedial capabilities allowed these two disciplines to come together, acting as a conduit that enabled the fusion and manipulation of pre-existing practice. The technology was new, in other words; but the creative uses to which it was put, were not. During the "first wave" of audiovisual work, which began in New York City in 1965, video was a facilitator rather than a genre, a technology that enabled music and art finally to join forces. Video, then, produced a unique moment in audiovisual history: able to create both image and sound concurrently, the new technology instigated the birth of the artist-composer and process-driven, interactive intermediality. For this reason, it makes more sense to refer to the genre as "video *art-music*," a term that better acknowledges the audiovisuality of the medium and the double capabilities of many of its practitioners.

The beginning of the twenty-first century is the perfect time to attempt a historical recontextualisation of video art-music. Whereas paint has been used creatively for thousands of years, the rise and fall of video as an artistic material took place within only forty. The format, with its easily operable, inexpensive, reusable design, did not become available until the mid-1960s and thus has recently reached its first half-century. The opportunity to make use of the new equipment was first explored by the so-called "father of video art," Korean-born Nam June Paik: in October of 1965, he travelled through New York City with a portable video camera (the Portapak) in a journey that kick-started an explosive revolution in art and music circles.[2] But although the video format quickly became one of the most innovative creative materials of the twentieth century, by 1995, the magnetic technology was already being superseded by the more resilient and reliable DVD system, with its longer playback capability and higher definition output. Only eight years later, DVDs were the preferred technology for weekly film rentals in America and today video is as obsolete as audiotape, with new films no longer released on the format and replacement cassettes for camcorders and home recording units increasingly hard to come by.[3] In what appears to be an even faster turnover, the DVD format is beginning to be pushed aside by Microsoft's High Definition DVD and Sony's Blu-ray technology (launched commercially in late 2007). It is clear to see that the development of artistic material has attained an unprecedented velocity, in which formats are developed and discarded in the blink of a historical eye. In terms of its technical rise and fall, then, analogue video can be considered a closed genre. As the digital age marks the demise of its usage, we are faced with an epoch that is almost already complete, a phenomenon rarely encountered before in the visual and sonic arts.

In one sense, however, this closure is a false one. Artist-composers, such as Bill Viola, may have swapped their material preference from magnetic to digital formats, but the fundamental aesthetic aspects of video have been retained. In fact, the shift between formats has been so seamless that moving-image work continues to be collected under the term "video art," despite the obvious technological inaccuracy. While it is true, then, that analogue video technology is now redundant in terms of recording and playback, the implications of audiovisual fusion that it enabled are still thriving. Many contemporary video practitioners, for instance, continue to embrace the audiovisuality of the digital medium and take charge of both image and sound: Sabrina Pena identifies herself as both "avant-garde composer" and "video artist," while Kathy Hinde prefers the term "interdisciplinary artist" to describe her video work with music and image.[4] The equipment may have evolved, then, but aspects of its technological basis and the opportunities for synthesis it affords continue to inform the new digital age.

Although occupying a comparatively tiny segment of visual and music histories, the various forms of video work have had a significant impact on the arts. The Turner Prize was won by video artists in 1996 (Douglas Gordon), 1997 (Gillian Wearing), and 1999 (Steve McQueen), for instance, while the Hugo Boss Prize, a biennial international award administered by the Solomon R. Guggenheim Foundation, frequently awards first place to moving-image artists.[5] As further recognition of video's integral and evolving position within the art canon, London's Tate Modern has recently completed phase one of its £215 million extension that will be dedicated to live art, video work, and installation: "[t]he world has changed rapidly over the last ten years, particularly in how we use technology. Tate Modern needs to respond to new developments," explains the published proposal outlining the changes.[6]

While contemporary video artist-composers, such as Pena and Hinde, continue to work with the audiovisual possibilities of the medium, composers, music directors, and concert venue managers have demonstrated an interest in including these "new developments" in their work with increasing frequency: *The Cave*, Steve Reich's collaborative project with video-artist wife Beryl Korot, a multi-screen, vocal-instrumental video opera (1993) and Viola's partnership with Peter Sellars for a production of Wagner's *Tristan and Isolde* (2005) are two of the most publicised examples of video practice being closely combined with music composition and performance. The use of video as part of an opera's staging has also become increasingly common: Katie Mitchell's production of Mozart's *Idomeneo* (June 2010) at the English National Opera, for instance, made use of video projections (by Fifty Nine Productions) to depict seascapes and landscapes, while Jocelyn Pook's *Ingerland* (2010), part of the OperaShots programme at London's Royal Opera House, included videoed images of football supporters (fig. i.1).[7]

Concert halls and opera houses are embracing video technology in a number of other ways: the San Francisco Opera has installed several high-definition video screens (known as "OperaVision"), for instance, to provide full and close-up shots of the stage for those occupying restricted-view seats; the Royal Opera House recently bought Opus Arte, a video production and distribution company to release and market film versions of its productions; and New York's Metropolitan Opera has begun to simulcast its performances in cinemas to those unable to

Figure i.1 Jocelyn Pook, still from OperaShots production of *Ingerland* at Royal Opera House 2 (2009). Photo by John Lloyd Davies.

acquire, or afford, its theatre tickets.[8] Since the dramatic rise of MTV in the late 1980s, the addition of moving image to music has become common practice for gigging bands, with U2 blazing the trail on their 1992–93 *Zoo TV Tour*, a massive, multimedia stadium production that mixed prerecorded visual footage, live television broadcast, and on-site VJing.

It is clear to see that video work, routinely collected by major art galleries and frequently included in music performance, now forms a popular and well-respected genre: it is difficult to imagine anything different. But such recognition was not always forthcoming and critical and institutional acceptance was hard-won. While it is important to note that many artists and composers working with video were actively opposed to institutionalisation and that, in some sense, the achievement of video in reaching into the heart of art and music establishments signals the loss of its early radical attitude, there are nevertheless a number of important issues that arise from the early combination of music and image.[9] The arrival of creative video work challenged the sanctity of music and art spaces by undermining conventions of listening and viewing already under threat from a radically evolving sociocultural context in the early 1960s, in light of contested civil rights, anti-war sentiments, feminism, and the anticommodity aesthetic. Rather than focusing on a single object (a painting, sculpture, or fresco) or a piece of music, video artists and composers were concerned with the movement, relationship, and sound existing *between* a number of elements.[10] As a mixture of moving image, sculpture, music, and sound, video work challenged both the neutrality of the gallery space and its viewing procedures or, rather, it revealed the neutrality to be an illusion, in three ways. First, a work could activate its surroundings by incorporating both performance space and the people within it into its composition. Second, the use of moving images placed the element of time into a space conventionally filled with static objects and, in so doing, presented the exhibition-goer with a dimension usually reserved for the concert hall or theatre. Finally, and yet most radically, video, as an audiovisual medium, introduced sound and music into the gallery environment, a space normally occupied by silent works. Expanding into the gallery space spatially, temporally, and aurally, then, video works required a radical re-evaluation of art exhibition practice (in terms of curation, preservation, funding, and patterns of audience engagement) and, to take one step further, the defining parameters of art itself. As a component of the concert hall, video was similarly hampered by aesthetic, financial, and practical concerns. Amid fears that the inclusion of image would detract from musical contemplation and appreciation were the difficulties of installing video screens and cameras in auditoriums created for live performance, problems only recently being confronted, as the San Francisco Opera's new inclusions demonstrate. As a result of such challenges, video art-music was the recipient of tough aesthetic discrimination and was forced to occupy new, audiovisual spaces.

These spaces are central to this book. The particular form of process-orientated synchronicity enabled by early analogue video gave rise to new ideas about music, art, and the possibilities for communal modes of creativity. During the 1940s, theories of architecture, mass media, and literature were reformulated according to physical and social spaces by László Moholy-Nagy and Siegfried Giedion, Clement Greenberg and Joseph Frank respectively: Giedion, for example, postulated "space" rather than structure or material as the real architectural medium.[11] We can treat video in a similar way, by investigating around the edge of art and music in order to explore not the video forms themselves, but rather the changing nature of the spaces in which they exist. Shifting the focus thus from object to spatial process promotes a contextual *audiovisual* engagement with early video work, while at the same time re-articulating the ways in which sound and image can communicate with each other. Such a theoretical relocation encourages a more syncretic approach to the medium by treating it as the nervous system of audiovisual interaction.

Once decentred, early video can be read as a rich and diverse network of interactions, a hub of influences that lie, only thinly veiled, beneath the medium's appearance of novelty. Outlining their theory of remediation, Jay Bolter and Richard Grusin propose an understanding of digital media predicated on a process of constant and progressive re-iteration:

> Digital visual media can best be understood through the ways in which they honor, rival, and revise linear-perspective painting, photography, film, television, and print. No medium today, and certainly no single media event, seems to do its cultural work in isolation from other media, any more than it works in isolation from other social and economic forces. What is new about new media comes from the particular ways in which they refashion older media and the ways in which older media refashion themselves to answer the challenges of new media.[12]

According to the authors, remediation operates via the self-reflexive and visible inclusion of "older media" into new work, a continuous refashioning that enables digital media to acknowledge and evolve from a diverse range of predecessors. Although all media are involved in the remediation process, digital technologies have become increasingly adept at erasing their perceptible influences, with computers operating like a "media-integrating machine" (Yvonne Spielmann), able to incorporate earlier forms with little or no obvious separation or fissure.[13] In older media, however, the process is clearly discernible. In early video work, preexisting audiovisual articulations, such as broadcast television, are constantly (and often explicitly) included and revoiced, a reuse of the prevailing cultural climate foregrounded through the grainy images that such transmission produces.

But remediation need not be restricted to visual reconfiguration: it can also be used to understand video's double, audiovisual constitution. The inclusion of sound and music into video's mixture was a natural extension from Fluxus, where artists had begun to unfold their work through time in Happenings and so on: simultaneously, composers both within the group and beyond were acquiring heightened awareness of the spatial possibilities of music first explored during the Renaissance. Just as artists were starting to investigate the temporal dimension of their work, musicians began to respond to performance spaces in new ways, creating art and music that overflowed, each into the realm of the other. Set against a historical backdrop of intense experimentation that ranged from the conceptual work of Duchamp and the performance-based practices of Allan Kaprow on the art side, to the spatialised soundworlds of Stockhausen and the aleatoric procedures of John Cage in the arena of music, video technology provided a new means to expand—and remediate—several strands of traditional practice.

Early video work rests, Janus-faced, at the intersection of these two spatially expanding disciplines. As the segregation between art forms became porous, the deeply embedded conventions of musical performance and art display became vulnerable, even fragile. Video could probe the boundaires between private and public spaces, combine mental and physical spatialities, and move the static arts into a temporal arena. It demanded a rethink of the traditional gallery environment, while also giving rise to alternative audiovisual performance/exhibition spaces that continue to operate today.

So it is a mistake to assume that video had no continuity with the past: rather, it harboured a double past. Arrival at the "new" genre was achieved neither by progressing in any one direction, nor by developing a particular form. Instead, early video enabled the disciplines of art and music to disband and recombine in new and hitherto unprecedented configurations. It follows that, once context is taken into account, music and art in the twentieth century cannot coherently be discussed as individual disciplines, but rather encourage a more lateral history, or spatial sensibility, that moves fluidly through the space between them.

In order to go some way towards such a revaluation, this book traces two intertwined genealogies for early video art-music: one audio, the other visual. The video work that emerged in 1965 is revisited from a number of angles which, when combined, form a complicated, but by no means exhaustive, set of parameters that enabled music and art practices to expand into video work. To achieve this, I follow the lead of early video artist-musicians by using video technology as a conduit into several other areas of discourse.

While the proliferation of disciplines and ideas that this creates is exciting, it has been necessary to delimit the discussion in other ways. My focus here lies in work created and performed in America during the 1960s and early 1970s; the time when video, which still required separate technologies for recording and playback, was used mainly as a live component of multimedia events. There are several reasons for this. During the first years of video work, many of the main protagonists were either American or alighted on US soil for political or artistic reasons. The Portapak, available in America in 1965, was only introduced into the

European market around 1970. British video practitioner David Hall recalls the subsequent blossoming of video work across the Atlantic:

> Some experimentation occurred with a few artists (including myself) and community groups around 1970, but I think the significant moment was when I made ten unannounced *TV Interruptions* transmitted by Scottish television in 1971. It has been claimed by writers that "these works have come to be regarded as the first example of British artists' television and as an equally formative moment in British video art."[14]

The globalisation of video work happened quickly around the turn of the decade and the medium was put to creative use by Hall in England, VALIE EXPORT in Austria, Ulrike Rosenbach in Germany, and Robert Cahen in France, amongst others. Woody Vasulka (who emigrated to America from his native Czechoslovakia in the 1960s) understands video's rapid integration into the international art scene as the direct result of technological development: "With tape, new networks of distribution were quickly established. Video became truly international. It was easy to duplicate, mail and view."[15]

Because this study is contextual and situates early video work within its wider artistic and musical communities, it has been necessary also to engage with the local cultural, social, and political environments (specifically that of New York City), which had a profound influence on the ways in which video pieces were configured: as Joan Jonas puts it; "Video as we used it was personal, and the personal was political."[16] As we have seen, the earliest examples of video art-music were found in America: but as my discussion progresses into the early 1970s, I have kept this geographical focus in order to navigate between the personal and the political, despite several strong voices from other countries joining the conversation. At the same time, however, we must recognise that early video cannot be described as representing a purely American sensibility as it has been infused with multinational voices from the outset. Although hailing from Korea, for instance, Paik came to New York City via the German Rhineland, where he spent the years between 1958 and 1963. It was here that he first met John Cage and began his transition from musician—via actions—to media artist-composer: "My life began one evening in August 1958 in Darmstadt. 1957 was 1 BC (Before Cage)."[17]

Paik's connection to the experimental creative scenes in New York City during the 1960s encouraged him to treat video as a powerful and subversive tool for intervention. After its first road trip with Paik, the medium was readily integrated into the actions and interactive events of other artists. And it was here, in the real-time, experiential mobilisation of a live audience, that video's audiovisuality most clearly arose. The refreshed spatial interaction facilitated by the technology locates video art-music at the intermedial intersection between visual and audio disciplines. As a result, although single-channel, installational, and sculptural video is considered alongside video documentary and work for broadcast television, my discussion centres primarily on video-in-performance between 1965 and 1971. For the same reasons, I remain particularly interested in those practitioners responsible for germinating (or at least setting into motion) both the images and the sounds that underpinned their performances, even though it was not uncommon for early video makers to visualise prerecorded music that may have been composed or performed by someone else. Following my call for a terminological change from video *art* to video *art-music*, I have chosen to refer to these audiovisual facilitators as "artist-composers." While I acknowledge that these designations—one who creates images; another who works with sounds, often in advance of exhibition/performance—can be problematic, I would like to recontextualise them within a refreshed discourse; to re-imagine each title as a fluid, expansive, and increasingly interchangeable designation. With this in mind, artist-composer is intended to suggest not simply a combination of interests, but rather a continuous creative experience that arises in the present tense.

Sounding the Gallery, then, decentres video and considers several different ways of locating the video medium and its artist-composers during its early years. The book is based on the belief that the linked nature of sound and image in the video signal was deeply significant to early video artist-composers, as it elicited a spatial form of engagement that gave rise to new relationships between art/music practices and their audiences. Chapter 1 sets out the technological specificities that enabled the rise of the audiovisual composer during the 1960s. With reference to the theoretical work of Gene Youngblood, André Gaudreault and Philippe Marion, and Yvonne Spielmann, the medium is situated within the expansive multimedia culture of the decade, and its intermedial qualities are considered alongside several video artist-composer biographies. Rethinking the material qualities of art and music helps to unpack the hypothesis that video is an audiovisual art form, which represents the coming together of two separate but related histories during the twentieth century.

The second chapter goes back in time in order to trace the different ways in which music and image have interacted in the past. With reference to the theories of Gotthold Lessing, Daniel Albright, Richard Leppert, and Nicholas Cook, the consideration of visual music, audible art, audiovisual instruments, colour-sound synaesthesia, and experimental film demonstrates that video does, in fact, have a long and fruitful lineage and should thus be understood as a facilitator for intermedial discourse rather than a brand new genre. With this audiovisual narrative in mind, the third chapter offers a comparative history of the consonant *spaces* that enabled such intermedial merging. The theories of László, Moholy-Nagy, Sigfried Giedion, and Clement Greenberg provide a useful starting point for an investigation into the expanding notions of art and music and the liberation from traditional viewing and listening procedures that such expansion entails. Drawing on the work of Christopher Small and Brian O'Doherty, a brief history of the conventions of exhibition and display, viewing procedures and audience behaviour in the gallery is compared with an overview of concert hall customs and the aesthetics of listening. This comparative study is contextualised by an overview of mixed media performance (music, Happenings, conceptual art, performance art, site-specific installations, and so on), with particular reference to their places and methods of display, exhibition, and/or performance. Here I argue that space, architecture, and the reconfiguration of gallery and performance venues, as well as issues of audience engagement, are vital to an understanding of video as a sonic, as well as a visual, medium.

Chapter 4 positions the rise of video art-music within these audiovisual and spatial genealogies. Identifying points of contact between musicians and artists during the 1960s and 1970s, this section situates the early years of video within their sociocultural context. In light of the reception and aesthetic problems (even resistance) encountered when bringing sound and the moving image into the gallery, the alternative performance/exhibition spaces sought by video artist-musicians are charted in order to produce a comprehensive outline of early video work. These four chapters, then, provide alternative audiovisual histories for video art-music and its performance/exhibition spaces and outline the arenas inhabited by early video practitioners.

The final chapter combines the multiple genealogies of audiovisuality and spatial expansion to posit a theory of the "nondiegetic" image. I theorise that the genre developed stylistic traits more akin to listening than viewing; and as a result, new forms of engagement were demanded of visitors to galleries and concert halls.Using film music discourse as a starting point, this section discusses the blurred boundaries between art and life and the consequent dismantling of exhibition containment in multimedia video work. Immersion, interaction, performative action, and the expanded consciousness of the mirrored and closed-feed environment are explored through the performance and surveillance videos of Joan Jonas, Bruce Nauman, Peter Campus, and Dan Graham. These ideas are then used to inform a reading of Paik's collaboration with Charlotte Moorman, with particular attention given to their *Concerto for TV Cello* (1971). This examination leads to consideration of the active dialogue now possible between audience, art work, and exhibition/performance space. Building from this discussion, early video is considered in relation to film space and the aesthetics of audiovisual realism.

The Epilogue then brings us back to the present day, tracing the various lines of influence that early video has had, not only on recent video work, but also on the development of gaming, audiovisual apps, and contemporary modes of music consumption.

1

Composing with Technology

The Artist-Composer

As soon as I had a video camera in my hand—
as soon as I had that majestic flow of time in my control—
I knew I had my medium
(Steina Vasulka)[1]

It is commonly believed that the birth of video art coincided with the commercial availability of the Sony Portapak in 1965, a large, yet portable, video camera. The widespread significance of this date was signalled by the travelling exhibition *Video: An Art, A History, 1965–2005*, a collection of video and multimedia pieces from the Centre Pompidou, selected by its Curator of New Media, Christine Van Assche.[2] Assche's "history" of video begins in October 1965, when legend has it that Nam June Paik travelled the streets of New York City with the Portapak. Resident by this time in America, the artist took a cab home with his newly acquired camera. When the journey was delayed by a traffic jam, Paik, with true Fluxus spontaneity, made his first video piece. Pope Paul VI was visiting the city to address the United Nations and Paik recorded the commotion caused as his convoy paraded the streets. Because the Portapak could be input directly into a television monitor, Paik was able to show his tape at the Café-au-Go-Go, Greenwich Village (a popular haunt of artists and musicians) that evening, thus bringing closer together creation and display in a way that was to characterise the work of many subsequent video artists. (Yvonne Spielmann has refuted the validity of this legend, arguing that it was not Paik, but rather Andy Warhol who, in August of the same year, presented *Outer and Inner Space*, a double-screen film in which a life-size, filmed Edie Sedgwick converses with her own videoed image [see video 1.1▶]).[3]

Because the video medium in its portable format only became available in 1965, it appeared to promise an art form without a clear ancestry despite its initial similarity to film: video "had no tradition," contends curator David A. Ross; "It was the precise opposite of painting. It had no formal burdens at all."[4] As there have been few instances in music and art histories in which a completely new resource has become available (examples that have had a profound effect on music practices include the piano and print technology), the technology's nascent quality was very attractive to video artist-musicians and critics alike. Paik, for instance, frequently praised video's promise of liberation from traditional art techniques: "As collage technique replaced oil paint" he writes, "so the cathode-ray tube will replace canvas…as precisely as Leonardo / as freely as Picasso / as colourfully as Renoir / as profoundly as Mondrian / as violently as Pollock and / as lyrically as Jasper Johns."[5] Elsewhere, he speculated that: "Someday artists will work with capacitors, resistors & semi-conductors as they work today with brushes, violins & junk."[6] While his reference to other artists and techniques postulates a familial connection with different media, Paik nevertheless speaks of "replacing" them with this brand-new material.

Filippo Marinetti, founder of the Futurist movement, admired variety theatre because it had "no tradition, no masters, no dogma."[7] Video, as a newly developed equipment, seemed to come with an even greater promise of historical independence. Like those working with broadcast television and film, video artists had often to learn how to use the equipment from scratch, and this was seen by many as a distinct advantage: in his influential book, *Expanded Cinema* (1970), Gene Youngblood argues that, "[t]o explore new dimensions of awareness requires new technological extensions," a completely new medium that could emancipate artists and musicians from old habits and learnt behaviours.[8] Regarded as having a definite beginning, then, video art did not need to break free from an established line of teleological development. As a result, artists felt able, when working with this newly available and rapidly evolving equipment, to choose their influences from anywhere: a freedom that charts, it is often claimed, the very "rise of Postmodernism." (Margot Lovejoy).[9]

The perception that video offered a space free from "tradition" and "burden" was taken to heart by many female artists. With no male-dominated lineage to fight against, many feminist performers adopted video, considering it a medium with which they could be truly influential without facing comparison to a hefty weight of male predecessors, a liberation from history apparent in the work of Joan Jonas, Steina Vasulka, Ilene Segalove, and Shigeko Kubota (wife of Paik). Video art-music's emergence coincided with the sexually liberated 1960s, an era in which feminism, with its aims to evaluate and redress women's position in society, was being pursued with renewed vigour: the appropriation of the new technology by feminist-minded artists ensured that video's newly emerging story was one in which, unusually, the woman's voice could clearly be heard.[10] The call for cultural revisionism in women's video of the 1960s and 1970s resulted in the recurrence of certain tropes; ones relating to the subversion of female stereotypes and identity.[11] Popular issues include the traditional representation of women as domestic homemakers and the media's frequent, yet discriminatory, portrayal of female characters as either sexual victims or femmes fatales. Because such topics, postulates Marita Sturken, were "threatening and hence ignored by their male counterparts," there developed for video a uniquely female language hitherto unfound in art practice.[12] Women artists, then, perceived the possibilities of video to extend beyond the physical innovation outlined by Paik above: video could also provide opportunity for a refreshed subject matter.

The personal nature of such discourse encouraged many female video artists, including those named above, to turn the camera on themselves. Performing the joint role of creator and model created a destabilising duality that enabled the artist to reclaim her body from the male artist's gaze. In order to counter accusations of narcissism, however, many artists problematised traditional representations of the female form by presenting it in unfamiliar, distorted, or grotesque ways. Operating as her alter ego "Organic Honey," for instance, Jonas performed her 1972 work, *Vertical Roll*, amidst mirrors and closed-circuit video projection (see video 1.2⏵). Her performance, in which she sported various symbols of female identity (a kimono, a belly dancing costume, a doll's mask, and a fan), was played through an intentionally malfunctioning television monitor, tuned to create a vertical roll—a black bar that rises repeatedly up the screen. As we shall explore further in chapter 5, Jonas' arms, legs, and torso were dislocated from one another, resulting in a fragmented and disturbing image of the female body trapped in, and manipulated by, media technology.

While artists such as Jonas attacked the physical objectification of women, other video practitioners addressed the cultural positioning of females within a domestic role. This second trope was explored so often that both the compilation and exhibition of early video work by women usually includes significant commentary on the problems of domesticity. The first disk for *I Say I Am* (1998), a survey of female video art between 1972 and 1980, is entitled "Desire and the Home," its intention to reveal how (to refer to the DVD liner notes) women artists "explore domestic issues such as motherhood, sexuality, death, familial relationships, control of physical space, and the preparation and consumption of food."[13] The protagonist in Martha Rosler's piece, *Semiotics of the Kitchen* (1975), for instance, demonstrates the use of kitchen utensils to her audience in such a threatening way that they become more like weapons than benign culinary aids (fig. 1.1; see video 1.3⏵). Likewise, the first section of the travelling exhibition organised by the American Federation of Arts (AFA), *Revising Romance: New Feminist Video* (1984–85), was called "Domestic Drama." Works in this section, such as Ann-Sargent Wooster's *House*, juxtaposed the domestic ideals perpetuated in daytime television programmes and advertisements with the reality of housework and domestic confinement.[14]

Unhampered by tradition, video was an open and as-yet-undefined arena in which the woman artist could occupy a strong and influential position. Although there were many occasions where women formed collective production, exhibition, and festival organisations—the first female video festival at *The Kitchen* in New York City (1972), for instance, or *The Feminist Studio Workshop* in Los Angeles (1973)—female artists also held pivotal roles in the larger video community. Julie Gustafson, a documentary video artist who concentrated on women's issues and the family, became co-director of New York City's Global Village, one of the first

Figure 1.1 Martha Rosler, video still from *Semiotics of the Kitchen* (1975).

arts centers for video documentary in America, while Kubota's *Nude Descending a Staircase* (1976) became the earliest example of video sculpture in the permanent collection at the *Museum of Modern Art*.

Heralded as one of the few really new art forms of the twentieth century, then, video attracted practitioners who resisted attempts to ascribe to their work a past, preferring instead to operate within the generic and historical free space that the medium seemed to offer.[15] To put it in the words of early video artist Scott Bartlett, "[t]here's a whole new story to be told thanks to the new techniques: we must find out what we have to say because of our new technologies."[16] But did the "new technologies" really enable a "whole new" form of artistic creativity that began only in 1965, as Assche would have it? If we look more closely at the cultural context of 1965, is it still possible to speak about audiovisual video work as having "no formal burdens at all," as many critics and artists have claimed? Or is it more productive to discuss video as a format that introduced "new techniques" into preexistent art and music narratives? Did video, in other words, enable expansion rather than replacement?

Film, Television, and Video: The Image as Process

As the "whole new story" began to unravel, it became clear that the most innovative aspects of video came from the opportunities for audiovisual synthesis that it enabled, an intermedial quality rarely encountered before. Although its syncretic nature provided an aesthetic draw for many practitioners, video's dual-channelled form was originally technologically determined. John Belton has defined video by its difference from television, pointing out that while television is a broadcast medium, its purpose to transmit prerecorded material without altering its form or content, video is a recording one, the medium of the surveillance camera.[17] This difference between delivering and preserving is an important one. Only coming into existence at the moment of its transmission, television—meaning literally "seeing from afar"—is a technology that can span great distances almost instantaneously, its signal passed through an antenna from transmitter to receiver, or decoder. Defined by its ability to send directly an audiovisual signal across the world, television cannot materially be considered an aesthetic medium: it is, as artist Les Levine has pointed out, "neither an object nor a 'content'."[18] Rather, it is a process that does not suggest any preceding substance. Speaking about the art of communication, or rather acknowledging that art is communication, Levine postulates television as an art form that acknowledges that the message between sender and receiver is more important than its content.

Although today material for television can often demonstrate a significant amount of postproduction skill, the medium's existence as process rather than content was emphasised by those using the technology artistically during the middle of the twentieth century. The first time a television set entered a gallery was in 1963. Paik's March exhibition at Galerie Parnass (Wuppertal), *Exposition of Music–Electronic Television* and Wolf Vostell's May show at the Smolin Gallery (New York), *TV Dé-coll/age*, both highlighted the reception aspects of broadcast by using the monitors as sculptural objects. Paik placed television sets around the gallery, manipulating them magnetically to influence the pictures on the screens; Vostell placed televisions on plinths, filing cabinets, and the floor, and *décollaged* the broadcasted images. The wave of video art that followed these exhibitions was characterised by a similar preoccupation with physical processes; with the transmission/reception aspects of the equipment rather than with what was in front of the camera, a move pre-empting the publication in 1964 of Marshall McLuhan's *Understanding Media: The Extensions of Man*, in which the author coined the phrase, "The Medium Is the Message."[19] Dieter Daniels has argued that this emphasis on process was a necessary one, as there was little or no chance of an artist gaining access to television broadcast at its source until 1968–69, when the first programmes involving cooperation between artists and studios began to appear: "artists do not work with television as a broadcasting station and institution but just with the terminal device, the television set." He argues further: "its institutional status as a media system remains unassailable, artists can only change it as a model at the point of reception."[20]

Film, on the other hand, "deliberates" (Belton). Unlike television, there is usually a delay between recording and final product, a period of postproduction (visual and narrative editing, audiovisual synchronisation, overdubbing, the addition of music and sound effects) that can often demand more time than the filming process itself. This delay is becoming more exaggerated as the film industry challenges itself to greater heights of technical achievement. During the eight years it took to produce *The Lord of the Rings* trilogy, for instance, only 274 days were spent filming. Each film then required an entire year of postproduction to complete the computer animation, miniatures, and digital programmes, while director Peter Jackson spent six weeks per film with composer Howard Shore advising on the score.[21] In a bid to achieve a greater "realism," or rather, to produce a less-processed product, some filmmakers have purposely highlighted the materiality of their work. Usually such examples come from those working beyond the mainstream narrative tradition, such as Warhol, whose films frequently expose their means of creation through a complete lack of editing and postproduction effects. Shots are often static, a stillness frequently compounded by an unmoving subject matter, such as the Empire State Building (*Empire*: 1964), while editing fissures and glimpses of the camera apparatus are frequently left in view (as in *Sleep*, *Haircut*: both 1963; and *Eat*, 1964 [see video 1.4 ⊙]).[22] More recently, examples can be found in mainstream cinema, with directors, such as Daniel Myrick and Eduardo Sánchez (*Blair Witch Project*, 1999), Matt Reeves (*Cloverfield*, 2008), and Lars Von Trier and Thomas Vinterberg, co-founders of the Dogme 95 movement, opting for a more spontaneous, "documentary" aesthetic through improvised dialogue and hand-held cameras (see video 1.5 ⊙).

Others have attempted to reduce the appearance of deliberation by working on the film stock itself. Rather than "filming" what is in front of the camera, artists have painted, scratched, or placed objects directly onto the celluloid strip. In his early work, during the 1930s and 1940s, for instance, New Zealand artist Len Lye developed a method later known as "direct animation." In his 1937 short, *Trade Tattoo*, with music provided by the *Lecuona Cuban Boys*, he enhanced black-and-white documentary footage with paint, stencilled patterns, and animated text to create a multilayered, technicolor collage. American filmmaker Stan Brakhage, in his silent 16mm short, *Mothlight* (1963), placed the wings of moths, dead leaves, and flowers between pieces of Mylar tape, which he then fed directly through an optical printer to produce a projectable, handmade film (fig. 1.2; see video 1.6 ⊙).[23] Nevertheless, despite the more instant quality of such work, direct production still takes time and requires an intermission between creation and presentation. The emphasis on "making" or "working on" a film—on the development of "content"—to be projected within a closed environment, then, differentiates the medium from the process orientation and immediacy of television's global transmission.

Such "deliberation" has much to do with film's genealogy. Photochemical and mechanical in construction, the flipbook-style delivery of film has its roots in photography. When Thomas Edison took his Kinetoscope to the 1893 Chicago World's Fair, he essentially displayed a slideshow of still images that changed fast enough to give the impression of movement. Even though film technology has developed rapidly during the last century, this basic principle

Figure 1.2 Stan Brakhage, film still from *Mothlight* (1963).

has remained constant and artist Walther Ruttmann's famous praise for film, founded on the opportunity it afforded "to paint with time," alluded to a flow that does not really exist.[24] When watching a film, the eye plays tricks on us, joining together the static images through a process known as critical flicker fusion, which creates the illusion of a continuous flow, a smooth movement from one picture to the other. At its most basic level, in other words, the filmic image is intermittent and halting, requiring completion by the audience to produce the desired effect, a continual cognitive mediation between technology and the mind's eye. The inclusion of sound and music in a film's final mix help create this illusion of motion (it is primarily for audiovisual synchronicity that the famous clipboard is used, a snapping visual gesture that requires a precise and easily coordinated sound by the engineer to kick-start the individually recorded tracks.) Able to move through time without hesitation, music and real-world sound can help lead the mind away from the perception of visual disjunction. Although filmmakers working within the "mainstream" tradition attempted to conceal this halting progression under the illusion of flow, many artists who experimented with film technology during the early twentieth century were intrigued by the relationship of stillness to movement. Cubist and Dadaist painting, for instance, with its preoccupation with capturing motion on the canvas, extended particularly easily into film: Duchamp's films provided kinetic solutions to pictorial problems encountered in his experiments with optics and his interest in the work of Eadweard Muybridge, for instance, while Man Ray's first film, *Retour à la raison* (1923), was a clear extension of his photographic compositions.

While film developed from mechanical visual forms, video shares its magnetic technology with that of sound recording and reproduction. Just as television evolved separately from film, its technologies and methods fundamentally different, so too did video develop along different lines. In fact, as a recording device whose images and sounds can be transmitted instantly via a closed-circuit feed, it is a totally different medium from its moving-image cousins.[25] Although video translates as "I see," a name that positions the format within the visual technologies, this designation is misleading. With no photochemistry and no moving parts (apart from the tape), video evolved from the transmission of coded, electric signals across a wire common to the telephone and the telegraph. Initially a device for recording sound, not image; video is an electromagnetic process closely aligned to audio, rather than visual technologies, as video artist-composer Bill Viola explains:

> Technologically, video has evolved out of sound (the electromagnetic) and its close association with cinema is misleading since film and its grandparent, the photographic process, are members of a completely different branch of the genealogical tree (the mechanical/chemical). The video camera, as an electronic transducer of physical energy into electrical impulses, bears a closer original relation to the microphone than to the film camera.[26]

Stemming from the electromagnetic tradition used for sound preservation and communication, video's heritage, or "branch of the genealogical tree" is that of audiotape, rather than film, technology.

During World War II, German engineers used Fritz Pfleumer's 1928 experiments with magnetic tape recording as the basis for developing a reliable means of recording their radio communications.[27] When the improved technology found its way to America after the war, it was readily seized upon by the entertainment industries as a means to prerecord material and so liberate programming from the fallibility of live broadcast, which, up until this time, had been the only option. In 1948, a version of the magnetic technology, refined and developed by American electronics company Ampex Corporation, enabled the first prerecorded radio material (*The Bing Crosby Show*) to be aired by the American Broadcasting Company (ABC). Investigations into the recording of image were closely connected to these improvements in sound recording. During the early years of television, film was used to record programmes for subsequent broadcast through a process known as kinescope. A time-consuming and expensive practice, kinescope required a film camera to record straight from a television monitor. It was clear that an alternative method was needed as a matter of some urgency and it was not long before television companies and engineers looked to magnetic audio technology for ideas. Although television ("video") and audio signals are similar, and thus could, in theory, share the same technological methods, the large amount of information carried by the visual signal compared with that of a sound broadcast demanded significant re-engineering of the equipment. An early prototype for preserving visual information on magnetic tape was demonstrated by Bing Crosby Enterprises, the entertainer's production company, in Los Angeles on 11 November 1951. But, although providing the first display of videotape recording, the procedure required a large amount of tape to produce only a short amount of low quality video. It would take several more years of experimentation before a workable method of audiovisual video recording was developed and it wasn't until 1956 that Ampex, already occupying the leading edge of tape recorder technology (a project worked on by Ray Dolby), demonstrated their cheaper and more practical broadcast-quality videotape equipment.[28] Known as the VR-1000, their Quadruplex technology used two-inch wide tape that, although mounted on reels in the same way as audiotape, could achieve a very high head-to-tape speed and so record the large bandwidth signals of video without using copious amounts of tape: this breakthrough was achieved by having a sweeping beam of electrical impulses continually scan the magnetic tape for information to produce a black-and-white picture with a mono audio channel. Within weeks CBS, followed closely by two other major networks in America, switched to the new technology, which would remain the industry standard for the next twenty years.

However, it was several years before the technology came within the price- and size-range of individuals. This time, the revolution was headed by Sony, who introduced the half-inch CV-2000 Portapak, a machine that, despite its hefty price-tag, was still able to record only twenty minutes of black-and-white footage with sound taken from an external microphone. Although advertised as being easily transportable, the CV-2000 was nevertheless cumbersome and heavy. In fact, it was another two years before Sony introduced a truly portable, battery-operated video recorder, the CV-2400. Armed with the knowledge that this equipment did not become commercially available until 1967, Tom Sherman has hypothesised that the machine Paik used for his mythical adventure in 1965 was in fact the CV-2000. This would suggest that Paik videoed the parade from the window of a building (for access to mains electricity) rather than from that of a car.[29] Arguing along similar lines, Spielmann points out that the 1965 Portapak did not have a rewind function: it follows that Paik must have made use of a video recorder to play his tape later that evening, a piece of equipment already used in the world of professional television.[30]

Sound and the Immediate

Whatever the true nature of the story, the physical components of video positioned it within a technological lineage that was aural rather than visual in nature, bequeathing to it physical attributes very different from those of film. Although videotape can be manipulated during presentation, as Paik demonstrated, it

cannot easily undergo the drastic postproduction transformations, or "deliberation," available to film, a complaint voiced by Viola, who frequently bemoaned the
laborious process of physically cutting tape and getting to grips with expensive
and awkward predigital editing machines.[31] Produced via a continual scanning
process, the video image is in fact not an image at all: it is a moving point of light
within a flowing stream of electrons.[32] To break this stream without rupturing the
audio or visual cohesion is therefore a complex business, a technical difficulty hindered further by the fact that the Ampex's two-inch Quadruplex system, although
modelled on the cut-and-splice method of film and audiotape editing, had no slow
reverse or forward function. The editing of prerecorded material was thus highly
imprecise. The playback machine had to be stopped as near as possible to the
desired cut and the tape transferred to a splicing block. A solvent containing fine
metal particles was then placed on the tape. Attracted to the magnetised sections
of the video, these particles, when the solvent evaporated, revealed separations
between tracks only five thousandths of an inch wide. Having identified these
separations, the editor was then able to cut the tape with a razor so as to mini-
mise any awkward visual jumps or stutters when two pieces of tape were joined
together with special adhesive tape. Until the video was played back, however,
there was no certainty as to how successful the edit had been: whether or not the
cut had been exactly right, or if there was any bleeding between shots. Although
the introduction of mechanical splicing stations, such as the Smith-Editor complete with microscope and roller that enabled tiny increments in tape movement,
helped to improve this process, the procedure nevertheless remained a fallible
one. Emmy Award-winning editor Arthur Schneider, for instance, described the
splicing of two-inch videotape as a process demanding perfect eyesight, a sharp
razor blade, and a lot of guts.[33]

As a branch of audio technology, and with problematic editing potential, videotape, during its first two decades, was used predominantly for live recording: as
a cheaper and less cumbersome device than film for capturing the moving image.
And yet, while both film and video produce the illusion that what they capture
is reality—what is in front of the camera—the nature of each illusion is unique.
Able to record and transmit movement electronically rather than mechanically,
video at its most basic level has a fluidity of motion very different from the flip-
book construction of film, a variation that can be reformulated as the difference
between stasis and motion. Robert Arns has described this difference in terms of
progress and stillness: "in film, movement is the basic illusion; really the succes-
sion of still images progressing after each other on the screen. In video, stillness
is the basic illusion as a still image cannot exist."[34] While the film image demands
mediation by the brain in order to place the stills within a flow that suggests
motion, the video image requires no such intervention: it is already in movement.
Furthermore, video cannot produce a complete picture—or still—at any one time:
"[v]ideo images are always in the process of their own realization" explains Belton;
"[t]heir association with immediacy and presentness is partly because they are

always in the process of coming into being."[35] As a continuous scanning motion able to deliver images without deliberation, then, video produces an immediacy difficult to achieve, at least at the most basic level, through the medium of film. Not only can video record and play back information easily, it is able to do so from within the shared time of its perceivers, an ability that so impressed Jean-Luc Godard that he once vowed to abandon his feature film career to make "instant newsreels" via portable videotape equipment.[36] Capable of recording and projecting instantly, video is a live medium. Roland Barthes famously argued that photographs offer a ghostly residue of what once was: a memory of something no longer there.[37] This, he maintained, prevents a full engagement with the person or subject presented and encourages only external contemplation of something now inaccessible. This ability to suggest another time makes a photograph appear unreal, even spectral. Film must, if we follow this through, be an endless progression of the past, despite the illusion of movement that Christian Metz described as the "transference of reality" into the filmic.[38] In video, on the other hand, like the ever-present Hindu Om, real movement ensures an endless present; a continual and fluctuating "now".

This sense of flow and contemporaneity is enhanced by the ability of video technology easily to record image *and* sound at the same time. While the finished film product is audiovisual, its process of construction often requires two different technological methodologies. Direct sound makes it possible to record image and sound live and in sync when shooting celluloid film, even though the two tracks will be processed separately; but this practice is usually the reserve of documentary film and filmed musical performances. In mainstream practice, both a visual director and a music composer are often employed, specialists in each area whose interactions can be limited (of course, close and productive collaborations have flourished under this dual-channelled operation: Alfred Hitchcock and Bernard Herrmann, Steven Spielberg and John Williams, Tim Burton and Danny Elfman, Peter Greenaway and Michael Nyman, to name but a few). Moreover, music in film does not operate alone but lies within a soundscape. Film theorist Rick Altman has convincingly argued that film sound should be taken as a single complex unit rather than as three or more separate components: music, sound effects, and dialogue.[39] The outcome of considering music thus as an element within a unified soundscape in large-scale film production multiplies the number of creative contributors involved: not only are composers, orchestrators, conductors, musicians, studio engineers, copyright staff, and audiovisual editors included, but now also sound engineers, editors and designers, effects producers and processors, Foley artists and Foley editors (the list goes on). Involving not only audiovisual relationships, but also those within the *mise-en-bande*, then, it is clear that film is the product of multiple, interacting authors. While mainstream cinema provides the illusion of audiovisual fusion, it is nevertheless both dual-channelled and multiauthored in construction. To put this another way: inherent in this medium is often a heterogeneity that belies the illusion of synchronicity and flow apparent in the final, sutured product. Similarly illusory is the suppression of film's "deliberation"—its Barthesian ghostly residue—for a sense that onscreen events unfold within the real, shared time of those seated in the cinema.

The Artist-Composer

Unlike film, the video medium allows for perfect synchronicity, as the visual and audio tracks are recorded and played back simultaneously as one signal. It is here, in the ability to instantly project a single audiovisual signal that video's material qualities translate into a new modality of immediate composition. As primary devices, Sony's early machines were largely shunned by the film industry as being an inferior alternative to film stock. Not only was the picture quality substandard, but the editing procedures demanded by the continual scanning movement of the video signal was far too inaccurate for film studios to entertain. However, many artists used to working with other materials (painters, sculptors, musicians) took the opportunity to handle the cheaper, more easily accessible moving image technology, with its unique promise of immediate yet transitory flow: "[t]he portapak was considered a revolutionary tool," remembers video artist Woody Vasulka; "almost a weapon against the establishment."[40] As a tool for recording home memories, video's capacity for co-recording sound and image has been greatly beneficial; as a tool for artistic experimentation, it has fuelled hitherto unprecedented intermedial work.

Unlike many other artistic materials—paint, stone, wood—video gave to artists the option of including sound in their work, the opportunity to combine into one strand image *and* music. Traditionally, image is static, visible, and silent: music, on the other hand, is temporal, invisible, and audible. To fuse these sensory impressions together into a single experience has been an exasperating mission and although there have been many efforts—Rimington's *Colour Organ* (1895), for instance—attempts have rarely managed more than the embodiment of a similar aesthetic (as in the work of Debussy and Monet), or the translation of one sensory experience into another (as in the synaesthetic experiments of Rimsky-Korsakov, Rachmaninov, Kandinsky, and others). Coexistence, or the simultaneous unfolding through time of both music and image, has been problematic, and the history of art music has thrown up only a few collaborative, audiovisual forms, as we shall see in the next chapter. Opera, with its mixture of music, text, and theatre is an obvious example, but the staging—the visual side—is most often the brainchild of a director and can change fundamentally from production to production. At first glance, film appears the perfect solution, as it allows image to burst into motion; "to paint with time." But, as we have seen, mainstream film is often multiauthored; its unity at a material level illusory.

Highly charged with combinative possibility, video allows the authorial gap inherent in film's construction to be closed, encouraging image and music into a symbiotic partnership rarely encountered before. Video, continually in the process of becoming, is infused with a sense of "immediacy and presentness" that repositions its images within the transitory realm of music, giving it an existence and decay that coincides with its moment of production. Able to unravel temporally, the video signal undergoes a sort of "aging," a "kind of irreversibility" (Paik) that is normally reserved for musical and theatrical experience.[41] This allows a rethinking of Metz's dictum quoted above: unlike film, the motion-based video offers not a transference of reality into the filmic but, rather, a transference of reality and image into the musical. Because the virtual image of video is immediate, it creates a sense of the "now" that enables it to coexist temporally with music, to be present in the same, as Stravinsky would say, "psychological" dimension.[42] This audio basis, together with its continual motion, posits for the video image an existence in the musical sphere and vice versa in a way not possible with other artistic media, and its meaning no longer needs to be emergent as it materialises, unified, at the moment of its creation.

Such material audiovisuality raises issues of reception and perception. To the viewer, film and video both offer a smooth and realistic progression of images, and the different ways in which the brain must create this illusion is not immediately obvious to most of us. But what is important is the creative possibility that such a difference allows. While Belton acknowledges that there are many bases for comparison between film and video, as mentioned, his investigation focuses largely on their technological divergences from each other. And yet, while the two formats are materially distinct, it is important to remember that each allows for a range of recording practices used by different kinds of artists and musicians. If we therefore extend this examination into the types of artistic practice that each format has encouraged, the results are compelling.

Derived from, and existing in, the musical sphere, the physical makeup of video has clearly influenced the aesthetic uses to which the medium has been put. Because the format is, at root, an audio one, practitioners have often to take charge of both the sonic and visual sides of their work. It is true that variations on this practice can also be found in mainstream film, whereby a director creates what Kevin Donnelly has termed a "composite score," a quintessential postmodern composition of disparate pre-existing pop, rock, and high art music: most famously, Stanley Kubrick favoured his temp track of pre-existent music by Ligeti and the two Strausses over Alex North's original score for *2001: A Space Odyssey* (1968) (see video 1.7▶).[43] Occasionally, a director is able to compose his own score, a phenomenon exemplified by Clint Eastwood, who has both composed for and directed several of his films, including *Million Dollar Baby* (2004), which earned him a nomination for Best Original Score at the 2005 Golden Globes. Similarly, David Lynch, always heavily involved in the music for his films, wrote and recorded some of the original tracks for *Inland Empire* (2006).[44] As Altman has pointed out, however, the large-production scale of mainstream film requires a considerable workforce to construct the soundscape, of which music is only one part.

Informed by cultural and economic forces very different from those of mainstream film, many examples of single-authored audiovisuality can be found in early experimental film. The early Berlin-based school of "absolute" filmmakers, for instance, often used musical forms to inform their visual structures. In 1919, Ruttmann described his work as "[a]n art for the eye that differs from painting in that it takes place in time (like music). Hence, a completely new type of artist than has hitherto been only latent will emerge, placed somewhere between painting and music."[45] As we shall see in chapter 2, the "new" types of artists that followed attempted to situate their work "between music and painting" by using musical form as a method of composing image. Hans Richter articulated his idea of visual music in a statement with Viking Eggeling:

> Music became a model for both of us. We found a principle that fitted our philosophy in musical counterpoint: each action produces a corresponding reaction. So we found a suitable system in counterpoint fugue, a dynamic and polar arrangement of conflicting energies.[46]

Such an "arrangement of conflicting energies" can be found in Richter's silent animated film *Rhythmus 21* (1921), in which black-and-white geometric shapes move across the screen, receding and pulsing to an unheard beat (fig. 1.3; see video 1.8⏵).[47]

Using different methods, Oskar Fischinger developed an audiovisual aesthetic that culminated in his *Tönende Ornamente* (Sounding Ornaments), or hand-drawn

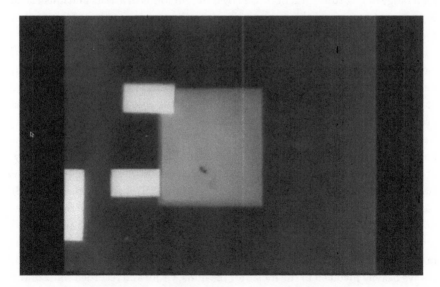

Figure 1.3 Hans Richter, film still from *Rhythmus 21* (1921).

optical soundtracks. While many of his films were based on preexistent music (visual interpretation of No. 5 from Brahms's *Hungarian Dances* (1931) for instance, or the first movement of Bach's Brandenburg Concerto No. 3 in his 1947 *Motion Picture No.1*), other work attempted a type of visual composition founded upon musical structures:

> Undoubtedly, the composer of tomorrow will no longer write mere notes, which the composer himself can never realise definitively, but which rather must languish, abandoned to various capricious reproducers. Now control of every fine gradation and nuance is granted to the music-painting artist, who bases everything exclusively on the primary fundamental of music, namely the wave—vibration or oscillation in and of itself.[48]

The idea of a silent type of visual music can be found in the work of later filmmakers working with sound technology. The films of Brakhage, for instance, demonstrate a similar progression towards a silenced music. Although his earlier work involved collaboration with James Tenney (*Interim*, 1953) and the music of Cage (*In Between*, 1955), his most experimental soundtrack is that of *Fire of Waters* (1965), in which a score composed at various points of slowed-down birdsong, the speeded-up sound of a woman giving birth, and a "wind-song" accompanies flashes of lightning over a suburban neighbourhood. Marie Nesthus has pointed out the similarities between the compositional techniques of Brakhage and those of Olivier Messiaen—indeed the director calls his exploration of the relationship between aural experience and colour in *Scenes from Under Childhood* (1967–1970), a "tone poem for the eye" and acknowledges the composer as his influence.[49] As we have seen, Brakhage began to produce silent films without a camera, preferring instead to scratch or paint directly on the filmstrip in order to create an image that symbolised the very act of perception.[50] In 1996, evoking ideas strikingly similar to those of the earlier German school, he explained that:

> I aspire to a visual music, a "music" for the eyes (as my films are entirely without sound-tracks these days). Just as a composer can be said to work primarily with "musical ideas," I can be said to work with the ideas intrinsic to film, which is the only medium capable of making paradigmatic "closure" apropos Primal Sight. A composer most usually creates parallels to the surroundings of the inner ear—the primary thoughts of sounds. I, similarly, now work with the electric synapses of thought to achieve overall cathexis paradigms separate from but "at one" with the inner lights, the Light, at source, of being human.[51]

In mainstream film, even if the conception of both aural and visual tracks comes from the same source, the technology demands that the two remain physically separated during the production stages (Kubrick flouted this necessity by playing his temp track aloud in the studio to create the correct atmosphere for the actors). Experimental filmmakers, however, working with a smaller budget and a different set of aesthetic codes, found ways to create single-authored "visual music": Richter and Ruttmann by creating silent films based on musical structures; Fischinger by constructing optical soundtracks in which image was translated to sound; and, later, Brakhage by evoking the "primary thoughts" of perception to produce "'music' for the eyes." The creation of such work demanded engagement with the materiality of film (to paint, punch holes in, or scratch the film strip) and a resultant "deliberation": and the results, at least in the early years, were visual translations, or interpretations, of music; or aural transformations of images.

The ease with which video's sound and image tracks can be recorded and projected simultaneously, on the other hand, encourages those working with the medium to take control of both audio and visual tracks not only conceptually, but also *concurrently*. Although it is easy at this point to over-romanticise the idea of the singular compositional voice, it is important to remember that authorial control in fact went against many of the fundamental aims of early video artist-composers, who created concurrent audiovisual works that, while enabled at a material level by a single person, were nevertheless used to create live, collective, collaborative, and interactive creative spaces. As we shall see in chapter 4, at a time when a semi-utopian discourse about television as a democratic medium was emerging, it was at the intersections between artist-composer, performer, audience, and environment that true intermediality arose.

The Audio-Image

In its early years, video's unique audiovisuality was particularly appealing to musically trained artists. Paik, for instance, was trained in music history and composition. First, in an act of rebellion, argues John Hanhardt, against the "conventions of his own culture," Paik studied music, art history, and aesthetics at the University of Tokyo, where he submitted a thesis on Schönberg.[52] He then continued to study music history under Thrasybulus Georgiades at the University of Munich before moving to the Academy of Music, Freiburg, to work with composer Wolfgang Fortner. He found the International Summer Courses of New Music, Darmstadt, particularly influential and it was here that he first met Stockhausen and Cage in 1957 and 1958 respectively. Furthermore, his subsequent work for the electronic music studio at the West German Radio Station, Cologne (WDR) brought him into contact with the work of composers such as Cornelius Cardew and Ligeti.

Paik's early compositional work demonstrates the way in which video practice could bring together artistic and musical elements. His style moved from the spliced tape technique that produced works such as *Hommage à John*

Cage (1959), in which screams and prepared piano playing were juxtaposed with taped excerpts of pre-existent music and sound effects, to produce what he called "action music" (fig.1.4).[53] Based on the concepts of improvisation, chance, and spontaneity that were informing concurrent work by Allan Kaprow, Joseph Beuys, Yves Klein, Yoko Ono, and others, the scores for Paik's "action music" described simple procedures that would demonstrate the physicality of performance: *One for Solo Violin* (1962), for example, asks the performer simply to smash a violin. Electro-acoustic composer Gottfried Michael Koenig explained that Paik's "concept of music [was] as something that intervenes and is not merely performed placidly. Music was by all means an energetic and violent matter."[54] Recalling a performance of Paik's violin piece by cellist Charlotte Moorman, film and video artist Jud Yalkut acknowledged that interventional gestures of "action music," even when contextualised within the arena of

Figure 1.4 Nam June Paik, *Klavier intégral*, 1958–1963. Photo courtesy MUMOK, Museum Moderner Kunst Stiftung Ludwig Wien, ehemals Sammlung Hahn, Köln. © Nam June Paik Estate.

intense experimentation in 1960s New York City, were highly contentious (and potentially violent):

> There was a very famous, almost infamous moment, when Charlotte was performing this piece by Paik, *One for Violin*, which involved smashing a violin, and she was about to smash it and some artist/activist—I think his name was Saul Goodman, or something like that—stuck his head right into the place where she was going to do this. It was a kind of protest to prevent her from smashing the violin. And what happened in the end was that somehow Charlotte actually completed the action, but he got hurt.[55]

Once performed, this music could not be repeated as the instrument had been destroyed: it was, literally, deconstructive music that rebelled against the musical canon and the nature of repeatable music performance. Highlighting the physicality of performance led Paik to reconsider the space that traditionally exists between performer and audience in the concert hall. Other works tried to activate the audience, to draw them across this space, a process demonstrated during a performance of Paik's *Etude for Pianoforte* (1960) at the Atelier Mary Baumeister in Cologne, where the composer jumped from the stage and cut the tie of audience member Cage and wet David Tudor with shaving cream.[56] Such multigestural performance was also envisaged for his unrealised *Symphony for 20 Rooms* (1961), in which he hoped to invite visitors to kick objects around the space and accompany his audiotape collages by manipulating various tape players themselves.

Although Paik did not turn his hand to the moving image until around 1961 and, as we have seen, only acquired his Portapak in 1965, his early performances and their inclusion of the tape deck apparatus clearly displayed the tendencies towards music performance and audience participation he would later adopt: "his movement between sound and videotape" surmises Hanhardt, "was a seamless investigation into the mechanics of sound and image reproduction."[57]

Such a seamless move between working with sound and videotape can be seen in pieces by many other artists, including Icelander Steina Vasulka, who, along with her husband Woody, founded "The Kitchen" in New York in 1971, an influential media arts theatre where people could interact freely with those working with video technology. Vasulka, like Paik, was a trained musician, graduating from the Prague Conservatoire and gaining a position as violinist in the Icelandic Symphony Orchestra before turning her hand to video work:

> My background is in music. For me, it is the sound that leads me into the image. Every image has its own sound and in it I attempt to capture something flowing and living. I apply the same principle to art as to playing the violin: with the same attitude of continuous practice, the same concept of composition. Since my art schooling was in music, I do not think of images as stills, but always as motion.[58]

Vasulka's interest in continual-motion images drew her to the transitory nature of video and her musical influence is often clear to see. The portrayal of something "flowing and living" is evident in her early performances of *Violin Power* (1970–1978), for instance, in which the artist was able to play the video image (fig. 1.5). For this closed-circuit performance, Vasulka used two cameras to record the movements of her bow moving across the strings as she played her violin. The soundwaves, recorded through a microphone and fed through a frequency shifter, spread the scan lines of the video image horizontally until they became visible. Vasulka then used a keyer (a device to combine two visual signals) and the Rutt/Etra Scan Processor to produce an audio signal able to manipulate the videoed images further: these images were then projected (see video 1.9 ⓑ). Spielmann understands the resultant convergence of music and video languages "in terms of their abstraction, when the sound stimulates the image's waveform. Music is connoted visually, insofar as video develops dimensions in time and space: the sound not only bends the scan lines apart so that these become horizontally visible and exhibit a temporal dimension. The *Video Violin* performance also uses the scan processor to modulate the sound's wave movement, until spatial forms of the image form themselves."[59]

Vasulka revisited this work in 1991, this time making use of a MIDI instrument—the five-stringed, electric ZETA Violin—and a PowerBook to interface her

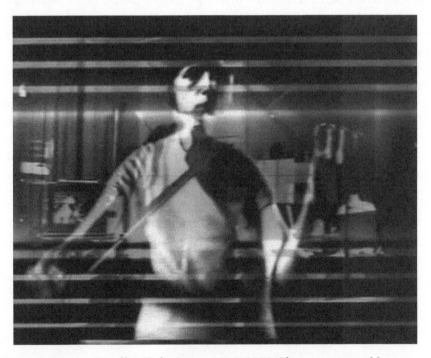

Figure 1.5 Steina Vasulka, *Violin Power*, 1970–1978. Photo courtesy of San Francisco Museum of Modern Art, Camille W. and William S. Broadbent Fund. © Steina.

sounds, thus providing "an instant access to any frame of video on the disk as well as access to fast/slow and forward/backward movements" (Vasulka):[60]

> The assignment at the moment is that stops on A and E string point to frame locations on the disk. The D and G strings control speed and direction and the C string is a master controller assigned to address segments on the disk. In another programming scheme, the C string controls which upper strings get assigned their function, as I experiment to make the performance more musical.[61]

While Vasulka created and shaped her images in a performative sound-image composition, a different form of audiovisual synthesis can be found in the work of French video artist Robert Cahen. Beginning his artistic life as an electro-acoustic composer, Cahen completed his studies in 1971 with Pierre Schaeffer and Michel Chion at the Conservatoire Nationale Supérieur de Musique (CNSM) in Paris, before becoming a member of the Musical Research Group of ORTF (Office de Radiodiffusion-Télévision Française). After his musical training, Cahen turned his hand to video work. While some of his pieces use music as narrative focus (including *Instantanés, trois portraits de compositeurs: Marco Stroppa, Philippe Manoury, Thierry Lancino* (1989) and *Blind Song* (2008)), others are informed by musical process. Just as composers of *musique concrète* created music from found sound, Cahen's video aesthetic was based on the translation of sound into image: "Everything that's done in concrete music can be done with electronic imagery. I wanted to do images that I had made with music."[62] To create such musical imagery, Cahen's video works manipulate images as though they were sounds, using colour, editing, and modelling to transform reality. In this way, objective images are removed from their original source and internalised: "Schaeffer taught me to edit sounds, to listen to a sound in itself, to know how to grasp what's in a sound independently of its original concept...that helped me to realise that you can look at an image without looking at what it originally signifies."[63] Sandra Lischi, discussing the influence of *musique concrète* on Cahen's video images, draws on the concept of decontexualisation:

> Processing disparate sounds and images, decontextualising and abstracting them, ultimately produced a new way of listening to "and therefore also looking at" things...That's why the shift from musical composition to visual work occurred with relative ease...The encounter of concrete music with the vast field of electronic music led to an extensive exploration in which the possibility of reworking natural sounds melded with the electronic production of completely artificial sounds.[64]

Although not single-authored (the soundtrack is by Chion), *Juste le Temps* (1983) is intensely musical. The piece depicts a woman's journey on a train: the French landscape that flicks past the window is electronically processed to abstraction, its slow motion making time visible and replacing the real landscape with an imagined one, independent (like the musical material of *musique concrète*) of its "original concept."

Despite the nuanced work produced by musically trained video artists, however, a working knowledge of composition or performance was not required to produce close audiovisual work. Tony Conrad, for instance, trained in mathematics at Harvard. Before he turned his hand to video in the 1970s, he became a member of the *Theatre of Eternal Music* (also known as *The Dream Syndicate*) alongside La Monte Young and John Cale. Working in "solid opposition to the North Atlantic cultural tradition of composition" (Conrad), the group developed a style known as "dream music," a highly repetitive soundscape based on the minimalist drones of just-intonation.[65] Conrad later collaborated with Krautrock group *Faust* (1972) and formed his own ensemble to record his album *Slapping Pythagoras* (1995).[66] The "principal motivation" behind his film *The Flicker* (1965–6 [see video 1.10▶]), was to create transmedial stroboscopic light patterns; "to explore the possibilities for harmonic expression using a sensory mode other than sound," an interest that infused his later video work (from the 1970s).[67]

Viola shares a similar background to Conrad. He studied visual art at the Experimental Studios, Syracuse University (although he also worked on electronic music with Franklin Morris), before joining David Tudor's avant-garde performance group, *Composers Inside Electronics* (where he became involved with Tudor's *Rainforest* project), from 1973 to 1980. As we have seen, Viola has been particularly vocal about the audio basis for video at a material level. But he has also repeatedly expressed the artistic consequences of such a basis; namely the possibility of audiovisual confluence, or interchangeability:

> One of the many things I learned from [Tudor] was the understanding of sound as a material thing, an entity. My ideas about the visual have been affected by this, in terms of something I call "field perception," as opposed to our more common mode of object perception. In many of my videotapes, I have used the camera according to perceptual or cognitive models based on sound rather than light. I think of all the senses as being unified. I do not consider sound as separate from image. We usually think of the camera as an "eye" and the microphone as an "ear," but all the senses exist simultaneously in our bodies, interwoven into one system that includes sensory data, neural processing, memory, imagination, and all the mental events of the moment. This all adds up to create the larger phenomenon we call experience...field perception is the awareness or sensing of an entire space at once.[68]

For Viola, the possibility of creating "field perception" by moving image into music's "psychological" dimension came from the physical peculiarities of video, a potential "unification of the senses" that was the most alluring aspect of the format. That video art is often sound-based, then, owes much to its audio genealogy, a lineage that has ensured that what could easily have become an image-based genre remained instead one highly aware of its audiovisual qualities. Moreover, this intermedial technology, according to Viola, led to the creation of a new, hybrid being: the artist-composer, or audiovisual practitioner.

Because sound was readily producible by video, those with little or no musical training were also able to include an aural side in their work. Many early exponents of video work developed an interest in sound through different disciplines: Jonas through her background in sculpture, for instance, Carolee Schneemann and Vostell through their training in painting, while Vito Acconci's first creative endeavours were through poetry, an interest in vocalisation that developed into a career-long preoccupation with sound and image combines: in *Stages* (1973), the artist sings to the audience acousmatically, while in *Theme Song* (also 1973), his face is seen in close-up as he uses tape recordings of Bob Dylan, the Doors, Van Morrison, and others to initiate an increasingly intrusive dialogue with the viewer (see video 1.11 ▶).

Others did not even have a background in the arts: as we have seen, Conrad graduated in mathematics, while Peter Campus trained in experimental psychology and Woody Vasulka as an engineer. Speaking about his works *Matrix I* and *II* (1970–1972), Woody explained that, at this time, he was "very much involved in changing the image in sound or controlling the sounds with images, and generating images from sounds and vice versa."[69] In his *Matrix 1, Black Sunrise* (1971), a multi-monitor video array, sound created from the video signal was transmitted to an audio synthesiser to form a transformational audiovisual work, as Spielmann explains: "The visual forms of a recorded disc converted into horizontal drift, and the sound, which is produced by the drifting, is the expression of video noise, the raw material of audiovisuality."[70]

Bruce Nauman was trained in mathematics and physics. Although many of his works, such as the video corridors, operate in silence (at least at the level of video's materiality), the artist became interested in sound early on. He met Steve Reich in 1968 and Philip Glass shortly afterwards: "This was really important for me. I was able to use their idea about time as a really supportive idea," he explains; "I was a musician. I played guitar and bass...The way I used the videotape was to incorporate their ideas about the way time should be...All these things were kind of cross-feeding into each other."[71] The spatial and temporal elements of early minimalism can be found in his *Audio Video Piece for London, Ontario* (1969/70), in which a TV monitor shows a live image of an adjoining room: although this second room is locked, visitors can hear a soft, looped knocking sound coming from within. And yet there is no clue on the monitor as to how this sound is being produced. The result is a rupture between sound and image. His investigations into spatialised sound culminated in *Raw Material* (2005) for the Turbine Hall in London's Tate Modern, where he discarded image altogether in favour of a collage of twenty-two spoken texts.

The Art of Noises

Video technology, then, enabled two things: first, composers were able to visualise their sounds; and second, artists were able to sound their visual work. Although video pieces by musicians could be considered "musical" in the traditional sense (*TV Cello, Violin Power,* and *Instantanés, trois portraits de compositeurs,* for instance), video work by artists, filmmakers, and dancers made use of the instant recording capacity of video to turn ambient or ubiquitous sounds into compositional material. In this sense, video work can be located at the edge of an expanding notion of musical material that had informed much twentieth-century compositional practice. Spielmann has positioned the material quality of video within the "descriptive category of noise," explaining that video, "considered precisely, does not present image and sound (like film) but instead forms of expression from both these signal states":

> Audio and video are interconnected noises with which the video signal can selectively produce the electronic noise aurally/auditively and visually. From the definition of the audiovisual qualities, it follows, in terms of categorization, that video in its radical media form has to be actually allotted to the category of noise rather than to a consistent type of image. In other words, electronic noise can also be moved horizontally and multiplied into a spatial object—different from a "fixed" moving image as in film—by means of feedback and delay.[72]

Although the literal visual spatialisation of electronic noise was explored by Vasulka in *Violin Power,* locating video within the "descriptive category of noise" also points towards an emancipatory effect on visual compositional strategies. Spielmann uses Woody Vasulka's *No.25* (1976) to illustrate her point. Like *Violin Power, No.25* is based on video noise visualised as scan lines: but whereas Steina's piece used scan processing to manipulate video lines, in *No.25*, the video signal audibly and visibly scans the raster field so that the image can be both seen and heard, thus exemplifying "the purest form of creating video by means of video noise": this piece, continues Spielmann,

> belongs to the category of "noise objects," for the transformations created by modulating the waveforms in the scan processor (with its oscillators) show an unfinished visual process consisting of the interplay of horizontal and vertical shifts. At the same time, they amplify the nature of the blank image as noise. When the blank image is curved, stretched, and compressed, we hear *video noise.* The video image has become the presentation of its audiovisual structure.[73]

Although such visualisation of video noise suggests the "unification of the senses" that so intrigued Viola, can these "noise objects" be considered as music or does video audiovisuality point towards a different aesthetic? When Jacques Attali described music as "the organization of noise," he did so with the knowledge that definitions of noise have shifted over time.[74] Thinking along similar lines, Paul Hegarty begins his history of noise music with the claim that "[n]oise is not an objective fact. It occurs in relation to perception—both direct (sensory) and according to presumptions made by an individual. These are going to vary according to historical, geographical and cultural location."[75] This idea is demonstrated by the reception of Beethoven's *Die Große Fuge*, op.133 (1825–1826), a work described by one confused critic present at its first performance as being "as incomprehensible as Chinese," but later praised by Stravinsky for being "an absolutely contemporary piece of music that will be contemporary forever."[76]

Margorie Perloff has since discussed the idea that noise and music are not separate entities but rather exist on a continuum in what she calls "The Futurist Moment."[77] When Luigi Russolo presented his manifesto, *The Art of Noises* (*L'Arte dei Rumori*) in 1913, he called for a musical response to the new soundscapes forged since the Industrial Revolution. As society is faced with a greater array of sounds, music, he reasoned, must expand to incorporate noise. In order to illustrate the expansion of musical material, Russolo invented a number of instruments— *intonarumori* (noise machines)—and wrote in his manifesto that he and his assistant Ugo Piatti, "enjoy creating mental orchestrations of the crashing down of metal shop blinds, slamming doors, the hubbub and shuffle of crowds, the variety of din from the stations, railways, iron foundries, spinning mills, printing works, electric power stations and underground railways."[78] Russolo put his manifesto into action in *Awakening of a City* (*Risveglio di una citta*, 1913), a piece for an ensemble of his *intonorumori*. A similar dissociation of real-world sounds from their mimetic function in order to create musical forms can be found in works by later composers. Varèse's *Ionisation* (1931), for instance, features sirens, anvils, and a lion's roar alongside the more traditional array of percussion instruments. Referring to the ionisation of molecules, the work is based on the variation of rhythmic cells: "I was not influenced by composers as much as by natural objects and physical phenomena," explained Varèse.[79] Works such as *Ionisation* counter the understanding that noise is a negative phenomenon or, as C. S. Kerse puts it, "sound which is undesired by the recipient"; "a sound without musical quality or an unwanted or undesired sound."[80] In this piece, the sirens—culturally understood as a warning signal—are placed within a musical structure, encouraging a redefinition of the traditional understanding of musical material.

While a similar form of sound recontextualisation was later explored by Xenakis, Helmut Lachenmann, and Cardew amongst others, a different type of manipulation can be found in the disembodied strategies of *musique concrète*, a type of composition particularly important, as we have seen, to Cahen. Schaeffer proposed that music could be made up of "sonorous fragments that have a real existence, and that are thought of as being clearly defined and complete sonic objects."[81] In his tape piece *Étude aux chemins de fer* (1948), Schaeffer organised sounds recorded at the Gare des Batignolles, Paris, according to what he perceived to be a musical aesthetic. During the 1950s, the Cologne studio produced further experimentation into the art of noises: Stockhausen used electronics to create a similar *acousmêtre* in *Gesang der Jünglinge* (1955–1956) in which the human voice is manipulated and (ideally) spread over five speakers. Electronically distorted and spatially presented, *Gesang* anticipates the video work of Cahen where the manipulation and separation of real-world sound and image is the primary motivation.

The expansion of musical material took a different turn in the work of John Cage, whose compositions for "junk" percussion ensembles and his work with radio receivers, such as *Imaginary Landscape #4* (1951) and the expansive *Variations VII* (1966), which required ten telephone lines, radio and television bands, geiger counters and an artillery of other noises (fig. 1.6), was particularly influential to video artist-composers such as Paik and Vostell: "If this word, music, is sacred and reserved for eighteenth- and nineteenth-century instruments," wrote Cage, then "we can substitute a more meaningful term: organization of sound."[82] Faced with "the entire field of sound" that marks the future of music, traditional musical techniques such as harmony will, he reasoned, be inadequate when faced with the "non-musical" nature of sound:

> Wherever we are, what we hear is mostly noise. When we ignore it, it disturbs us. When we listen to it, we find it fascinating. The sound of a truck at 50 m.p.h. Static between the stations. Rain. We want to capture and control these sounds, to use them, not as sound effects, but as musical instruments. Every film studio has a library of "sound effects" recorded on film. With a film phonograph it is now possible to control the amplitude and frequency of any one of these sounds and to give to it rhythms within or beyond the reach of anyone's imagination. Given four film phonographs, we can compose and perform a quartet for explosive motor, wind, heartbeat, and landslide.[83]

Cage's notion of "organised sound" called for a change in approach to composition. His expanded and inclusive concept of music that came together with an interest in process-orientated art not only engaged and activated temporal and physical spaces, it also drew attention to auditory perception. In much the same way as Duchamp's found art (not only in terms of sourcing artistic material, but also in the importance of its new context), there was an increasing emphasis on seeing afresh, or listening anew. Rather than highlight the regulated system in which his "musical instruments" were placed, Cage drew attention instead to the different listening strategies that his work encouraged. Hegarty explains hearing as "less reflective" than listening, "a physical process we can do nothing about."[84] Much of Cage's aleatoric music required its audience to listen to sounds ordinarily only heard.

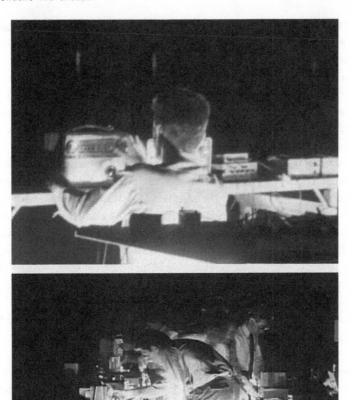

Figure 1.6 John Cage, *Variations VII*. Nine Evenings: *Theatre & Engineering* (1966). Photo courtesy of Experiments in Art and Technology.

The emphasis on perception and listening opened up composition to the non-musician. By the 1960s, the first generation of what would later be known as sound artists, were beginning to take the compositional use of noise into another area: Annea Lockwood's burnt pianos and Max Neuhaus's soundwalks used sound as compositional material that could exist outside of the concert hall, for instance, while the acoustic art and sound sculptures of Bill Fontana were, like the work of Cage, created with the aim to "challenge all of the old historical definitions of noise and the resulting preconceptions that most people have about the sounds they live with."[85] Alan Licht has distinguished between sound art and music in terms of dramatic trajectory : music, he contends, "sets up a series of conflicts and resolutions, either on a large or small scale."[86] Sound art, on the other hand, is not time-based: people do not have to experience the whole narrative, but can experience these works like the plastic arts; they can dip into an aural experience at any time and stay as long as they choose. For this reason, "[s]ound art belongs in an exhibition situation rather than a performance situation—that is, I would maintain, a necessary correlative in defining the term."[87] As a result, the work of sound artists is rarely informed by musical processes or based upon a linear construction of sounds.[88] While the lack of narrative drama may well be the "necessary correlative" in the definition of sound art, however, it must be remembered that many early minimalist works were conceived according to a similar aesthetic. Many of Reich's early compositions demonstrate a peculiar stasis, as the sense of teleology is replaced with an emphasis on the immediate; although often rejecting the term minimalist, Morton Feldman's works of extended duration (such as his one-movement String Quartet II [1983], which can last for up to six continuous hours), were often premiered in art galleries rather than in concert venues. And yet, despite encouraging strategies for engagement similar to those required for minimalist music, sound art often lacks visual support and began with the "invisibility of sound through recording and radio and telephone transmission and continued through the *disjunction* of sound and image" (Licht).[89]

"Noise in particular," argues Licht, "may come under the heading of 'sound by artists'."[90] With little or no music training, artists interested in process-driven work have, throughout the twentieth century, explored the creative qualities of sound: Duchamp's aleatory *Erratum Musicale*, for three voices (ca. 1913), in which notes could either be drawn from a hat, or randomly selected via numbered balls dropped through a funnel into model railway cars, Man Ray's *Lautgedicht* (*Sound Poem*, 1924), or Kurt Schwitters's sound poem *Ursonate* (1926–1932). With the path already paved, artists in the 1960s, including those who would later work with video, produced an array of pure soundworks that were not bound by compositional strategies: Joseph Beuys made an hour-long recording *Ja Ja Ja Ne Ne Ne* of himself saying "yes yes yes yes yes no no no no no" (1968); Acconci recorded himself counting while jogging in Central Park (*Running Tape*, 1969); and Nauman made *Record* (1969), a painful recording of him sounding a violin (an instrument he cannot play). Moving even closer to video were works that combined aural and visual elements. In *Voice Piece for Soprano*, (1961), for instance, Yoko Ono required the performer to scream into a microphone (situated in a gallery), against the wind, against the wall, and against the sky (see video 1.13▶). In a similar vein, La Monte Young produced poetic actions to be performed as music (in *Piano Piece for David Tudor #1*, the performer is asked to bring the piano a bale of hay and a bucket of water to eat and drink, 1960), whereas the sounds in *Poem for Tables, Chairs and Benches* (1960) were created by moving furniture across the performance venue floor.

The sounds recorded and manipulated by the video camera were not always musical, in the traditional sense: as we shall see in chapter 3, they included real-world sounds, accidental noise, recorded music, and static feedback. But if we consider them as sounds intentionally collected and meant to be "heard," then many video pieces come close to the aesthetics found in all three types of expanded music—noise music, sound art, and sound by artists. Understood in this liberated context, the audio part of video can be seen as an expansion of musical material into visuality: "video noise" can then be read as a form of audiovisual composition.

Multiple Histories

Despite the newness of its voice, then, video art did not operate in creative isolation. Video could readily reproduce sound, which enabled those with no musical training to become composers and sound artists as well as visual artists. It is here, within the interdisciplinary possibilities of the medium, that the key to understanding video's history lies. Using cinema as an example, André Gaudreault and Philippe Marion have highlighted the problem of pinpointing the "birth" of a new medium in purely physical terms, arguing that before media specificity can be formulated, the technology must first establish itself in relation to preexistent disciplines, institutions, and other artistic media.[91] The cinematograph was invented at a particular time, for instance, yet initially the technology was used to help develop well-established entertainment genres such as plays and other public performances: "despite its historically demonstrable irruption as technology," argue the authors, "[i]t wasn't until cinema's practitioners arrived at a reflexive understanding of the medium and until the cinema achieved a certain degree of institutionalisation that the medium became autonomous."[92] This *genealogy of media* results in a problematic identification, in which the film medium is born not once, but twice:

> The first birth is when a new technology is used to extend earlier practices, to which it was at first subservient. The second birth is when it sets out on a path that enables the resources it has developed to acquire an institutional legitimacy that acknowledges their specificity. Our perspective has led us to think that instead of talking about the birth of a medium, or at least its second birth, we should instead be taking about its *constitution*.[93]

It is easy to map the genesis of video onto such a model of genealogical constitution. The first wave of video work that followed its "first birth" (from 1965 to 1971, when portable video technology became available with "playback," "rewind," and "fast forward" functions), was characterised by an interest in the technology itself, its sculptural possibilities and its integration into existing artistic investigations. As mentioned, those who first got to grips with video were most often already working in other disciplines—film, music, dance, poetry, performance art, and so on.

Along lines similar to those of Gaudreault and Marion, Spielmann has argued that video cannot be considered an "aesthetically independent genre" until the 1970s and speaks instead of the "integrating birth" of the format.[94] Before the mid-1970s, video became an increasingly significant part of other creative events, such as Happenings and multimedia performance art, but its process of constitution towards media specificity was relatively slow. While the notion of genre is often problematic, early video art-music repels categorisation almost entirely: not only did its materials constantly change, but they also included audio *and* visual elements. The enlarged possibilities of reuse, along with a renewed ability for spatial expansion, make a unifying style for early video work highly difficult to identify. In fact, so prevalent was the literal and conceptual borrowing of early works that Kaprow, in 1974, went against the grain and placed creative video in an old and tired history:

> The use of television as an art medium is generally considered experimental. In the sense that it was rarely thought of that way by artists before the sixties, it must be granted a certain novelty. But so far, in my opinion, it is only marginally experimental. The hardware is new, to art at least, but the conceptual framework and esthetic attitudes around most video as an art are quite tame.[95]

Heterogeneous in nature, eclectic and plural in perspective, early video work operated like a "meta-media," a multi-incorporative genre that reflected the media overload of television—what Jean Baudrillard referred to as the "obesity of information."[96] For this reason, video, during its period of constitution, acquired a mobility of meaning: as critic Sean Cubitt argues, the extreme diversification of the form means that it cannot be considered as any one thing, but rather as a set of relationships around the uses of video; in other words, "a culture."[97]

In this early phase, then, video culture was in the process of becoming, acting more like an adhesive that pulled together hitherto disparate strands of art and music practices than as protagonist in its own story; a facilitator of intermedial discourse rather than a genre. Dick Higgins, who, in 1966, appropriated the term intermedia from Samuel Taylor Coleridge (1812) in order "to define works which fall conceptually between media that are already known," later described the difference between multimedia and intermedia in terms of conceptual fusion (although it is important to remember that intermedia can be included in, or arise as the result of, multimedia).[98] Although mixed media allows artists to include one form of media within another (opera, theatre, Fluxus performances, and so on), thus encouraging a synchronous dialogue between different practices, each medium nevertheless retains its distinctive qualities. Spielmann has described this multimedia practice as "accumulation."[99] An intermedial expansion, on the other hand, involves a "transformation"—or conceptual fusion—of two traditionally separate media, as in concrete or visual poetry: it is a new emergent form that occurs as the result of a collision between media, and, as such, needs to be constantly redefined. Spielmann defines such a fluid merging as "the exchange and transformation of elements that come from different media":

> Intermedia therefore is a formal category of exchange. It signifies an aesthetic encompassment of both form and content. In an intermedia work of art, content becomes a formal category that reveals the structure of combination and collision. The related meaning of content is to express such modes of transformation that are effected by the collision of painting and film, of film and electronic media, and so on. The contextual meaning of intermedia is to reveal the media forms themselves. The making visible of elements that are considered media specific can be performed by ways of comparing and transforming elements such as the interval.[100]

During its constitution period, video acted intermedially as a conduit that enabled the conceptual fusion and manipulation of preexisting elements. In so doing, it mobilised ideas already under investigation by musicians and artists and thus encouraged the expansion (constitution) identified by Gaudreault and Marion. Such mobilisation can be found particularly in the early work of Acconci, Paik, John Baldessari, and Dennis Oppenheim, who were preoccupied with video as a physical medium that enabled other ideas to be more thoroughly explored. Like visual poetry and performance art, then, video was initially used as an agent of "transformation" and it makes little sense to divide its early period into genres such as installation, performance or sculpture, categorisation which, explains Spielmann, "scarcely contributes to determining the specifics of video."[101] Such designation only became viable when video developed its specificity in the 1970s and became a genre easily delineated (although not in all cases) from other media, especially in its single-channelled form. This delineation was enabled by the technology's development: "With the introduction of the video cassettes in 1973," explains Woody Vasulka, "it became even easier, and harmonized with the exhibition purposes of video. By the mid-1970s, video as art was fully entrenched in the galleries, with many developed genres, forms and concepts."[102] Many artists and critics believe that video's line of development has been governed by advances in the equipment, giving its evolution, according to Chris Meigh-Andrews, a "technology-dependent relationship."[103] British video artist David Hall has gone so far as to correlate the history of video technology directly with that of the video aesthetic:

> [D]eveloping technology has undoubtedly influenced the nature of the product at all levels and wherever it is made. These developments have inevitably affected aesthetic criteria as well as making life easier. In the

early days of basic black and white portapaks, extremely limited editing facilities and no special effects, the tendency was towards fairly minimal but nevertheless profound pioneering work. This was necessary and appropriate at a time when concerns were generated in part by reductive and "cerebral" preoccupations. If it can be said that now, in this so-called post-modernist phase, an inclination has developed towards more visually complex, even baroque art work, then the timely expansion of technical possibilities in video allows for greater image manipulation.[104]

Able first to recontextualise television (as demonstrated by Paik and Vostell), then to create recordings of current events, early video artist-composers demonstrated a preference for basic material that was in a constant state of change; material rooted in, or moving closer to, the live. This interest in immediacy was a defining style of Paik's entire career, which, in support of Hall's chronicle of video, evolved in direct relation to technological advances. Paik's style was able to develop a video specificity as it moved from the manipulation of television at its "point of reception" to the "greater image manipulation" of global communications via satellite, as in his 1984 piece, *Good Morning Mr. Orwell*, in which a live dialogue between WNET TV in New York and the Centre Pompidou, was enabled by instant satellite transmission. A similar development can be seen in the two versions of Vasulka's *Violin Power*.

Early video technology was most often used to create intermedial connections between several disciplines—music, sculpture, performance and interactive art, and so on—and can thus be considered installational. Moreover, video's early freedom to reuse and combine material from any era resulted in an eclectic discipline suspended in a high-energy state of change. Marking the "rise of Postmodernism," video's early eclecticism can be read as the quintessential twentieth-century desire for originality, a search for novelty voiced by Paik's admission that "[m]y experimental television is not always interesting, but not always uninteresting: like nature, which is beautiful not because it changes beautifully, but simply because it changes."[105] Wittgenstein described art as a game whose rules are made up as the game is in process, and nowhere does this seem more apt than with the use of analogue video as an art form.[106] With each video artist-composer (and, further, with each piece made), the form appeared typified anew. In this respect, early video technology and its aesthetic uses were analogous: the technology with its endless process of becoming; and the ever-changing uses to which it was put.

The Double Lineage

In the discourse surrounding this "culture," there is a consensus that video represents a new beginning, or, at least, the beginning of new and radical possibilities. And while it is clearly linked to tendencies operating concurrently in music and art circles, it would seem that to define video art-music in a way beyond its technological basis is a confounding task. But a definition based on its materiality acknowledges only an equipment-orientated sphere of influence and postulates video as a closed system. Clearly this is not the case. Despite the fact that the early preoccupation with the television monitor as a sculptural object seemed to lead readily to this material-focused definition, the uses to which the equipment was put linked it clearly to concurrent work in other disciplines. Although Kaprow's rather scathing attack on video above seems to bow to the recurrently problematic relationship music and art hold with technology, he nevertheless makes an interesting point: beneath the technology, there lies an art form that connects itself to multiple well-trodden avenues. In support of video, John Wyver, a British TV producer, contends that when the format was newly available, its lack of funding, gallery support, or broadcast airtime meant that those working with the medium had to argue for its acceptance, a situation that pressed them into highlighting its novelty over its inclusive or symbiotic possibilities: such "concentration on video as video cuts the forms of video creation off from the rest of an increasingly dynamic and richly varied moving image culture."[107] Daniels argues further that striving for a definition based on video's materiality not only cuts off video work from the rest of "moving image culture," but actually holds negative connotations when considered against the multimedia embrace prevalent at the time in Fluxus events, expanded cinema, performance art, Happenings, and so on in fact, it encouraged "a retrograde step into terrain that has clearly been cordoned off again."[108]

Within contemporary art, argued Susan Sontag in 1966, there are "two principal radical positions" that remain irreconcilable. One supports the blurring of distinctions between disciplines in order to encourage a "vast behavioural magma or synaesthesis"; the other seeks to maintain discrete genres by highlighting "the intensification of what each art distinctively is."[109] Her statement is mirrored in the attempts to historicise early video work. While some voiced concern that the term "video art," as a definition based on equipment, prompted a "retrograde step" in an era of inclusivity, it is nevertheless important to remember that it was this technology that facilitated a flow of influence between media. From the outset, video's dialogues with other disciplines encouraged inclusivity, not isolation. The concerns of Daniels and others above that a label such as "video art" may suggest closure and autonomy are silenced once the complexity of video's multiple genealogies is considered.

However, with little to restrict the definition of video culture beyond its physical makeup and fondness for recontextualisation, the form has acquired an instability that poses a problem for philosophy of art, cultural studies, and aesthetics. Any critical attempt risks getting lost amongst video's multidisciplinarity: as Douglas M. Davis explains, "the new combine, art and technology, falling as it does between academic departments and between 'isms', particularly daunts us."[110] Indeed, whilst television culture, its power mechanisms, markets, ideological control, and representations of race, gender, and class, have been extensively dissected, only passing, fragmented evidence of video's fifty-year existence has appeared in media literature until recently. This silence is beginning to be addressed, with some major monographs on the better known video artists recently published, and the appearance of an increasing number of nuanced anthologies exploring and theorising video work.[111]

Perhaps it is better to speak about video's contextualisation in a different way: video offered to the world of twentieth-century music and art practices a new and syncretic way of voicing its ideas. Its revolutionary aspect lies in the ability to set ideas previously held in stasis or silence into motion and audibility; to combine audio and visual elements. The technology was revolutionary, in other words, precisely because of the expansion it enabled in preexistent disciplines. According to his discussion of "field perception" and his belief that "all the senses exist simultaneously in our bodies, interwoven into one system," Viola would perhaps see this coalescence as a humanisation of video. It is not, then, that video has no history: rather, because a single, traceable line of development is impossible to find, those working with video are able to claim an ancestry of assorted disciplines. It follows that the technological art form operates within a zone of maximum hybridity that gives it, in the words of Julie H. Reiss, a "resistance to historicization."[112] But this does not mean that it is an isolated, technology-dependent media that cannot be historically contextualised. In fact, such multidisciplinary "magma or synaesthesis" is every bit as revolutionary as the absence of a past.

Video's contextual and ancestral multiplicity can be simplified by channelling its diversity into two pathways—one visual, the other musical—two lines that echo the duality inherent in the technology. Distilling video thus will demonstrate that it is not the word "video" that becomes problematic when referring to the genre, but rather the word "art." To situate the genre etymologically within the visual arts is responsible for cordoning it off from its dual past and audiovisual present. What is needed is a reappraisal of the connotations of the term "art" in order to establish the audio as equal in importance as the visual. As we have seen, technologically speaking, the form is a sound-based media. While defining video work solely according to its technological peculiarities is inaccurate and belies its cooperative nature and achievements, as Wyver and Daniels warn, it is nevertheless undeniable that video's material quality has influenced the uses to which it is put. It led to an immediacy and dependence on live realisation akin to music; it allowed image to "burst into motion" and exist in music's "psychological dimension" to produce direct musico-visual emergence; and its ability to record music and image simultaneously gave birth to the hybrid being, the artist-composer. Moreover, video enabled an osmosis-like flow between disciplines, a flow particularly well suited to the multimedia sensibility prevalent during the early 1960s.

Given the clear audiovisual nature of video, it is rather astonishing that sound is often ignored in critical discussion. The tendency has been to approach the area from one standpoint at the exclusion of others, discussing, for example, video's Fluxus basis, digital mastery, analogies with film or sculptural tradition, and its similarity to other intermedial forms such as Happenings, performance art, site-specific installation, and so on. Usually this position is a visual one: rarely is music approached in a substantial manner. And yet an all-encompassing theory of video requires consideration beyond its visual and sculptural qualities into its synaes-thetic properties. The exceptions to this silence have already been noted. Belton, Viola, and Spielmann have identified the audio basis of video, for instance, while Hanhardt's monograph on Paik begins with an exploration of his musical back-ground. Refreshingly, he continues:

> Paik's shift in interest in composition and performance to an engage-ment with the material site of television as an instrument must be viewed less within a visual art context than in relation to the modalities of temporality and impermanence, as well as the conditions of industrial and postindustrial artistic production. It was at the juncture where the means of fabricating sound and image intersected that Paik struck a stra-tegic position in late-twentieth-century art.[113]

This is an important point: Paik's "strategic position" was not only an aesthetic one, it was also physical; *Exposition* represented the first time a television set was included in a gallery and marks the beginning of a sound-based genre into the art institution. And it was this convergence with music that provided the capac-ity for art to reach beyond its conventional limits in the mid-twentieth century, both creatively and institutionally. On the back of such a statement by one of Paik's most supportive curators, then, the critical silence surrounding the sound and music of video is astonishing. Although passing and fragmented analysis of video's sound can be found in art theoretical discussions of the genre as an open and fluid system, there has been hardly any engagement with the genre by musicologists.

But once video is recognised as a receptive intermedial system, a link to the historical lineage of each discipline it envelopes is established. These links can be visual and musical although, as shown above, the critical reception of video has tended to err on the side of the former. Yet even Paik himself seemed to suggest that video's immediate ancestry lies not in the visual arts, but rather within a musical lineage when he claimed that "[i]t is the historical necessity, if there is a historical necessity in history, that a new decade of electronic television should follow the past decade of electronic music."[114] While there is little precedent for an audiovisual art form, music and art practices can nevertheless be considered to have been working towards this fusion for many centuries (as we shall see in chap-ter 2). The story of video's hybridity, then, can be loosely plotted along two lines: one visual, the other musical. Far from having no past, the genre has a double his-tory and represents the cultural syncretism of music and art ancestries.

Nevertheless, any historical investigation into the origins of video art-music must acknowledge the *desire* for pastlessness espoused by many practitioners and critics. To put this another way: a theoretical approach to video's "culture" must acknowledge these multiple yet elusive histories, while at the same time treating them with a suspicion similar to that of the video artists and composers themselves. And yet, it is also important to note that these two positions are not mutually exclusive. Video *was* a new medium that enabled advances in terms of audiovisual dialogue: but behind the promise of synthesis lurked a dual aesthetic evolution. Resituating early video art at the intersection of music and art histories will recognise this double evolution without devaluing the unique syncretic ability of video: it will also prevent the "retrograde step" into discrete categorisation threatened when labelling video according to its technology by identifying the genre's multifarious ancestors and contemporary colleagues. As a culture—a "meta-media"—then, video art-music becomes compromised if viewed from only one perspective: rather, it necessitates a criticism that is as interdisciplinary as its subject, a theoretical approach that takes into account both the diversity and the historical/progressive duality of video. With this in mind, it is possible to rephrase Bartlett's enthusiastic exclamation that "a whole new story was about to be told thanks to the new techniques." If we relocate his emphasis from the tale to the telling, it can be suggested that, during the 1960s, there developed a whole new *way* of recounting well-known stories.

2

Silent Music and Static Motion

The Audiovisual History of Video

> We want to incorporate the universe in the work of art.
> Individual objects do not exist anymore.
> (Gino Severini)[1]

In 1965, video was a new technology. When used as an artistic tool, it extended existing experimentation in conceptual and process art, music composition, and sound art to produce fresh forms of intermediality and expanded modes of collective creativity. In chapter 1, we saw how those working with video during its earliest years used the audiovisual technology to extend their existing work in other disciplines, such as music, sculpture, painting, and even engineering, leading to a "genealogy" of the medium that André Gaudreault and Philippe Marion have called its period of "constitution" and Yvonne Spielmann its "integrating birth."[2] According to Gaudreault, Marion, and Spielmann, a medium's constitution is the time it takes for a technology to assert its media specificity in relation to contemporary practices. During its journey of self-reflexivity, video, acting as a facilitator of intermedial discourse, presented a solution to the boundaries between art and music that had existed—and been challenged—for centuries. While video provided audiovisual opportunities for artists and musicians during the late '60s, then, the medium can be placed on an old and well-trodden path that goes back to the earliest recorded artistic endeavours.

Audiovisual interaction now pervades our home life via film, television programmes, music videos and computer games: the internet is saturated with musical pop-ups; many websites include a soundtrack when opened; and phone and tablet apps allow us to participate in interactive audiovisuality wherever we are. The interaction of music with moving image has become a part of our daily lives, with a prevalence and power that makes it difficult to imagine a time when it did not exist. But although attempts at sound-image fusion can be found long before the advent of film, video art-music, the internet, gaming or apps, these endeavours were often thwarted by technological restrictions, aesthetic challenges, or both. Throughout history, the *desire* to achieve artistic synthesis has moved in and out of favour. While medieval and early modern artists, musicians, and architects sought a transmedial holisticism defined in part by parallel philosophical objectives working towards theological harmony, Enlightenment thinkers, such as Gotthold Lessing, promoted a separation of the arts into discrete entities. Although an obvious exception to this separation was music for the stage, in which the practice of fusing together music, image, and literature can be traced through French grand opera and at least back to the late eighteenth century, in other disciplines a certain specialisation occurred as the arts became more and more isolated, their uses and places of execution becoming increasingly distinct from one another. Music and art, in other words, became less amenable to mixture. The search for a *Gesamtkunstwerk* (or total work of art) by Wagner and others during the nineteenth century saw a move back towards a merging of disciplines, a search for a unity larger than the sum of its parts. Wagner considered opera a unity in which no one art was subservient to another. For him, the separate branches of the arts—music, architecture, poetry, dance, and painting—when united around drama, could produce a synthesising, or "totalising" effect:[3]

> In this Drama, each separate art can only bare its utmost secret to their common public through a mutual parleying with the other arts; for the purpose of each separate branch of art can only be fully attained by the reciprocal agreement and co-operation of all the branches in their common message.[4]

Wagner's theorising of the *Gesamtkunstwerk* took into account not only the compositional coexistence of all his materials, but also the staging of the final score. So important did he consider the realisation of his music drama, that in 1876 he opened his own theatre (*Festspielhaus*) in Bayreuth, in which he could control every aspect of the performance, as we shall see in the following chapter. Important innovations in this theatre included the placement of the orchestra out of sight, the dimming of the lights in order to focus attention more thoroughly on the stage action, and a preference for Greek amphitheatrical seating in order to focus all eyes on the stage. Wagner's ideas had a profound effect on subsequent art forms as diverse as film (in the 1950s, cinematographer Morton Heilig proposed a "cinema of the future" that would "faithfully reproduce man's outer world as perceived in his consciousness"), the immersive and virtual worlds of video art-music and cyberspace, and the audiovisual interactivity of computer games.[5] Moreover, histories of installation art (such as that in the *Grove Dictionary of Art*) frequently cite Wagner and his notion of "immersion" as providing a fundamental step towards the multidimensional art form.[6]

Coexisting with these drives to produce a "mutual parleying" of the arts during the twentieth century, however, were numerous counterattacks and retreats into autonomy. In his book, *Untwisting the Serpent: Modernism in Music, Literature and Other Arts*, Daniel Albright weaves the ebb and flow of media coordination into the reception chronicle of the mythical Greek character Laocoön.[7] One of the best sources for the myth is the *Aeneid*, where Laocoön, a Trojan priest of Apollo (although some think Poseidon), famously warned the people of Troy against bringing the wooden horse into the city: "Have no faith in the horse! / Whatever it is, even when Greeks bring gifts / I fear them, gifts and all." Hurling a spear into the giant horse's leg, however, Laocoön enraged the gods, who sent two giant sea serpents to strangle the priest and two of his sons:

> At the same time he raised to the stars
> hair-raising shouts like the roars of a bull
> when it flees wounded from a sacrificial altar
> and shakes the ineffectual axe from its neck.[8]

In 1506, a marble statue depicting the horrific death, thought to have been created during the Hellenistic age, was discovered in Rome. Known as *Laocoön and his Sons*, the sculpture depicts the Trojan priest facing death with face uncontorted, his mouth only slightly open. At the start of his book, Albright reviews the critical literature that has focused on the visual and textual depictions of this anguished character, beginning with Lessing's *Laocoön: An Essay on the Limits of Painting and Poetry* of 1766.[9] The first to highlight the Laocoön problem, Lessing contrasted Virgil's screaming protagonist with the calmer, less-contorted sculpted version, noting that the half-open mouth of the statue rendered impossible the production of "hair-raising shouts." Why do the poem and the statue depict Laocoön's death cry so differently? Lessing used these opposing evocations to highlight the difference in artistic and aesthetic ability between the visual and literary arts. According to him, a scream cannot be portrayed sculpturally because the result would be too ugly for an art form dedicated to beauty: "The wide naked opening of the mouth—leaving aside how violently and disgustingly it distorts and shoves aside the rest of the face—becomes in a painting a spot and in a sculpture a hollow, making the most repulsive effect."[10] Poetry, however, not bound by the same visual customs, could well evoke a character roaring like a bull.

Lessing used this comparison as a basis by which to divide the arts into complementary domains whose borders, according to him, should remain intact: the temporal, sequential media like music or poetry, or what he called the arts of *Nacheinander*; and the juxtapositive forms such as painting and sculpture, or what he called the arts of *Nebeneinander*:[11]

> This essential difference between [poetry and the visual arts] is found in that the former is a visible progressive act, the various parts of which take place little by little [*nach und nach*] in the sequence of time; whereas the latter is a visible static act, the various parts of which develop next to one another [*neben einander*] in space.[12]

While sculpture and painting must observe the decorum of space, Lessing maintains, poetry is necessarily bound by the teleological thrust of its delivery. This space-time divide prevents the arts from accurately coalescing: to attempt fusion is futile. Subsequent critics who have also highlighted the Laocoön predicament to voice disdain for the crossing of medial borderlines include Irving Babbitt who, in *The New Laokoon: An Essay on the Confusion of the Arts* (ca. 1910), attacked Strauss's dependence on extramusical imitation and Wagner's drive for a mystical and unified *Gesamtkunstwerk*.[13] Even more stringent in its attack of transmedial fusion is Clement Greenberg's 1940 paper, "Towards a Newer Laocoon." Greenberg condemns as "artistic dishonesty" the practice of one medium taking the effects of another in order to escape the problems and limitations inherent in its own materiality: as an example of such dishonesty, he cites Shelley's exaltation of poetry as a medium that came closest to "being no medium at all."[14] Against this he posits avant-garde art, praising its emphasis on the substantiality—or "opacity"—of its materials without recourse to a secondary medium for elucidation:

> The history of avant-garde painting is that of a progressive surrender to the resistance of its medium; which resistance consists chiefly in the flat picture plane's denial of efforts to "hole through" it for realistic perspectival space.... The motto of the Renaissance artist, *Ars est artem celare* [Art is the concealing of art], is exchanged for *Ars est artem demonstrare* [Art is the manifesting of art].[15]

Such "surrender to the resistance of its medium" can be found not only within single-media works, but also within multimedia collaborations from both before and after Greenberg's attack. The 1917 ballet *Parade* is an example in which, rather than draw holistically together, the many elements collide in intentional discord. The sets (Picasso), scenario (Cocteau), choreography (Massine), and music (Satie) retain their "opacity," appearing on the surface to have little to do with one another, a dissonance that Apollinaire, in his programme notes, famously describes as "a kind of super-realism [*sur-réalisme*]"; "an integral schematization that would seek to reconcile contradictions while sometimes deliberately renouncing any rendering of the immediate outward aspect of the object."[16] Instead of seeking a higher unity, or *Gesamtkunstwerk*, in other words, the creators of *Parade* allowed each art form to resonate in autonomous dissonance with the next when performed by Diaghilev's Ballets Russes, an example not of artistic convergence, but rather of a dialogical divergence. Although underpinned by a different aesthetic, the Fluxus events that began appearing during the 1960s used a similar method of eclecticism and media antagonism: music, chance actions, found objects, the spoken word, the guttural utterance, noise, paint, sculpture, and video commingled in an interactive multimedia environment that operated through the "accumulation" of contradictory elements (Spielmann).[17]

While Lessing's argument is operable in the specific—his comparative reading of poem and sculpture *is* convincing—he nevertheless fails to recognise the innate interpermeable nature of all arts. According to him, music, as a "progressive act" that takes place "in the sequence of time" exists in a dimension fundamentally different to that of arts of *Nebeneinander*, such as painting and sculpture, which are "visible static" acts: these dimensions, he claims, cannot be united without recourse to what Greenberg, along similar lines of reasoning, later described as "artistic dishonesty." Yet Lessing's reading is one based on an aesthetic assumption that the arts exist beyond the real world; that they somehow transcend their own modes of execution. But if we take the creation of music and image into account, then it becomes much harder to separate the audio from the visual.

Live music performance (at least before the digital age), for instance, is always gestural, requiring at least one performer and her movement to sound the music (recording of course negates the gestural, but back to this later). As Richard Leppert explains:

> [T]he slippage between the physical activity to produce musical sound and the abstract nature of what is produced creates a semiotic contradiction that is ultimately "resolved" to a significant degree via the agency of human sight. Music, despite its phenomenological sonoric ethereality, is an embodied practice, like dance and theatre.[18]

An integral part of the live experience, the sight of music is emphasised differently by different traditions. The use of notation—a different sort of musical imaging—in Western art music has led to the belief, for instance, that here, gesture is not as important to the notion of the "work" as it is to orally transmitted traditions such as traditional and popular musics or jazz, a notion recently contended by musicologists. Several radical denunciations of this position can be found in the 1960s and 70s. Taking gesture to its extreme, Helmut Lachenmann experimented with making the physical production of sound the content of his work. His theory of a *musique concrète instrumentale* proposed unorthodox playing techniques in order to create a form of found sound from traditional instruments ("the musical sound," he said in an interview, "may be bowed, pressed, beaten, torn, maybe choked, rubbed, perforated and so on") that would defamiliarise traditional technique, a manifesto according to which the materials and energies used to create the music became equally, if not more important, than the sonoric result: "the classical base-parameters, such as pitch, duration, timbre, volume, and their derivatives retain their significance only as subordinate aspects of the compositional category which deals with the manifestation of energy."[19] To produce such music often required of the performers extraordinary exertion, such as that of the cellist in Lachenmann's *Pression* (1969), who is asked to sound the instrument by drawing the bow across the body, bridge, and muted strings to produce screeching, scrubbing noises. The production of sound, in other words, is highlighted (see video 2.1▶). As we shall see in chapter 5, Nam June Paik took the emphasis of gesture one stage further in his work with Charlotte Moorman at around the same time. The video artist-composer clad his performer in television screens wired up to look and sound like a cello—the *TV Cello* (1971)—thus closing the gap between gesture and sound by making Moorman both performer and instrument.

Withholding a performer from view can also have a profound impact on an audience. The offstage trumpets ("placed in the far distance") announcing the Apocalypse in the fifth movement of Mahler's Symphony No. 2 ("Resurrection", 1888–1894), the acousmatic boys' choir in Britten's *War Requiem* (op. 66, 1961), and numerous examples of "unsung voices" in opera, for instance, were used to suggest emotion too big to encounter unmediated, or an ethereality that could suggest a higher presence.[20] In a way akin to Pythagoras's method of teaching from behind a curtain to hide the frailty of the human form (a method famously flouted in *The Wizard of Oz*, 1939 [see video 2.2▶]) while mimicking the invisibility of God, such *acousmêtre* could attain great power. However, in other instances, an absence of visible gesture could leave an audience disquieted. When gestural necessity was resisted in the electronic music of the Cologne School, where works such as Stockhausen's tape piece *Studie 1* for sine tones (1953), his self-proclaimed "first purely electronic piece," required no human stage presence (apart, perhaps, from someone to press "play"), the action needed to create the music (even electronically) was displaced to a previous time.[21] This absence led to a greater sense of unease in the audience and performances by the School were widely criticised for their lack of human qualities. Conlon Nancarrow's work for the player piano came under similar scrutiny. The rhythmic complexity of much of his music made it impossible to perform with any accuracy. In response to the technical demands, Nancarrow wrote much of his work for the mechanical player piano, a move that dehumanised the performance of the music and made the pianist notable by her absence (see video 2.3▶).[22] However, in this case, it was not only the visual lack of a human presence during a performance that created unease; the absence of performer nuance also generated auditory difficulties. Research has shown that listeners find perfectly realised rhythm unsettling: "the ear perceives absolute regularity as awkward and artificial" explains Jonathan D. Kramer, an accusation Nancarrow found difficult to understand:

> I am amazed that most people who object to the nonhuman element in computer music or in the player piano have no objection to a Shakespeare sonnet, for example. That sonnet has remained the same over the centuries. No one suggests it should be changed by a new performance. A painting stays the same forever. The same is true of other works of art. But somehow music is supposed to be different all the time.[23]

The desire for difference has recently been articulated by several musicologists. Carolyn Abbate, for instance, has called for a "drastic" rather than a "gnostic" conception of music. According to her, retreating to the "souvenir" of music (the work) is a "way of domesticating" the "wild" experience of the individual acoustic instantiation. More exciting would be to replace analytical interest in the score (what Abbate calls the "supra-audible") with the sensual immediacy of live performance.[24] Latent in her plea is a call for performativity, an inclusion of the tangible and visual side of music within score-based analysis.

When the recording industry enabled home listening, similar issues were raised: what would happen when performance became disembodied, when the visual gesture was made acousmatic? Paradoxically, as recorded music became popular, the result was, for many traditions, an increased emphasis on a performer's image. Particularly true in popular music, this was apparent from the early appearances of rock 'n' roll musicians on television. Two "wild" and gestural performances of "Elvis-the-Pelvis," on *The Ed Sullivan Show* (1956) led to such a barrage of viewer complaints that when the singer returned for a third performance in January 1957, the show refused to film below his waist. During the 1980s, the popular music trade responded to the image-crazed masses with the music video, an artificial and highly creative reimaging of a song's performance that thrust appearance and dance routines into the forefront of the music community's consciousness. To some extent, the visual side of popular music can be said to have equalled, if not overtaken, the sonic side, a point bemoaned by Liam and Noel Gallagher of *Oasis* who, in their 1995 appearance on *Top of the Pops*, highlighted the absurdity of being asked to mime to their own song ("Roll With It") by exchanging roles and instruments to produce a clear audiovisual rupture. Nevertheless, the image of a popular musician in particular remains of paramount importance to their success, as their prominent presence in the fashion magazines attests: for many, Lady Gaga's outfits are more memorable than her music, while the platform shoes sported by Ginger Spice in the '90s were influential in raising many of the UK's teenagers (this author included) an extra foot off the ground. The performative gesture—or the embodied performance—then, remains a highly desirable element of the musical experience.

Static Music

Traditionally, visual art has had less to do with performance. But just as music is visual as well as auditory, art does not exist in a silent vacuum: on the contrary, both its exhibition and creation produce and encourage audible accompaniment. People do not view artwork in total silence, for instance. While galleries tend to be hushed places, they are nevertheless awash with voluntary and involuntary sounds. In his project *Audio Recordings of Great Works of Art: The Aural Aura of Masterworks* (1989–1999), sound artist Ed Osborn investigated the acoustic/sonic environment of silent objects. Making the "silence" of the art gallery the substance of this sound piece, Osborn recorded the noises surrounding thousands of artworks chosen according to certain criteria, including fame and location.[25] His recording of the *Mona Lisa*'s environment in the Louvre was particularly noisy:

generating large crowds, the painting was constantly surrounded by the sound of chatter, footsteps, camera shutters, and zoom lenses.

In terms of creation, the sound of painting has been highlighted in many films depicting the lives of artists including Derek Jarman's *Caravaggio* (1986), Ed Harris's *Pollock* (2000), and Peter Webber's *The Girl with the Pearl Earring* (2003); all of which feature the amplified, even musical, noise of brush strokes on canvas heard as though through the ears of the artist (see video 2.4▶). These sounds of production have even been embodied, or distilled in works themselves: Jackson Pollock's action paintings visually signify the process used to create his pictures, for instance, as for him the canvas was a place not for the reproduction, analysis, or expression of an object, but rather as a place in which to perform and record an action.[26] Similarly, when working, the artists themselves are enveloped in sound: people outside, music on the radio or, as Peter Blake once claimed, an endless soundtrack of The Beach Boys, a sonic ambience that complimented his pop art style. Others made their own soundtrack; Delacroix and Mengs famously whistled while painting to create the right atmosphere for their images.[27] Surrounding sound has also been distilled within paintings to visually conjure forth the acoustic ambience that engulfed the working artist: Umberto Boccioni's *[The Noise of] the Street Enters the House (La Strada entra nella casa)* (1911) is an obvious example (fig. 2.1).

Figure 2.1 Umberto Boccioni, *La strada entra nella casa* (1911). Photo by Michael Herling/Aline Gwose. Courtesy of Sprengel Museum Hannover.

Leppert has made several studies of music's visual representation in art: "[m]usic's effects and meanings, which in performance are produced both aurally *and* visually, in painting must be rendered visually only. The way of seeing hence incorporates the way of hearing."[28] As such, paintings of music performance can be a richly informative iconographic tool, not only in terms of performance practice, but also as a sociological resource. While unable to replicate, or represent, a particular piece of music (unless a title or decipherable notation is discernible), visual art can nevertheless "provide an invaluable hortatory account of what, how, and why a given society heard and hence in part what the sounds meant."[29] Through his reading of William Holman Hunt's *The Awakening Conscience* (1853), Leppert demonstrates how a "range of semiotic possibilities for specific compositions performed under conditions similar to those represented" is offered, with clues to music's role in society embedded in the images.[30] It follows that we can invert his previous statement: art, despite its silence, can be a sonically "embodied" practice.

Music, then, is gestural: when disembodied, it can be revisualised, the audio-visual "relationship or dialogue" repaired. Similarly, the soundworld of an artist can be rendered visually through a painting latent with residual sound. But what of the practical attempts at uncovering a transmediating thread between media? What of the less literal rendering of visible music and audible art: the translation of pure sound into static image? Despite Lessing's dislike for the mixture of the *Nacheinander* and *Nebeneinander* arts, many attempts were nevertheless made to cross the borders between spatial and temporal media, often with very positive results. Such attempts seek what Albright calls "*figures of consonance*" that operate on the assumption that there is "a deep concord" among artistic media, or what Francis Picabia put somewhat more simply in the title of his 1914–1917 piece, *Music is Like Painting* (*La Musique est comme la peinture*).[31] While music performance can be "rendered visually" and used to reconstruct a socially motivated music-making practice, painting can also encapsulate the more ethereal, less referential, even structural qualities of music itself. In 1895, for instance, Paul Gauguin theorised the distinct lack of media "opacity" in his work:

> Everything in my work is calculated and long considered. This is music if you please! Through arrangements of lines and colours, under the pretext of some theme from life or nature, I arrive at symphonies and harmonies that evince nothing absolutely real in the usual sense of the word and express no ideas, but are meant to provoke thought, like music...simply through mysterious affinities between our brains and such arrangements of lines and colours.[32]

In the necessary abstraction of visualising metaphorical sound rather than musical gesture—the invisible "drastic" event—such works became more prominent during the twentieth century. Many paintings were entitled with symbolic and abstract allusions to musical types, forms, or genres: Augusto Giacometti's *Chromatic Fantasy* (1914); Johannes Itten's *Bluish-Green Sound* (*Blaugrüner Klang*) (1917); and Hans Richter's *Orchestration of Colour* (*Orchestration der Farbe*) (1923) to name but a few.

While these examples can be seen as offering a rather vague audiovisual discourse predicated on what Gauguin referred to as "mysterious affinities" between media, other artists attempted to translate, or transpose, specific compositions into visual representation.[33] Perhaps the most precisely translated is Gustav Klimt's *Beethoven Frieze* (1902) housed in the Secession Building, Vienna, a visual response to Beethoven's Ninth Symphony that traverses what he calls a "coherent sequence" spread over three panels, taking the viewer from "Longing for Happiness," through "The Hostile Powers" and onto "Longing for Happiness finds Repose in Poetry" (fig. 2.2).[34] By producing a "coherent sequence," or chronology, Klimt gave directions to the viewer, who, in order to experience the entire work, is required to move along these panels. In this way, the artist attempted to resolve the incompatibility between the sequential and spatial arts: although the various parts develop next to one another in space, the *Beethoven Frieze* also takes place, "little by little" through time, as Lessing would say.

However, Lessing had voiced his disdain for attempts by one art form to move artificially into the realm of another. A lengthy poem describing a flower was, according to him, an unnatural use of the poetic medium, as its simulation required great labour, whereas a painter could achieve the same description with ease.[35] Later, Adorno would voice a similar sentiment. While the contributions of Lessing, Greenberg, and others to the Laocoön debate centred largely on the literary and visual arts, they included negligible discussion of music: in fact, it was not until Adorno's *Philosophie der neuen Musik* was published in 1949 that the interaction between music and the other arts was critically considered. Voicing his dislike for the music of Stravinsky, Adorno claimed that the composer worked like a cubist

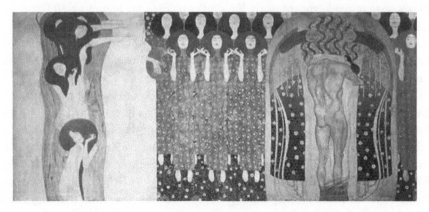

Figure 2.2 Gustav Klimt, *Beethoven Frieze* (1902) at the Vienna Secession Building.

painter: "the spatialisation of music is witness to a pseudomorphosis of music to painting, on the innermost level an abdication."[36] His concept of "pseudomorphosis" succinctly sums up Lessing's criticism of poetry that attempts to conjure forth clear visual images: the derisive term was used to describe the endeavour of one art form to use the tools of another without regard for the media specificity of the word, image, or sound. It was pseudomorphosis that silenced Laocoön's sculptural scream. In terms of content, however, the mediation between the abstraction of Beethoven's symphony and Klimt's detailed visual narration is more a response or homage than a simple reiteration. Such homage can also operate conversely, as was demonstrated in Debussy's 1903–1905 symphonic sketch *The Sea*, inspired by Hokusai's woodblock print *The Great Wave* (1830–1832): although working from the same common denominator, the artist and the composer did not continue to tell exactly the same tale; rather, each transmedial interpretation was unique to their respective tools.

A less literal attempt to distill a piece into an image occurred several years later between two contemporaries. Kandinsky allied his stylistic abstraction to the newly emerging compositional style of Schönberg, in particular his Quartet No.2, op.10 (1907–1908) and his *Three Piano Pieces*, op. 11 (1909). Upon hearing the quartets performed, Kandinsky wrote to the composer (18 January 1911):

> In your works, you have realised what I, albeit in uncertain form, have so greatly longed for in music. The independent progress through their own destinies, the independent life of the individual voices in your compositions, is exactly what I am trying to find in my paintings ... I am certain that our own modern harmony is not to be found in the "geometric" way [of cubism] but rather in the antigeometric, antilogical way, and this way is that of "dissonances in art," in painting, therefore, just as much as in music.[37]

In response to the keyboard work, Kandinsky painted his *Impression III (Concert)* (1911), in which the overpowering black section signals both at a representational level (as the piano on which it was performed) and at a more nonreferential level as, in his own words, "like a dead void after the extinguishment of the sun, like a profound silence....It is, in musical terms, a full, concluding rest."[38] In Kandinsky's reading of Schönberg, there is an attempt to embody time in a single instant rather than to stretch out his images along a linear trajectory as Klimt had done. Instead of attempting literally to move painting into the temporal, in other words, Kandinsky condensed *Three Piano Pieces* into a single spatial moment that was nevertheless alive with movement and a *sense* of time. In 1914, Ezra Pound, when considering the possibility of instantaneity in a long poem, looked to Japanese Noh theatre for inspiration: "In the best 'Noh' the whole play may consist of one image," he explains; "I mean it is gathered about one image. Its unity consists in one image, enforced by movement and music."[39] Albright describes the

Noh play as a "*magnified version of a single aesthetic particle*" and this is a good way in which to view Kandinsky's concurrent representational and nonrepresentational reaction to Schönberg's concert.[40] This is perhaps what Karajan meant when he claimed that he knew Beethoven's Fifth Symphony so well that, in his mind, the piece collapsed into simultaneity, observable in an instant.[41]

To a certain extent these translations, however well explained and rationalised, nevertheless remain metaphorical. Similarly metaphorical is the appropriation of musical forms into painted compositions; structural attempts at combining *Nacheinander* and *Nebeneinander* arts. Such endeavours elucidate Lessing's fears and Adorno's scathing idea of the pseudomorphic to a greater extent than the interpretative, narrativising examples above, as they are concerned with the translation of technique, rather than idea, from one medium to another. One way to do this involved the use of musical structure as an aesthetic organisational device: Marcel Duchamp's *Sonata* (1911), or Franz Marc's Sonatina for Violin and Piano (*Sonatine für Geige und Klavier*) (1913) are just two examples. More concrete was the attempt to paint according to musical form and, in particular, according to polyphonic types, such as the fugue. Such efforts were certainly not a twentieth-century phenomenon, but can be seen as early as the turn of the nineteenth century, when Philipp Otto Runge experimented with painting a figurative image according to the fugal principle of imitation: in a letter to his brother, 4 August 1802, Runge claimed that his work in progress, *Lesson of the Nightingale* (completed 1804–1805) represented "the same thing as a fugue is in music."[42] Nevertheless, during the twentieth century, the possibility of creating a visual fugue really took hold (Mikalojus Konstantinas Čiurlionis, *Prelude and Fugue* (1907); Kandinsky, *Fugue (Controlled Impression)* (*Fuga [Beherrschte Impression]*) (1914); Adolf Hölzel, *Fugue (on a Resurrection Theme)* (*fuge [Über ein Auferstehungsthema]*) (1916); and Alexei von Javlensky, *Fugue in Blue and Red* (*Fuge in Blau und Rot*) (1936) are but a few examples). In 1912, František Kupka theorised the kinetic dimension that informed paintings such as his *Amorpha: Fugue in Two Colours* (*Fugue à deux couleurs*) (completed in 1912), in which red and blue "voices" intertwine to create metaphorical motion: "By using a form in various dimensions and arranging it according to rhythmical considerations, I will achieve a 'symphony' which develops in space as a symphony does in time."[43] Kupka here talks about spatialising the fugal concept rather than temporalising the painted surface, his notion of rhythm manifesting itself in purely metaphorical terms. As such, these quasimusical paintings can be differentiated from the work of artists intent on capturing as closely as possible movement and time on canvas. In the same year as Kupka completed his *Amorpha*, for instance, Giacomo Balla introduced *The Hand of the Violinist* (or *Rhythm of the Violinist*) (*La mano del violinista-Ritmi del violinista*) (1912), a painting clearly intent on exploring the Futurists' concept of the "multiple-phase" image, whereby the movement of a subject is depicted in sequential, superimposed, stills.[44]

Slightly later, yet in a similar vein to Kupka, Klee theorised the transition from musical to visual structure in terms of "polyphonic painting." By layering areas of colour on top of one another to create "many voices," Klee developed diagrams of three- and four-part polyphonies, visible in *Swinging, Polyphonic (And a Complementary Repeat)* (1931) and *Dynamic-Polyphonic Group* (1931). Speaking about his earlier watercolour *Fugue in Red (Fuge in Rot)* (1921), he described how the idea of visual polyphonic imitation worked (fig. 2.3). The picture, he explained:

> shows a floating progression of colours and forms, including both rec-ognisable objects and forms abstracted from them (leaf, vase, rhombus, rectangle, triangle, circle) overlapping in many layers, in colour values ranging from light to dark. The temporal element is clearly indicated by the way the mass of forms looms out of the dark background, becom-ing increasingly more brilliant until finally achieving the brightest of colours.[45]

Had Greenberg considered *Fugue in Red*, he would surely have deemed it a case of "artistic dishonesty," condemning it, as he did Shelley's poetry, for being like "no medium at all." And yet, Klee's "polyphonic painting," while attempting to emu-late temporal and simultaneous linearity, nevertheless pertains to Greenberg's

Figure 2.3 Paul Klee, *Fugue in Red (Fuge in Rot)* (1921).

preference for the motto *Ars est artem demonstrare* over that of the Renaissance *Ars est artem celare*. Here, Klee highlights the painted surface, his rhythms not only clearly articulating the manifesting of art, but also the manifesting of the *process* of art. In attempting to capture fugal movement, in other words, Klee highlights, rather than disguises, the "opacity" of his medium, using music as a secondary media not for elucidation, but rather in order to draw attention to the specificity of the painted form and its limitations.

Hearing Sound and Seeing Colour

While the above examples are largely metaphorical, many artists and composers attempted a more systematic audiovisual correspondence. One correlation came in the form of tone and colour associations, a relationship with a long and complex history that encompasses esoteric, cognitive, and quasiscientific scrutiny. Tone-colour connections have been important to many cultures, and early colour-cosmic-numerical associations can be found from Indian philosophy to Isaac Newton's *Optiks* (1704), for instance. However, there are those biologically enabled few whose cognitive wiring allows such tone-colour correspondence to occur naturally. For synaesthetes, this relationship is not a matter of rational or esoteric theorisation, but is, rather, the result of a natural conjoining of the senses.[46]

A phenomenon first recognised by the ancient Greeks, synaesthesia is the cognitive connection between any two senses that occurs spontaneously. The concurrence of music and colour is the most commonly experienced, with Scriabin, Rimsky-Korsakov, Messiaen, and Ligeti amongst those displaying (or at least claiming to experience) symptoms of the condition. Messiaen explained that:

> I am affected by a sort of Synaesthesia of the mind rather than of the body, which allows me, when I hear a piece of music, and also when I read it, to see internally, through the mind's eye, colours which move with the music; and I feel these colours extremely vividly, and sometimes in my scores I have even indicated precisely the correspondences.[47]

Mentions of blue and orange chords can be found in the piano part of the second movement of his *Quatuor pour la fin du temps* (1940–1941), while a footnote in *Catalogue des oiseaux* (1958) explains that "The chords ought to have a sonority akin to a stained-glass window with orange dominating and complimented by specks of blue."[48] In his research into Messiaen's colour-sound works, Jonathan Bernard discovered that the associations proved largely consistent between pieces, although he also found a disparity between the composer's early works, in which the sound-colour relationship was one predicated on absolute pitch, and his later music, where colour is linked with specific chord spacings.[49] In the preface to *Couleurs de la cité céleste* (1963), the form of which "depends entirely on colours," Messiaen set out instructions for the conductor: "I have noted the names of these colours on the score in order to communicate the vision to the conductor, who will, in turn, transmit this vision to the players he is conducting: it is essential, I would go so far as to say, that the brass 'play red', that the wood-wind 'play blue', etc."[50] The composer's desire was for an audience to experience his music in the way that he had done during its creation; to be able to feel the visual hues of his piece. Distinctive here is the notion of a single-authored work: Messiaen's music does not provide a reaction to a preexistent work, as in Klimt's *Beethoven Frieze*; nor does it base itself around a structural device borrowed from a different discipline, as in Klee's *Fugue in Red*. Rather, united at its point of creation, the problems inherent in the combination of the arts of *Nacheinander* with those of *Nebeneinander* are sidestepped.

However, Nicholas Cook points out that, in fact, Messiaen enabled his listeners to experience "only half of the multimedia experience he imagined, a kind of one-dimensional shadow of a multidimensional whole."[51] While the composer considered his work an audiovisual coalescence, the audience nevertheless encounters only the sounds, whether or not they are based on visual relationships: "Where does that leave us, the listeners?"[52] Cook asks what happens if we, as an audience, fail to "hear these colours;" if they have no aesthetic influence on our aural experience, "can we really claim to have heard the music at all?"[53] The same question can be asked of Klee's polyphonic paintings, or Klimt's *Beethoven Frieze*: if we fail "to see these sounds," have we really seen the art?

Earlier, Scriabin had attempted to address this problem in performance. Unlike Messiaen, Scriabin's association of colour and music was not based on individual notes, but rather on keys (key areas came with a long history of emotional responses). The colour scale was placed on the cycle of fifths, running from C major (red), G major (orange), D major (yellow), and so forth.[54] Leonid Sabaneev, however, hypothesised that Scriabin saw only three colours naturally: red, yellow, and blue (which he heard as F-sharp); the others "he deduced rationally."[55] Not only did he predicate his compositional process on (at least some) synaesthetic correlations, he also required that colours be projected in performance so that the audience could also experience the correspondence: so that they could not fail to "hear these colours." The composer described his synaesthetic colour-classification system, in which the tones of the chromatic scale were linked to specific colours, as enabling a "reunion of the arts separated over the course of time."[56] Although the validity of his ability has been questioned, one of Scriabin's most clearly articulated tone-colour experiments is found in his last orchestral work, *Prométhée, le poème du feu* (op. 60, 1910), a piece for orchestra, piano, voice, and a *clavier à lumières*.[57] At the top of his score, Scriabin notated two lines for the *clavier* on a light stave (*luce*). Although *Prométhée* was premiered in Moscow in 1911 without visual accompaniment (the equipment was not ready), its first performance in Carnegie Hall, New York on 20 March 1915 by the Russian Symphony Orchestra, conducted by Modest Altschuler, included projections by a coloured bulb light-manual on a small screen. The reviews, however, were not enthusiastic:

> During the performance the lights in the auditorium were extinguished, and a white sheet at the back of the platform and above the heads of the players was illuminated by streaks and spots of light of various colours which had no possible connection with the music, but which served to divert the sense of the audience from a too concentrated attention on the music.[58]

Another critic described the premiere as merely a "pretty poppy show."[59]

The first reviewer's comment—that the "various colours" had "no possible connection with the music"—is a feature to which Cook also turns his attention: "the very fact that the *luce* part is notated on a musical stave subordinates colour to musical principles," he writes.[60] In fact, Cook fails to find any convincing "internal rationale" for Scriabin's colour sequence, reading the lack of association between the two *luce* parts as suggesting that the composer "has simply subordinated his colours to a principle that is not so much musical as notational, and that he has done so without regard to its perceptual effect."[61] This lack of correlation between work and its realisation could be due to Scriabin's partial synaesthesia, which required the composer to rationally deduce audiovisual connections from the outset. Regardless of these problems, however, attempts to realise the *luce* part have been diverse, ranging from each member of the audience holding a piece of reflective tin foil (Yale Symphony Orchestra, under John Mauceri, 1971), a twenty-five-foot inflatable balloon lit from within (The Residentie Orkest under Michael Gielen in the Scheveningen Kurzall, The Netherlands, March 1973), onto a forest of suspended, moving chords (Leeds Town Hall, October 1983), and computer images projected on five screens showing both lines of *luce* notation (Håkon Austbø and the Luce Foundation, September 2005).

Although Kandinsky has also been deemed a pseudo-synaesthete, his efforts to translate Schönberg's music into colours and shapes mentioned above nevertheless resulted in intriguing audiovisual analogies that were different again from the cognitive conjoining of Scriabin and Messiaen.[62] In his Bauhaus lectures, he compared human nerves to the strings on a piano: if a note is hit on one piano, he explained, then the corresponding string of another situated nearby will also vibrate.[63] Kandinsky took this idea further in his autobiographical paper, *Rückblicke* (1913), in which he compared his memory of a Moscow sunset with a performance of Wagner's *Lohengrin*:

> *Lohengrin* seems to me to be a perfect realization of this Moscow. The violins, the deep bass tones, and especially the wind instruments embodied the entire force of the early evening hour for me back then. I saw all my colors in my mind, they appeared before my eyes. Wild, almost mad

lines drew themselves in front of me. I did not dare to state in so many words that Wagner had painted "my hour" in music. But it became absolutely clear to me that art in general was much more powerful than I had thought.[64]

Those powers were evoked in his subsequent painting through the association of colours with certain instruments or sonorous qualities: for him, orange evoked the sound of a viola, with its "warm alto voice"; yellow conjured up the strident and declamatory nature of the trumpet; and green suggested the "sustained meditative tones of the violin."[65] Kandinsky predicated his sounding colours on the theosophical theory of electrical vibrations emitted from particular thoughts or feelings, vibrations that could be experienced through colour and shape. According to the artist, for instance, trumpet yellow has an aggressive character and "may be paralleled in human nature with madness."[66] When an artist composes a picture, his or her feelings manifest themselves within it; the colours and shapes then broadcast such vibrations to the viewer, who experiences the painting as though it were a musical source transmitting sound: "Colour is the keyboard, the eyes are the hammers, the soul is the piano with many strings. The artist is the hand which plays ... to cause vibrations in the soul."[67] However successful Klee's translation of polyphonic unravelling onto canvas was—his "floating progression of colours and forms"—it nevertheless remained just that; a translation. Kandinsky on the other hand, upon hearing music, such as *Lohengrin*, experienced colours in motion: similarly, when he created a painted response, as he did to Schönberg's *Three Piano Pieces* in *Impression III (Concert)*, the painting, although a static object, became animate with "powers akin to those of music." For him, such colour-tone work, far from producing a pseudomorphic paraphrase, vibrated in and through time in a way reminiscent of Abbate's "supra-audible" sounds.

Perhaps, then, it is not accurate to categorise and separate the arts according to their immediate temporal or spatial qualities. Rather, something extra comes into play when they combine, something similar to Pound's "ideograms," or the *gestus* described by Brecht and Weill: an ideogram or a *gestus*, explains Albright, "is not an element within any specific artistic medium; it is not an icon, not a word, but a chord, vibrating between media, abolishing the distinctness of media."[68] Albright's understanding of these gestures able to speak across genres is reminiscent of Cook's hypothesis concerning audiovisual dialogues in film: for him, the crux of the question is not whether or not music and image can say the same thing but, rather, what their "emergent" language is when combined. Cook believes that the juxtaposition of image and music creates a new form, which demands a new interpretation of each.[69] As a result, he invites us to treat film as operating through a type of synaesthesia, whereby an input in one sensory mode excites a response in another, constructing meaning as the film progresses, rather than reproducing it. Music is never "alone," he declares: instead, it combines with other filmic elements (and personal histories) to create a cumulative meaning, one that could be achieved by neither music nor image alone.[70]

The Sounding Image

Despite this "emergent" intervention—this vibrating "chord"—however, the end product is most often a translation of one sensory input into another rather than a simultaneous audiovisual flow: time can vibrate within a painted instant, but it nevertheless remains without actual teleological motion. While it is true that the graphic scores of some synaesthetic works allow the performer to experience the semblance of colour music as they play—as in Ligeti's coloured scores, or Scriabin's *luce* diagram—attempts such as Scriabin's to create a synaesthetic sensorium that provides for the audience a tone-light symbiosis often failed, as it did for his unrealised (and unfinished) *Mysterium*, an enormous, participatory work that had to be enacted in the Himalayan foothills over the space of a week. But history has thrown up several attempts to bring this holistic sensory experience to a wider audience, to stimulate all senses simultaneously in a way that could mimic the unique ability of the human mind. The colour organ, immortalised by Aldous Huxley in *Brave New World* (Lenina and Henry witness, on the domed ceiling of the Abbey hall, that "the colour organ had momentarily painted a tropical sunset") is one example.[71] As we saw with Scriabin's ill-fated use of the instrument in *Prométhée*, many considered the organ little more than a gimmick; a machine that had less to do with the possibilities of fusion than it did with display, spectacle, and bravado. Nevertheless, the spectacle produced some interesting results. Developed first by French Jesuit Louis-Bertrand Castel with the encouragement of Rameau, around 1730, the idea of the *clavecin oculaire* (harpsichord for the eyes) involved attaching the keys of a normal harpsichord to a row of coloured glass ports. It is unclear whether the *clavecin*, which Castel described as the "universal instrument of the senses," was realised during his lifetime, however;[72] there is also significant doubt as to whether a full-size model was ever achieved, despite several attempts shortly after the inventor's death (a later model employed 500 candles and numerous small windows hidden behind small curtains, which were pulled open when a note was played to reveal a "flash of colour.")[73] After encountering a prototype of the machine, Telemann was so impressed that he described it in a small pamphlet. But despite Telemann's interest in the *clavecin oculaire*, the organ received a special mention in Babbitt's 1910 text as being a perfect example of Laocoönian misadventure.

After several more attempts at the colour organ, including an instrument unveiled in America by Bainbridge Bishop, British Alexander Rimington experimented with the newly developed technology to further advance the mechanics of the instrument and so provide for its recipients a sense of audiovisual immediacy more akin to the synaesthete's experience than the static experiments of the painters mentioned above (fig. 2.4). In 1895, he developed an organ, followed several years later by a corresponding book, *Colour-Music: The Art of Mobile Colour* (1912). In it, he writes that: "upon depression of any note, the corresponding colour by these mechanical means is projected upon the screen at the end of the great hall. Thus each note of the keyboard has its own distinct and personal colour, corresponding to the proper interval on the spectrum band, just as each note of the pianoforte has its own distinct musical sound. The keyboard is, in fact, a large palette from which we can paint with instantaneous effect upon the screen the colours being at will combined into one chord, or compound tint, upon its surface."[74]

Despite the size and complexity of Rimington's colour organ, the instrument could produce no sound: the music thus had to be provided by an external source. In a lecture-recital in London, June 1895, the designer presented his machine to the accompaniment of several musical instruments, including a piano and a normal organ. Kenneth Peacock has pointed out that this instrumentation was the same that Scriabin would later choose for performances of his *Prométhée*.[75]

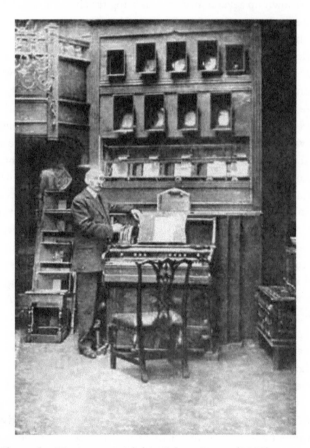

Figure 2.4 Alexander Rimington with his Colour Organ (1895).

The possibilities of the colour organ, with its simultaneous audiovisual flow, were exhaustively investigated as the twentieth century unfolded. The public presentation of the Optophonic piano in Moscow during the early '20s by the Russian painter Vladimir Baranoff-Rossiné, an instrument that simultaneously generated a varying tone and projected patterns through revolving glass disc filters and painted lenses and mirrors onto a nearby surface, was heralded by the artist as being one of the most highly attuned audiovisual instruments to date. Perhaps the most well-organised research into producing colour-music was performed by the *Prometheus* group, founded in 1962 at the Aviation Institute in Kazan. Compiled of musicians, artists, and engineers, the group aimed to explore the physical ways of creating a correspondence between music and the kinetic image:

> In the manner of sound cinema, the music-kinetic art medium is directed simultaneously to the eye and ear. In the latter medium, however, the kinetic (actually kinematic) images projected onto a translucent or opaque screen that we use are not representative of familiar actual objects, but are of a non-figurative kind. We consider our work with this medium as *instrumental choreography*.[76]

While Kandinsky, Klimt, and others experimented with the direct translation of specific music into visual representation—programmatic painting as it were—battling all the while with depicting the temporal within a static image, those working with colour organs and light projections were able to transpose sound into image during the unravelling of specific pieces. In the late 1920s, Swiss painter and "Musicalist" Charles Blanc-Gatti (a friend of Messiaen), for instance, used his synopsia to create visual transpositions of Bach and Stravinsky. He later created a Chromophonic Orchestra in 1933, a colour organ that was designed to "represent mobile, multicoloured lighting effects on a screen...in absolute synchrony with a musical piece."[77] In 1939, he made *Chromophonie*, a short abstract animation based on his orchestra, in which each note of Julis Fučik's *Entrance of the Gladiators* (Op.68, 1897) was given a corresponding colour. In his analysis of the film, William Moritz writes that "the insufficiency of Blanc-Gatti's theoretical assumption is mirrored in the film's poverty of movement: a stylized trumpet may emit a ray-wedge of red, but after that it often has nothing else to do."[78] Also coming into play in the first half of the twentieth century, however, were composers writing specific colour-music pieces in a manner after Scriabin. Hungarian composer Alexander László went so far as to create an instrument and theoretical colour-tone framework to support his compositions in a way much more densely articulated than that of Scriabin, although not synaesthetically devised. His sonochromatoscope, based on ideas presented in his theoretical text, *Farblichtmusik* (Colour-Light-Music, 1925), was a device by which projectors attached to a "colour-light piano" cast colours onto a darkened stage.

László performed *Farblichtmusik* concerts from 1925, conjoining images from his sonochromatoscope with his own compositions, as well as with the music of Rachmaninoff, Chopin, and his light-music predecessor Scriabin. In his preludes for coloured light and piano, each of the eleven pieces is governed by a single colour, which dominates the piece throughout, changing shade according to the rhythmic, motivic, or modal transformations of the music. However, critics present at the shows described the result as unsatisfactory, claiming that the visual display did not achieve the same level of fluidity as László's music.[79]

An interest in audiovisual interchange was also clearly evident in the early filmic avant-garde, where the visualising of music was no longer confined to a colouristic interpretation, but rather could be a complete cinematic image, a mixture of early colour organ experimentation and the abstract, yet static imagery of the painters mentioned above (it is important to note that, due to the capacities of early film technology, these pioneers worked largely in black and white, although there are a few examples of hand-coloured works). In his 1916 manifesto, "The Futurist Cinema," Filippo Marinetti proclaimed film the highest art form, praising its potential for unification, despite writing in an era dominated by the technical nonsynchronicity of silent film and its musical accompaniment. Using language similar to that of Wagner, he claimed that film alone had the ability to contain all other art forms, a capacity for unity that created a "totalising" effect on the human consciousness: it was able to produce what he called "*polyexpressiveness*," or a "POLYEXPRESSIVE SYMPHONY."[80]

Although early film throws up several examples of visualising music in film, it was members of the "absolute" school of filmmaking that developed most fully the idea of visual music. Richter, for instance, perceived the analogy between music and painting to be so close that they could be embodied within the same gesture. During his time working with Viking Eggeling in Zurich in 1918, Richter aimed to produce film that, like music and abstract painting, could work directly on the viewer. As we saw in the discussion of single-authored film in chapter 1, Richter explains that musical counterpoint—and fugue in particular—became a "model" for their work because "each action produces a corresponding reaction," which helped to create "a dynamic and polar arrangement of conflicting energies."[81]

Situated on the back of Scriabin's synaesthetic experiments in *Prométhée*, Klee's *Fugue in Red*, the Optophonic piano of Baranoff-Rossiné, and the first performances of *Parade*, Richter's references to art-music correspondence, fugue, conflicting energies, and counterpoint resonate with the audiovisual experimentation of his contemporaries. In particular, the idea of creating image through the aesthetic strategies of music composition became the guiding principle for his series of silent films, *Rhythmus 21* (1921) and *Rhythmus 23* (1923/4 [see video 2.5▶]) (although these dates have recently been questioned).[82] Considering his images to be "instrumental themes" able to acquire accumulated energy, Richter orchestrated his work through the rhythmic principle of opposites: "a vertical line was accentuated by a horizontal," he explains, "a strong line connected with a weak one, a single line gained importance from many lines, etc."[83] The resulting abstract forms, then, like some kind of figurative notation, are visualised representations of musical structure.

But although musical principles informed every aspect of Richter's process, music itself was not vital to the end result. Sound, he theorised, had been translated into another voice, or language, through rhythm and its aural residue was no longer needed: to both see and hear something would be patronising to an audience. Rather, he hoped that through these images, he "could touch the spirit more directly than conventional filmmakers did" (Scott MacDonald).[84] Richter's experimentation with the representation of music through image enlarged the possibilities latent in Runge's eighteenth-century fugal painting through to the distillation of musical form and structure via the "many voices" of Klee's polyphonic canvases.

Other "absolute" filmmakers preferred to embrace the tensions created when music and art were simultaneously presented. In fact, one of the earliest abstract films to be given a public performance with live musical accompaniment was created by German artist Walther Ruttmann, a former student of painting and music at the Academy of Fine Arts, Munich.[85] *Lichtspiel* (Light Play) *Opus 1* (1921) is a purely objective display of moving shapes created by filming single frames of the artist's brushstrokes as he painted on layers of glass: these images were then combined with cut-out animation (see video 2.6▶).[86] For the live presentation of his painted film, Ruttmann performed the cello part in a string quintet he commissioned from Max Butting.[87] Witnessing this audiovisual show was Oskar Fischinger, another German artist, who, also trained in music, was to become one of the most significant audiovisual artists of the early twentieth century. Inspired by Ruttmann, although keen to avoid the elder artist's painted film style, Fischinger developed a method of creating visual music that was to be greatly influential to video artist-composers. In his visualisations of preexistent music, images were made to fit with, and respond to, particular pieces of music in a way reminiscent of Blanc-Gatti's colourisation of Bach and Stravinsky around the same time. Fischinger's charcoal animated adverts, for instance, offered audiovisual synchronisations to various well-known tracks, precise rhythmic echoes that prophesy the editing techniques of much music video: in the seventh study (1931), the flicking and curving of Fischinger's drawn shapes across a dark space are intricately choreographed to Brahms' Hungarian Dance No. 5, while the Minuet from Mozart's *Eine Kleine Nachtmusik* provides the rhythmic coordination for the eleventh study (1932).[88] This technique of close synchronisation was later introduced into mainstream practice after Fischinger worked on Bach's Toccata and Fugue in D Minor for a sequence of optical music in Disney's *Fantasia* (1940: he later demanded his name be removed from the credits after his designs and sketches were altered; although his influence can be seen in this passage, his actual work cannot).[89] Using the newer (yet uncommon) oil-on-plexiglass animation technique in 1947 (fig. 2.5), Fischinger set the images of

Figure 2.5 Oskar Fischinger with a panel from his film *Motion Painting No.1* (1947). Photo © Fischinger Trust, courtesy Center for Visual Music.

his *Motion Painting No. 1* to Bach's Brandenburg Concerto No. 3, describing the resultant relationship between music and image as similar to a stroll along a river bank:

> [W]hat you see is not translated music, because music doesn't need to be translated on the screen—to the Eyes music is in itself enough—but the optical part is like we walk on the side of the river—sometimes we go a little bit farther off (away) but we come back and go along on this river, the concerto by Bach. The optical part is no perfect synchronisation of every wave of the river—it is a very free walk, nothing is forced, nothing is synchronised except in great steps. The film is in some parts perfectly synchronised with the music, but in other parts it runs free—without caring much about the music—it is like a pleasant walk on the side of a river. If the river springs, we on the side do not necessarily spring to it, but go our own free way—sometimes we even go a little bit away from the river and later come back to it and love it so much more—because we were away from it.[90]

Rather than the optical rhythmic replication in his earlier work, Fischinger here strives for a deeper, more nuanced unity between the arts—a relationship achieved only via "great steps" (the artist considered those who regarded his work as mere "illustrations of music" to be "poor in their imagination").[91] Such steps necessitate an interpretative gap that harks back to works by painters translating music into pictorial representation rather than the rhythmic correspondence sought by the early colour organ protagonists: Max Klinger's etched response to Brahms's vocal works in his *Brahms-Fantasies* (1894), for instance, or Klimt's linear interpretation of Beethoven's Ninth Symphony; visual responses that allow the artist to "go their own free way" despite following the music's course. The difference here is that Fischinger's experiments, enabled by the newly available film technology, were able to move through time: to actually coexist in music's "psychological dimension."[92]

However, Fischinger's concern with the delivery of his optical music, his attention to performance, and his three-dimensionality, which began with a commission from László in 1926, were of even greater interest to video artist-composers. After the composer had received poor reviews for his own attempts at manifesting his music visually, he approached Fischinger to produce a filmed accompaniment to the slides and spotlights of his *Farblichtmusik* shows, which began with slides, but with no film in 1925. The collaboration produced the first simultaneous unravelling of music and abstract film within an environment dimensionally enlarged by László's colour organ (or what Fischinger referred to as a "spectrum-piano") light show. Unfortunately for László, however, reports of the *Farblichtmusik* performances again criticised the composer's audiovisual attempts, this time attacking not the visual aspect, but rather the musical, comparing unfavourably his romantic, "old fashioned" score with Fischinger's highly contemporary filmed images.[93] For whatever reason, László did not give adequate credit to Fischinger and the two had stopped working together by mid-1926.[94]

Fischinger, having tasted the potential for intramedial interplay, however, continued to produce several solo multiple-projector film shows that were performed with music from 1926, including *Fieber I, II, III* (Fever), and *Vakuum*, which was accompanied by a percussion ensemble. He referred to his sculptural audiovisual art form first as *Raumlichtmusik*, then later as *Raumlichtkunst* (space-light-art).[95] In his paper, "Eine neue Kunst: Raumlichtmusik" ("The New Art: Space Light Music"), Fischinger wrote: "[o]f this Art everything is new and yet ancient in its laws and forms. Plastic-Dance-Painting-Music become one. The Master of the new Art forms poetical work in four dimensions.... Cinema was its beginning...Raumlichtmusik will be its completion."[96] Interestingly, Fischinger, unlike many video practitioners working towards similar ideals several decades later, was sure to acknowledge the lineage of his "new art," an ancestry whose tendrils lay in areas far beyond the purely cinematic: as we have seen, his new audiovisual space reactivated and combined the static, dramatic, and musical arts. In Fischinger's early quote, for instance, he brings together music and image as he mentions not synchronisation, but rather a conversation between two independently willed, yet compatible, narrative companions. But the success of these pieces is in doubt if we are to believe the rather scornful comments of László who, after attending a public performance in Munich, complained that the noise produced was far from musical and seemed instead present solely for the job of concealing the mechanical din emanating from Fischinger's seven projectors.[97] Whatever the motives behind László's comments, they did not represent the general view: in fact, *Die Zeitlupe München* magazine complimented Fischinger's "original art vision which can only be expressed through film."[98]

Fischinger, like the video artist-composers to come, was enticed by the possibilities of producing single-authored work. In his statement, *Sounding Ornaments* (1932), the filmmaker explains a method for encoding graphic sounds, or what he calls "graphic sound ornaments," along one edge of his film strip, "ornaments" that could broadcast tones when played through a machine, thus allowing the composer's work to "speak for itself directly through the film projector" (fig. 2.6).[99] As we saw in chapter 1, the filmmaker spoke of a "music-painting artist, who bases everything exclusively on the primary fundamental of music."[100] In many ways, Fischinger's "graphic sound ornament" technique inverted Kandinsky's earlier quasi-synaesthetic method of converting Wagner's music into shapes and colours.

Figure 2.6 Oskar Fischinger's display card of strips from his ca. 1932 Ornament Sound experiments. Photo © Fischinger Trust, courtesy Center for Visual Music.

Here, the aim was to sound the abstract images. After initial experimentation, the "music-painting" filmmaker made several observations:

> In reference to the general physical properties of drawn sounds, we can note that flat and shallow figures produce soft or distant-sounding tones, while moderate triangulation give an ordinary volume, and sharply-pointed shapes with deep troughs create the loudest volume. Shades of grey can also play a significant role in drawn music-ornaments.[101]

Although the result, based mainly on dynamics, was not quite Wagnerian, it nevertheless provided a similar way of playing a picture, or capturing the sound of music in paint. But the drawn music-ornaments also highlighted several differences between the work of Kandinsky and Fischinger. First, the filmmaker was working alone, rather than interpreting the work of another artist; and second, yet most important, the result was physically determined rather than subjectively produced.

By paring down music to its most basic element—the wave—Fischinger's method enabled the filmmaker to compose and extract unmediated sound from the filmstrip without recourse to "capricious reproducers": but this mechanical technique also negated the opportunity for the more "capricious," heuristic human interpretations that had informed Kandinsky's work. Rather than a translation of abstract image into music, then, Fischinger here *converted* it. In this way, the "graphic sound ornaments" preempt the work of more recent media artists such as Yasunao Tone, who, in his 2000-piece *Wounded Man'yo 2/2000*, made use of audio software *Sound Designer II* to transform the movement of his mouse as he traced Japanese characters into acoustic oscillation sequences. In both cases, the exchange from optical to audible phenomenon was possible without immediate interpretative intervention.

Fischinger's close audiovisuality was of great influence to the next generation of experimental filmmakers, including New Zealand artist Len Lye and Scottish-born Norman McLaren, who spent most of his productive film-making career working for Canada's National Film Board (NFB). In the 1930s, McLaren and Lye had each independently hit upon the idea of drawing, painting or etching directly on the picture area of the film stock. McLaren's recollection of his first attempts at removing the live-action images from sequestered spools of commercial film stock by immersing the film in his bath (an attempt that prevented any family member from bathing for a week), underscores the intimacy of the discovery and the process.

Later, at the NFB and with the help of Evelyn Lambart, McLaren took the cameraless—or direct animation process—a step further. In his work on McLaren, Terence Dobson points out that the filmmaker, who had previously created direct animation films by using purely abstract imagery, largely ignored frame divisions when using his predominantly abstract images to produce the 1949 piece, *Begone*

Dull Care.[102] By the skilful placing of different types of imagery and movement with different phrases in the music track, McLaren and Lambart produced a film with a remarkable accord between the visual elements and a jazz soundtrack. After devising the film's structure, McLaren then worked with Oscar Peterson to select and assemble appropriate passages of music provided by the Oscar Peterson Trio. Then, section by section, McLaren and Lambart created the specific visuals to work with the music.

McLaren developed two methods of creating strict visual synchronisation to music—or what he called "animated sound"—that operated in a way more akin to Fischinger's sounding ornaments.[103] Hand-drawn synthetic sound involved drawing directly onto blank film or etching into the film stock with razor blades and needles in order to produce sound, a technique discovered by accident when working on *Book Bargain* in 1937, which he later employed for films such as *Scherzo* (1939), *Dots* (1940) and *Loops* (1940):

> I draw a lot of little lines on the sound track area of the 35mm film. Maybe 50 or 60 lines for every musical note. The number of strokes to the inch controls the pitch of the note: the more, the higher the pitch; the fewer, the lower the pitch, the size of the stroke controls the loudness...the tone quality is the most difficult element to control, it is made by the shape of the strokes. Well rounded forms give smooth sounds; sharper or angular forms give harder and harsher sounds. By drawing or exposing two or more patterns on the same bit of film I can create harmony and textual effects.[104]

McLaren's process enabled him to produce both sound and image at the same time, while ensuring that neither track was afforded creative primacy. Moreover, the filmmaker's animated, or synthetic, sound could produce a range of pitch, timbre and dynamic that was so nuanced as to allow NFB composer Maurice Blackburn to combine them with the sounds of conventional acoustic musical instruments when he worked on the soundtrack score of McLaren's 1955 film *Blinkity Blank*.

The second method of audiovisual composition included the camera. The artist drew, painted or collaged cards, each with a black pattern (depicting pitch, timbre and tone) on a white background, which were then photographed onto the soundtrack area of the film stock, where the projector could read and realise them sonically. First explored in *Now is the Time* (1950–51) and used for McLaren's Oscar- winning *Neighbours* (1952) amongst other films, this photographic method was developed (with Lambart) to enable a compositional range of five octaves (a patterned card was created for each semi-tone). In *Synchromy* (1971), the same coloured pattern cards were placed on both the picture and sound areas of the film: "The pattern that makes the sound is seen on the screen simultaneously with the auditory presentation of the sound." (Dobson; see video 2.7▶)[105]. Like Fischinger, then, McLaren moved from visualising music (via audiovisual collaboration) to single-authored work that operates as an important precursor to video's "constitution" (Spielmann).

Located on the West Coast of America, filmmakers James Whitney, Hy Hirsh, Jordan Belson, and Harry Smith—a group that Moritz referred to as the "Californian Visual Music Artists"—continued to explore different audiovisual relationships. Belson, for instance, experimented with recording equipment in order to find a way to compose his own electronic film music. "Pieced together in thousands of different ways," (Belson) the images for *Allures* (1961) were inspired by work he had done for his Vortex concerts (a series of multimedia events held at the Morrison Planetarium in San Francisco): the electronic music was produced by the filmmaker in collaboration with Henry Jacobs.[106] Ethnomusicologist Smith, on the other hand, experimented with different types of audiovisuality in his film work. On several occasions, his early hand-painted films were modulated through a multispeed projector in order to provide a type of light show for jazz performances in San Francisco's Bop City night club. However, Smith composed many of his nonobjective films as pure visual music along the lines of the early "absolute" film of Fischinger, Ruttmann, and Eggeling. *Film No. 7: Color Study* (1950–52), for example, was a silent experiment in synaesthesia and has been described by Moritz as being "like a moving Kandinsky" (See video 2.8 ▶).[107] Although based on musical principles rather than specific compositions, Smith encouraged an aleatoric musical response to these films: at some screenings, he would put on the radio or random records to accompany the images; at other times, he would ask people to accompany his work with any music of their choice.[108]

While both Belson and Smith acknowledged the influence of Fischinger on their work, it was the Whitney Brothers—John and James—who developed his line of thinking most directly, although the German's choice of well-known, preexistent music seemed to them old-fashioned. John had studied twelve-tone composition with René Leibowitz in Paris (1937–1938) before he returned to America and was keen to link his compositional techniques with the visual interests of his brother. In 1942, John created a system of pendulums, which could be swung at precise speeds. A slit at the top of the device exposed the vibration equivalent of each swing directly onto the soundtrack area of a filmstrip to create an array of electronic tones. At the same time, James worked optically, painting (or stencilling) shapes onto index cards in order to create hand animation; capable of producing visual inversions, counterpoints, chord clustering, and retrogressions, these images could function like Schönberg's musical structures.

The five animations that made up *Film Exercises* (John created numbers one and five; James the middle three: 1943–1944) illustrate the evolution of Fischinger's "drawn music-ornaments." An animation stand allowed direct light to shine through the openings of drawn stencils in order to expose various areas of the soundtrack strip: the resultant translation of oscillation into synthetic sound enabled the simultaneous creation of sound and image. As a result, the series operated through the primary elements of serial composition. Each exercise represented a variation of the same basic materials, the audiovisual conversation sometimes in precise synchronisation and at other times operating in counterpoint.

Anticipating some of the discussion surrounding video art-music outlined in chapter 1, John believed that technical innovation would enable a fine art for both eye and ear: the computer, he continued, is:

> the only instrumentality for creating music inter-related with active color and graphic design, and though the language of complementarity is still under-examined and experimental, it foretells enormous consequences and offers great promise.[109]

Expanding his work first through an analogue computer (using the mechanism of a World War II M-5 Antiaircraft Gun Director Design), John later moved into the digital processes in order to explore more thoroughly his belief that motion graphics could be ordered according to the mathematical properties of music, an idea he unpacked in his 1980 book, *Digital Harmony: On the Complementarity of Music and Visual Art*. In this text, the artist outlined his theory of the "complementarity" between music and filmmaking, a "digital harmony" based on the laws of consonance that could be applied to images in motion as well as to sound: "[w]hat I knew about music confirmed for me that emotion derives from the force-fields of musical structuring in tension and motion. Structured motion begets emotion. This, now, is true in a visual world, as it is a truism of music."[110] *Digital Harmony* begins with a critique of earlier visual music on the grounds that it often failed to conjure forth a temporal-spatial whole, or a "liquid architecture":

> Twentieth-century abstract art has been a training ground for visual response to musical experience, but in the mind's eye, architecture in motion lies at the root of our enjoyment of music. Many people, with closed eyes at a concert, are "watching" the music, but after all these centuries, there still exists no universally acceptable visual equivalent to music! It should exist and it will soon.[111]

Whitney's *Arabesque* (1975, with input from programmer Larry Cuba), based on the santur (Persian hammered dulcimer) music of Manoochelher Sadeghi, goes some way towards creating this "liquid architecture" (fig.2.7). Computer and oscillograph combinations create abstract sine waves and parabolic curves, which transform into patterns inspired by eighth-century Persian design and architecture. Later in his book, Whitney makes it clear that he was not seeking to create direct audiovisual synthesis in his work, but rather desired abstract graphics ordered according to the fluidity and structural qualities of music in a manner reminiscent of Fischinger's "giant steps":

Figure 2.7 John Whitney, film still from *Arabesque* (1975).

An early intuition about how to control total dynamics led me to activate all graphic elements through a motion function that advances each element differently. For example, if one element were set to move at a given rate, the next element might be moved at two times that rate. Then the third would move at three times that rate and so on. Each element would move at a different rate and in a different direction within the field of action. So long as all elements obey a rule of direction and rate, and none drifts about aimlessly or randomly, then pattern configurations form and reform. This is harmonic resonance and it echoes musical harmony, stated in explicit terms. I tried this procedure in several films, and was gratified by the consistency of the confirmation it demonstrated.[112]

Faster computer technology allowed Whitney to create more complex digital harmonies: he wrote, in collaboration with Jerry Reed, an audiovisual composition program called the Whitney-Reed RDTD (Radius-Differential Theta Differential) and, while he continued to use other music (by Terry Riley for *Matrix III*, 1972), he also began to compose his own soundtrack for works such as those in the *Moon Drum* series (beginning 1989). Whitney's long exploration of visual music takes us right into the 1990s and has had great influence on subsequent audiovisual experimentation. The contemporary direct films of Bärbel Neubauer, who composes her own music and Richard Reeves, whose *Linear Dreams* (1997) also includes hand-drawn sound, continue in the tradition set out by Fischinger and the Whitney Brothers, while the kinetic light sculptures of Paul Friedlander demonstrate new possibilities for the evolution of visual music (see video 2.9▶).

The examples charted here, then, provide a strong case for audiovisual dialogues that were occurring before and during the "constitution" of video art-music. They also demonstrate that the desire to combine music and image, whether the desired result is unity or dialogical opposition, has a long and complicated history plagued by accusations of pseudomorphosis and redundancy. This lineage is predicated on the understanding that, although Lessing's observation that music is inherently temporal (a *Nacheinander* art form) and the traditional visual arts are spatial yet static (as arts of *Nebeneinander*), these distinctions are not exclusive to each type of media. In fact, music cannot help but be spatial and gestural: it is, to recall Leppert, "an embodied practice" despite "its phenomenological sonoric ethereality," a point driven home in the work of Lachenmann and by the enormous success of the music video. Art, on the other hand, can embody and spatialise time within stasis through certain methods, such as Klee's "polyphonic painting". With advancing technologies, the static image has even been able to burst into motion, either through bizarre contraptions such as the colour organ, or via film technology. The questions thrown up by such interaction, however, have been difficult to answer. What is the nature of music that artists have tried to embody? Although each is able to exist in the dimension of the other, music and art nevertheless operate through distinct sign systems and their combination necessitates hermeneutic consideration: what does music mean and what does an image sound like? One wonders how the audiovisual Laocoön would manifest himself.

Towards Video Art-Music

Whether audiovisual correspondences occur through involuntary cognitive association, planetary singing, scientific logic, or learnt responses, it is clear that music and image have a long history of interaction. The synergetic aspirations of video artist-composers, then, were old in both concept and practice. But as a new medium, video allowed for a more thorough investigation of music-image dialogues, its technologies enabling the mechanical problems encountered with earlier attempts at synchronicity to be resolved. As we saw in chapter 1, video's intermedial qualities are operable at many levels. At its most basic, it is an audio technology able to simultaneously record (and project) music and image; at its more complex, performative level, it can synergistically unite many other disciplines, such as music, painting, sculpture, poetry, dance, and other forms of performance. The development of video technology, in other words, enabled possibilities previously only imagined. Paik's *TV Cello*, for instance, provided opportunities for externally constructed synaesthetic experiences in a much easier and more eloquently expressed way. Three television screens playing a mixture of close-circuit feed and prerecorded video footage were placed one on top of the other and strung to produce a cellolike shape. When the *TV Cello*'s string was bowed, sound was produced: simultaneously, the images on the screens were warped and distorted by the playing to produce a concurrent audiovisual reaction (more on this in chapter 5).

Of course, video's potential for engaging with, or reactivating histories is no new thing. In all eras, artists and musicians have shown a fondness for allusion and recontextualisation: the contrapuntal style of Beethoven's late quartets, which alludes back to Bach and beyond, the neoclassicism produced by Stravinsky (in *Pulcinella*, 1920), the mixture of plainchant and triadic tonality in Arvo Pärt's tintinnabuli style, or the appropriation of Deep South music by Elvis are but a few eclectic examples. More specific instances range from sixteenth-century contrafact to the obvious quotation of Nono and Schnittke. Direct quotation is clearly evident beyond the art-music tradition in the form of the cover song, as exemplified by the Easy Star All-Stars' penchant for filtering whole albums by other artists through their reggae vibe (most notably, *Dub Side of the Moon*). Visual referencing is just as common, moving from the general, as in Brancusi's references to the art of ninth-century B.C. Cyclades, or Howard Hodgkin's mélange of quotation in *After Degas* (1993), to the specific, as in Cezanne's *A Modern Olympia* (1869–1870) inspired by Manet's scandalous *Olympia* (1863) or Picasso's *Las Meninas* series (1957) after Velázquez's canvas of the same name (1656). Referencing taken to the extreme can be seen in Robert Rauschenberg's *Erased de Kooning Drawing* (1953) or the rewrite, without change, of *Don Quixote* in the Borges parable ("Pierre Menard: Author of the Quixote", 1939). As we have seen, referencing has also been a popular choice for audiovisual artists, who frequently chose to image preexistent pieces of music: those working with colour organs, Fischinger's engagement with Bach, or the more recent practice of VJing.

A connection to the past in video art-music can be gleaned in similar ways: from the obvious (a work's content) to the subtle (its physical placement, or remediated installation). In 1970, Gene Youngblood pointed out that it was "common sense" that artists must work with what exists: "he could produce no art at all if he relied exclusively on information that is totally new."[113] While the technology is fresh, in other words, the information, or content, can include reclaimed material. As we saw in the previous chapter, some early video works offer new perspectives on old clichés, connecting themselves to previous visual histories through subversion: the seditious treatment of domesticity in the work of Martha Rosler, for instance, or the dislocation of a women's body from its traditional role as muse or object of beauty in the performances of Joan Jonas. While such refreshed perspectives attach themselves to previous practice through negativity, other video trends provide a more positive extension to ideas generated in other media, a connection visible in the *TV Cello*, which clearly expands upon the evolution of the colour organ and the visual music of experimental, direct film.

Other video works create a more discernible connection to an ancestry by quoting specific pieces or alluding to the style of certain schools, a trend that seems to oppose the claim of critics, such as David A. Ross mentioned in chapter 1, who maintain that video art is without tradition and represents the "precise opposite of painting."[114] Rather, the problems are tackled via a complementary voice; one that enables a different answer to be offered. Such recontextualisation of earlier visions resemble the reimagining of pieces of music (by artists Kandinsky and Fischinger for instance) or the sounding of preexistent images (by Blanc-Gatti amongst others). It has also become a common feature of experimental film, as seen in Jarman's temporal and spatial reworking of Caravaggio's paintings and the modified expressionism and abstract expressionism obvious in many films of Stan Brakhage. Steina and Woody Vasulka's reworking of René Magritte's painting *La légende dorée* (*The Golden Legend,* 1958) in their video piece *Golden Voyage* (1973) and Luis F. Camino's referencing of Velázquez's *Las Meninas* in his audiovisual piece *Velazquez Digital* (1989) demonstrate a similar sort of referencing, this time via the synergistic nature of video. Current artist Bill Viola often speaks of his penchant for referring to a long line of influence that includes the work of Goya, Bosch, Vermeer, and others: "I consider myself to be part of a long tradition of art-making," he states; "a tradition that includes my own cultural background of Europe, as well as the late 20th century's expanded range of Oriental and ancient Eurasian culture, and even embraces our current 19th-century French model of the post academy avant-garde and its rejection of tradition."[115] Viola's famous piece, *The Greeting* (1995) pays homage to Pontormo's *The Visitation* (c.1528–1529), while several triptychs in his 2003–2004 exhibition *The Passions* at the National Gallery in London contemporised their surroundings by referencing the styles displayed in other rooms, a perfect example of *détournement* (see video 2.10▶).[116] Through such borrowing, Viola's connection to art history was unmistakably stated. But the National Gallery exhibition also engaged clearly with its surroundings, referencing works from the gallery at large, linking itself to its location and initiating a degree of site-specificity as well as acknowledging its family tree.

A common trait of more recent video work, then, has been for artists to show an increasing awareness, or "remediation" of their past; moreover, a willingness not to "replace" it or to evolve from it, but rather, the desire to interact with and be immersed in it.[117] Maureen Turim has argued that when video work references earlier artwork, the result is not "kitsch citation, with no new imagination" or documentary, but rather art history criticism in performance.[118] In such cases, videography becomes a discourse on the artworks that prefigured it, inviting the audience to critically engage anew with pieces they may previously have been familiar with. Rather than passively citing the past, video quotation reactivates it, promoting, in Turim's words, the "artistic reinvention of discourse": "the import of one art inscribing our looking at the other arts, by which emphasis I mean that the process asks for new attention to the spectator and to the techniques that inscribe our observation.... [not] a simple debt to that history; rather, they engage that history."[119] As performative criticism, video acts as a type of ersatz painting, as palimpsest, or a reawakening; a continuation, but also an interaction.

Paradoxically, video art-music's innovative potential lies in its very ability to reuse existing images and sound: it can connect itself to, while simultaneously fragmenting and disintegrating, any area of art and music histories. Artists and musicians are free constantly to refer to and yet violate their predecessors; to choose their own history.

At first glance, it appears as though video practitioners demonstrate a preoccupation with revisiting a visual, rather than a musical past: but in fact, the addition of sound and music to the reimagining of preexistent paintings is a critical factor. Treating art as process necessarily takes it into the musical realm; its "psychological" dimension as Stravinsky would have it.[120] So when Turim focuses her thesis entirely on the graphic arts (her discussion of *Velazquez Digital*, for example, only briefly mentions Camino's soundtrack), she misses a fundamental aspect of video's engagement with history.[121] Unlike the referencing of Schnittke and Cezanne mentioned above, video can reinvent an image or section of music through a different discipline. Works such as *Las Meninas* can be reinterpreted aurally, its images relocated into music's temporal dimension in order to appeal to a sense not ordinarily activated by painting. It follows that, although not all video work, despite its distinct fondness for recontextualisation, is infused with a critical revoicing of a particular artistic moment, the format's technological connection to its multifaceted past is almost always apparent. Video's link to earlier audiovisual experimentation, in other words, lies in its physical, material basis as an audiovisual medium. The technology's evolution from early twentieth-century artists and musicians as diverse as Klimt, Kandinsky, Scriabin, Baranoff-Rossiné, and the Whitney Brothers is clear: all mark an important step towards video art-music. The genre's apparent lack of a history, then, creates a type of art concerned primarily with the past, whereby video artists and composers appear to produce an evaluation of, even a solution to, the existing physical and conceptual barriers of art *and* music. Such a transfer moves video beyond the reach of an Adornoesque accusation of pseudomorphosis.

Interest in video as a physical, audiovisual medium was particularly apparent in its earliest creative appearances, from the video sculptures of Paik, to the performance-generated events of Joan Jonas. Viola has often complained that the term "video artist" defined him by the materials he used, and not the uses to which he put them. Rather, he considers his materials to be of secondary importance to his work, the means by which he expresses himself rather than the expression itself; a means, moreover, that is predetermined because of the technologically based world in which he and other creative videographers work. This displacement of attention by content is one of the distinguishing features of the second period of video art-music as opposed to the first and demonstrates the fundamental change between early and later styles of work: a move back from context to content (we'll come back to this in chapter 5). The first wave of video work (approximately 1963 to 1971), on the other hand, was characterised by exploration of the new technology, a preoccupation with the physical processes of videoing—the transmission/reception aspects of the equipment—rather than with what was in front of the camera. As we saw in chapter 1, early video artist-composers such as Paik, Vostell, and others, were interested both in television's existence as process and the monitor's sculptural possibilities: their fascination with video, in other words, stemmed from the medium's temporal dimension and ethereality combined, somewhat paradoxically, with its physical presence as an object that could exist in and spatially command its environment.

Paik's two-fold formalism was the most significant stylistic innovation during the early years of video art-music, evidence of which can be seen in the work of many other artist-composers at the time (such as Vostell, whose first exhibition was held in the same year as Paik's and, on the other side of the Atlantic, British David Hall, whose first multiscreen installation show, using live broadcast television and performance, was included in the 1972 *A Survey of the Avant-Garde in Britain* exhibition, Gallery House, London). First, rather than create work from scratch, Paik placed magnets in or on monitors tuned to receive broadcast television, manipulating the sound and images to produce kaleidoscopic shapes, luminous colours, and electronic noises. While his choice of primary material suggests that Paik, unlike Viola, viewed his work as brand-new, instantaneously generated from live, commercial, mass culture rather than art history, his borrowings were nevertheless subjected to a play with sound and movement suggestive of a wider sphere of influence.

Paik then combined the distorted transmissions with his own video footage, running the fast moving montage through a series of programmes and plug-ins. The process foregrounded the mechanics of reproduction by exposing the medium's scanning components, an exposure that Paik hoped would demystify the "invisible" nature of broadcast technology. Second, he created "video walls" by extending his montages over up to three hundred "altered television sets."[122] These installations were frequently placed in contexts alien to normal television usage in an attempt to subvert the viewer's relation with the familiar screen: in *Fish Flies on Sky* (1975), monitors were hung from the ceiling, for instance, while for *TV Garden* (1974) screens were embedded within large leafy plants. Despite its synergetic abilities (or what Greenberg would call "artistic dishonesty"), video art-music simultaneously undergoes "a progressive surrender to the resistance of its medium": Paik's sculptural treatment of the television screen and his penchant for magnetically manipulating broadcast image are obvious examples of this.

At first glance, both the early and late schools of video practitioners, whether their references are predominantly contemporary (television) or older, use the recording and copying properties of video to quote, allude to, and recontextualise existing images directly, making them into primary material for new work in a way not possible before. A cynical reading of Paik's and Viola's "history criticism in performance" could interpret their technological reimagining of previous artworks and styles as an effort to gain institutional acceptance. As we saw in the previous chapter, amongst those under this impression was Kaprow who, in his viciously entitled article "Video Art: Old Wine, New Bottle," condemned the conceptual framework around video art as "tame."[123] But just as it is inaccurate to discuss video as representing the "precise opposite of painting" (Ross), it is also unfair to accuse those working with the magnetic technology of experimental docility. A more favourable reading of such recontextualisation takes into account the expansion that investigational video works allow, a growth into both audio and spatial territories that lurk beyond the reach of the painted image. Through its audiovisual capabilities, combined with its expanded use of space, video art-music shatters the space-time divide separating Lessing's *Nacheinander* and *Nebeneinander* arts, providing opportunity for a transmedial holisticism rarely encountered before.

3

Towards the Spatial

Music, Art, and the Audiovisual Environment

> The static architecture of the Egyptian pyramids
> has been superseded—
> our architecture revolves, swims, flies.
> (El Lissitzky)[1]

Film made giant leaps towards intermedial audiovisuality during the twentieth century by enabling images to become temporally and aurally active. But while experiments such as Norman McLaren's "animated sound" and the "digital harmony" of the Californian Visual Music artists moved towards single-authored audiovisuality, the results were usually projected onto a single screen.[2] By contrast, early video work was often installed as part of a three-dimensional environment in which live performers interacted with numerous screens, multiple speakers, and members of the audience. These multidimensional environments situated video's period of "constitution" (André Gaudreault and Philippe Marion) not only within an audiovisual lineage, but also within a spatial one.[3]

In the decades before video technology became available, the presentation of artwork and music became an increasingly important component of the creative process, a spatial interest that called into question conventional concert and art venue decorum. Creative attention slowly shifted from object to environment— from artefact to presentation—renegotiating the relationship between creator, receiver, and context. As a result, the *space* of reception—of listening and viewing—became a material entity, an ethereal, creative substance that lay at the heart of early video work. By the time Nam June Paik shot his first video in 1965, artists and writers had already begun to experiment with the idea that art was not a fixed object that demanded a single interpretation, but rather was something that encouraged a continually shifting engagement between itself, other objects, and the subjective recipient. As an integral member of the Fluxus alliance, Paik's earliest experiments stemmed directly from the group's aesthetic, with its emphasis on the blurring of art and life, humorous anti-art gesture, and impermanent

events and situations. In 1964, George Maciunas explained that "Fluxus is definitely against art-object as non-functional commodity—to be sold and to make
[a] livelihood for an artist. It could temporarily have the pedagogical function of
teaching people the needlessness of art including the eventual needlessness of
itself. It should not therefore be permanent."[4] As we have seen, the ability of the
portable camera to record and process live sounds and images in real time enabled
artist-composers to manipulate their environment in order to create an impermanent, performative and audiovisual space. This space became a fundamental compositional tool for early video artist-composers in their search for intermediality.

Chrissie Iles has separated the spatial evolution of video into three phrases: "The
first phase can broadly be termed the phenomenological, performative phase; the
second, the sculptural phase; and the third, current phase, the cinematic."[5] Although
these distinctions are useful, it is difficult to dislocate the performative from the
sculptural during video's "integrating birth" (Spielmann), as many pieces, such
as Paik's *TV Cello* (1971), operated as both transient performance *and* sculptural
object.[6] Similarly, the spatial implications of phenomenological, sculptural artwork
remain a common point of discussion for contemporary video artist-composers
whose work also encompasses the "cinematic." When discussing his recent work,
for instance, Bill Viola frequently speaks of the dynamic spatial forces at play
between sound, image, and visitor. Using the Duomo in Florence as an example,
he describes how sound, with its ability to travel "around corners, through walls,
or totally immerse, even penetrate the observer," can physically sculpt a space by
creating a sense of "aural architecture."[7] As we saw in chapter 2, understanding
space in acoustical terms was vital for Viola's belief that "all the senses [are] unified," a cohesion that enables "field perception," or "the awareness or sensing of an
entire space at once."[8] As with Paik's performative video sculptures, Viola's notion
of "field perception" moves the emphasis of video work from its materiality to the
expanded space of its presentation; from object to interactive process.

The interest of video artist-composers in spatialising their work has encouraged historians to place the genre within a sculptural, installational lineage. This
has resulted in the popular designation "video installation art," a tripartite label
balanced in the middle by a spatial designation. In their book on installation art,
for instance, Nicholas de Oliveira, Nicola Oxley, and Michael Petry identify four
categories of the spatial genre: Site, Media, Museum, and Architecture.[9] While
they acknowledge that the categories have "no ultimate authority" and that any
one artist can be (and often is) involved with more than one group, it is nevertheless important that "media" use, including video, is significant enough to warrant
a section to itself. Similarly, in an article in *Sculpture*, Nancy Princenthal identifies
four different substrands of installation art: "theatricality, a claustrophobic sense
of intimacy, the use of advanced media technologies, and obsessive composite
pieces (accumulations)."[10] Although three of her groups differ from the categories
identified above, as they are more sensory, video still features prominently.

However, while video works are included in some current commentaries on installation art, they are not always analysed in any great depth. But what has caused this omission? One possible answer lies in the numerous combinations of disciplines and styles enabled by the merging of installation with video, as we shall see below. But another is video's inclusion of sound. While the etymological triad "video installation art" reflects the genre's eclecticism, it nevertheless omits any musical association in favour of three visual connections: "video" (meaning "I see" despite the form's physical basis in audio technology), "installation" (a term employed primarily to indicate a sculptural form of visual art), and "art" itself. But, as we know, video work is able to command several levels of audio engagement: first, it is aural in makeup and demands an audiovisual command by its user; second, when displayed, it becomes intermedial, requiring no postproduction conjoining; and third, when installed, it encourages an audio response by artist, performer, and audience, who can all be thoroughly immersed in the piece. And yet these aspects are commonly forgotten. Here, I argue that video's audio qualities offer another form of spatiality not inherent in the term "installation"; and to ignore this audio element results in an impoverished understanding of early video work. Like the paradox of the chicken and the egg, it is problematic to determine whether the progression towards video intermediality led to expanded notions of performance space; or whether intermedial video was created in response to the ongoing spatial experimentation that characterised visual and musical creativity during the early twentieth century. What is clear is that the two forms of experimentation were symbiotically intertwined.

As an experiential arena in which individuals and communities interact, a physical site, a virtual place in film and media, and a theoretical ideal, "space," assumed a key role in modernist culture. In 1974, a decade into video art-music's period of "constitution," Henri Lefèbvre noticed that "the word 'space'," which until the years immediately preceding his writing, "had a strictly geometrical meaning," was experiencing an ideological and cultural shift in significance.[11] Architects were among the first to engage with the rethinking of space. Although the discussion can be traced as far back as architect Gottfried Semper in the nineteenth century, the concept of artistic spatiality began to take centre stage during the first decades of the twentieth. As part of his vision for the Bauhaus in 1919, Walter Gropius, founder and director of the first school in Weimar, called for a harmony between architectural function and design in order to achieve a new *Gesamtkunstwerk*; a refreshed articulation of space in which all disciplines could fuse in a synthesis of art and technology. This "architectonic spirit" took the form of cuboid design and a preference for the "dematerialising quality" of glass, which created "the impression that the structures were floating over the site": the result, explained theorist Siegfried Giedion, was an "unprecedented many-sidedness" that repositioned interest onto the spatial reconfiguration that the building created, rather than on its structural or material qualities.[12]

In 1929, Gropius's colleague László Moholy-Nagy produced *Von Material zu Architektur* (*The New Vision: From Material to Architecture*), in which he proposed a form of design that considered space itself to be a dynamic material. Moholy-Nagy suggested that the real medium specificity of modernist architecture was not the building materials, but rather the space that they shaped; according to his approach, the structure was a shell that designated only the boundary of the architecturally shaped environment: "Building material is an auxiliary, just so far can it be used as [the] medium of space-creating relations. The principle means of creation is the space itself."[13] For him, the early twentieth-century city demanded an understanding of space predicated on simultaneity, an idea reminiscent of the cubist belief that an image should not attempt to represent a single instant, but rather should embody multiple experiences, times, and viewpoints. This, stated Moholy-Nagy, would allow the architect to emphasise "relation, instead of mass."[14] In his theoretical text *Space, Time and Architecture: The Growth of a New Tradition* (1941), Giedion used Moholy-Nagy's ideas to formulate an architectural history that repositioned attention from material structure to spatial inflection:

> The essence of space as it is conceived today is its many-sidedness, the infinite potentiality for relations within it. Exhaustive description of an area from one point of reference is, accordingly, impossible; its character changes with the point from which it is viewed.[15]

Moholy-Nagy's concept of space informed his other diverse endeavours: the "theatre of totality," for instance, provided a performance arena in which all elements—sound, lighting, stage design, actors, and the spoken word—were placed on an equal footing. Within this theatre, the audience were not allowed to be "silent spectators" but were encouraged "to fuse with the action on the stage."[16] Like the "dematerialising" use of glass, Moholy-Nagy's mixed media pieces served to blur the porous distinctions between private and public spaces by placing in the foreground the "relation" between elements. This relational interest helped to dissolve the separation between art forms promoted by Gotthold Lessing and others by taking emphasis away from the object and placing it instead on the space in which it resides. With this refreshed spatial awareness in mind, several artists moved from the Bauhaus to join the mélange of artists, musicians, writers, playwrights, poets, and dancers who gathered at the Black Mountain College, North Carolina from the '30s to the late '50s. After his move, artist Josef Albers explained that "art is concerned with the HOW and not the WHAT; not with literal content, but with the performance of the factual content. The performance—how it is done—that is the content of art."[17]

In my introduction, I suggest that one of video art-music's biggest innovations was the physical and audible shattering of the gallery space that it encouraged. But it was not as simple as this: just as video's audiovisuality can be traced back centuries, so too can the engagement of art and music with its environment and the activation of its spectators and listeners. Like intermediality, then, the creative engagement with performance space was not a phenomenon born with the video medium. Rather, the new technology represented the peak of a spatial expansion that had been gathering pace throughout the twentieth century, an expansion clearly articulated in architectural theory and practice.

Sonic Spaces

The spatialisation of sound can be understood in various ways: the environment in which music is performed; where the players are positioned; and how the audience is placed. With the developments in surround sound and stereophony, the spatiality of live music, home sound systems and the cinematic experience has become commonplace, while personal music devices and locative media enable a continual acoustical re-mooding of a listener's environment. But the spatialisation of sound is nothing new. Many early medieval churches, for instance, provided the perfect physical layout for the antiphonal textures of liturgical music, and the dialogue between choir and congregation in responsorial psalm settings. On occasion, architecture and compositional practice entered into a symbiotic dialogue, a reciprocal influence that determined the Venetian polychoral style of Adrian Willaert and Andrea and Giovanni Gabrieli during the sixteenth century. It is believed that their *cori spezzati* (separated choirs) method of composing developed in direct response to the specific acoustical resonance of the San Marco di Venezia, a large space that physically split the choir into different groups: writing for successive antiphonal sections rather than a tutti continuum resolved the performance difficulties of having singers situated in organ lofts separated by a large, reverberating space (this evolutionary symbiosis has been contended by Iain Fenlon, who argues that the *cori spezzati* style existed before Willaert brought it to San Marco, and that evidence—such as Canaletto's sketch of the church (1766)—suggests that the choirs were in fact situated in the same space).[18] In a recent project, Deborah Howard and Laura Moretti explored the relationship between sacred music and architectural form in Renaissance Italy, hypothesising that not only did preexistent spaces influence compositional form as suggested above, but new building styles were created with acoustical ambience in mind.[19] To support their theory, the authors use circumstantial evidence to suggest that, during the 1590s, architect Jacopo Sansovino designed changes to the chancel of San Marco in order to better enhance the multidirectional presentation of Willaert's double-choir psalm settings, while it appears that the building of the *Ospedale degli Incurabili*, also in Venice (destroyed in the nineteenth century), was planned with its acoustical abilities firmly in mind.

Although similar instances of reciprocal influence were rare until the twentieth century, many other techniques of spatialising sound can be evidenced throughout music history. Awareness of the sonic peculiarities of performance spaces by composers is continually evident in terms of instrumentation, the use of pauses to prevent reverberant tone clusters, and so on. But more formal techniques of spatialisation can be found in specific pieces intended for preexistent, traditional concert halls. Stereo effects resound in many orchestral works, from the battle between two timpanists positioned on either side of the orchestra in the Allegro Finale of Nielsen's Fourth Symphony ("The Inextinguishable", 1916), or the bouts of antiphonal exchange between the two identically sized ensembles that drive Michael Tippett's Concerto for Double String Orchestra (1938–1939). Other works require performers physically to move as the piece unfolds. During the final Adagio of Haydn's Symphony No. 45 (the "Farewell", 1772), the musicians perform a final solo before leaving the stage one by one. The visual gesture is supported by a decreasing textural density until only the first-chair violins remain onstage to utter the final *pianissimo* passage. As we saw in the previous chapter, hiding the source of a sound can also draw attention to the physical staging and acoustic spatialisation of a piece, and there are numerous examples of musical acousmêtre that range from the offstage trumpet and horn calls heard in the fifth and final movement of Mahler's Symphony No. 2 ("Resurrection," 1888–1894), the unseen women's chorus that closes Holst's orchestral suite, *The Planets* (1914–1916), and the chilling offstage boys choir in Britten's *War Requiem* (1961–1962).

As the twentieth century progressed, musico-spatial gestures became more pronounced. Berio's *Circles* (1960) includes detailed stage directions for the performers, including "frantic gyrations" from the two percussionists and a "half circle" rotation from the singer in order that she is "absorbed into the ensemble."[20] Berio's spatial directions are not, however, "simply surface gesture": Robert Adlington identifies how the visual absorption of the singer is accompanied by a corresponding musical unification between voice and instruments, thus "visually articulate[ing] the musical relationship between the participants."[21] A similar relationship between space and musical structure can be found in Boulez's *Domaines* (1968), in which a solo clarinettist is free to wander between the six small ensembles surrounding her. As she enters into the physical "domain" of a group, a musical interaction is initiated, a mobile form of communication that creates a spatial and changeable soundscape that can be followed both visually and aurally. *Domaines* requires an articulation of spatial dynamics for its successful realisation, as the nature of the musical journey is determined by the physical movements of the clarinettist.

Referring to the work of composers such as Mauricio Kagel, Peter Maxwell Davies, John Cage, Berio, Stockhausen, and Cornelius Cardew, Eric Salzman speaks of newly emerging "experimental forms of interaction between the concert stage and theatre"; "musico-theatrical performance works that clearly did not belong in the opera house, the Broadway theatre or the traditional concert stage."[22] Despite the focus on staging, however, works by these composers are still (most often) intended for performance in traditional venues, as Chris Salter points out: these "theatrical works were small-scale, chamber-based events that, while pushing the theatrical envelope, were still situated in a concert setting."[23] While the audience receives a refreshed spatial experience, the standard transaction between performer and audience is still negotiated across a bifurcated performance space, a *modus operandi* that has been stable since the nineteenth century. Barry Blesser and Linda-Ruth Salter identify in the conventional music concert a "performing space and a listening space," two areas that remain physically separated from each other, even when an audience is encouraged into conversation in certain liturgical settings.[24] A similar spatial distinction is visible throughout the history of drama: Greek theatre had a "special place" for its performers, for instance, while medieval theatre troops would perform from their wagons to audiences in the street; this divided space can also be found in classical Eastern theatre.

In his investigation into the ways in which people interact within the bifurcated performance space of drama, Richard Schechner identifies three "primary transactions" that comprise the traditional theatrical event and, by extension, the music recital: the relationships between performers; between performers and members of the audience; and between individual members of the audience.[25] While all those involved in theatrical and musical performance must engage in at least one of these transactions, Schechner points out that the weighting of each relationship differs between cultures, ideologies, and eras; and these changing emphases have affected the spaces in which these events take place. The relationship between performers is perhaps the easiest to identify as it is played out on every stage, from the interactions between conductor and orchestra to the intricate manoeuvres of Boulez's clarinettist in *Domaines*.

Charting the other transactions is more complicated. R. Murray Schafer has contrasted the methods of musical consumption in Europe and North America with that of other cultures, noting that in many languages there is no distinction between the words "music" and "sound." This, he argues, encourages communal spaces for music making, in which the processes of performing and listening can be interchangeable: as we saw in chapter 1, closing the conceptual and creative gap between "music" and "sound" in early video work encouraged a similar merging of art and life. Compared to this, the rigid physical distinction between player and receiver in Western art music results, according to Schafer, in a music separated from everyday, interactive life:

> Music has become an activity which requires silence for its proper presentation—containers of silence called music rooms....In fact it would be possible to write the entire history of European music in terms of walls, showing not only how the varying resonances of its performance spaces have affected its harmonies, tempi and timbres, but also to show how its social character evolved once it was set apart from everyday life.[26]

Although it is true that the performance spaces of Western art music have had a significant impact on musical style, Schafer's understanding of music as sounds that are "set apart from everyday life" is not quite accurate: in fact, before the nineteenth century, music spaces formed an integral part of everyday life; and they were rarely "silent."

Although requiring "special places" for performers and listeners, the performance of sacred and secular music in Europe before the nineteenth century was not guaranteed the level of attention common to the modern audience. In her study of the reception of the cantata in Leipzig church services at the turn of the eighteenth century, Tanya Kevorkian hypothesises a "Baroque performance and reception aesthetic, which involved a layering of visual, aural and social experiences," noting that even Bach's music frequently failed to command the attention of a Leipzig audience preoccupied with complex social manoeuvring.[27] According to her study, congregants "made use of nearly every element of the liturgy, or seating arrangements, and of a range of behaviours to articulate their social status" and that, during the cantata performance, there was a certain level of noise from the stalls as people came and went, or chatted to their neighbours.[28] Here, there was very little separation between music performance and everyday life, although the lack of interaction between audience and performers prevented a truly "communal" space for music making.

The same was often true for secular music. Christopher Small draws our attention to a painting by Canaletto, *London: Interior of the Rotunda in Ranelagh* (1754) that depicts an orchestral performance held in Ranelagh Gardens, Chelsea. As the orchestra, seated on a platform to one side of the imposing, three-storey circular "music room," plays, the audience can be seen strolling around the space, deep in conversation: "It appears that the building has not caused socializing and enjoying music to be divided into two separate activities as does a modern concert hall.... Most of those present seem, at least to our eyes, to be treating the performance as background to their other social activities."[29]

Similar strategies of engagement are described by James Johnson in *Listening in Paris*, a reception history that charts the evolution of French concert life from the *ancien régime* to its modern form. Through the music of Gluck, Haydn, Rossini, and Beethoven, Johnson identifies a gradual change in audience behaviour from the loud, rowdy listeners of eighteenth-century opera to the attentive public of today: the transformation in musical experience from social event to a "new attentiveness" that begun to emerge during the 1770s.[30] Johnson describes the eighteenth-century audience of the Paris Opéra as a "busy, preoccupied public, at times loud and at others merely sociable, but seldom deeply attentive."[31] For the opera-goer in 1750, he continues, it was "unfashionable" to arrive on time:

> In the Old Regime, attending the opera was more social event than aesthetic encounter. In fact, eighteenth-century audiences considered music little more than an agreeable ornament to a magnificent spectacle, in which they themselves played the principle part.[32]

Although not as symbiotic an evolution as the acoustical architecture of the *cori spezzati* tradition, seventeenth- and eighteenth-century architectural design responded to the demands of the sociable visitor. For two and a half centuries, the Italian Baroque ring-balcony auditorium style remained the popular model for theatrical and operatic spaces, a design that gave preference to the ample viewing of fellow spectators over a clear prospect of the stage, which, in some cases, could be glimpsed only after a certain amount of bodily contortion. The longevity of this architectural aesthetic is demonstrated by one architect writing in 1760, who explained that "One has to stand to see the stage in all our theaters. It's as if they placed the partitions there intentionally to obstruct one's view of the stage."[33]

However, by the 1770s, things had begun to change and there emerged a new aesthetic sensibility that resembled "genuine attentiveness."[34] Johnson observes how the "notables of the Old Regime" began to seek higher boxes, which not only provided a better acoustic, but also made the occupier less visible to the rest of the auditorium:[35]

> By the 1770s there was growing interest in the artistic element of the spectacle. More and more, spectators were favouring the seats that faced the stage over those along the sides of the hall.... The artistic considerations of sight lines and sound were a growing preoccupation among spectators in the closing decades of the century.[36]

Moving away from the communal, social consumption of music towards a more individual, private reception prompted a change in architectural design. The modern concert hall, which evolved during the nineteenth century, demonstrates what Small describes as a gradual "mythologisation" of performance space that operates in the way more akin to that identified by Shafer above.

Breaking from the ring-balcony auditorium design, the Bayreuth *Festspielhaus* (opened 1876) represents what Michael Barron has described as a "great break in theatre design."[37] After finding Bayreuth's existing *Markgräfliches Opernhaus* inadequate for his vision of a total work of art, Wagner embarked on a building project that would create a space designed for the exclusive production of his own works. His *Festspielhaus*, appropriated from Semper's unrealised plans for an opera house in Munich, made several important innovations: the traditional horseshoe shape was replaced by steeply raked rows of seating facing the stage; the orchestra was placed under the stage and hidden from sight by a hood; and a double proscenium framed the performance area in order to create a greater illusion of depth (fig. 3.1). While these changes were determined in part by physical concerns (the acoustic balance between instrumentalists and singers was improved by placing the orchestra under the stage), they also responded to, and encouraged, new audience behaviour (the raked seating and absence of boxes helped to eliminate social distinctions, for instance). When the house lights were dimmed during a performance, these innovations induced what Wagner described as a "mystic gulf," or

Figure 3.1 Wagner, *Festspielhaus*, Bayreuth (1875).

"mystic chasm" between audience and stage, a "floating atmosphere of distance" between the spaces: "[t]he scene is removed as it were to the unapproachable world of dreams."[38]

Barron points out that, although Wagner's *Festspielhaus* was very influential to theatre style, its impact is less obviously visible in subsequent opera house construction.[39] But despite Wagner's theatre proving a one-off in terms of specific design, many of his ideas—placing focus on the stage and discouraging audience interaction—have informed the modern, purpose-built concert venue. The concert hall, Small claims, has become a highly sectionalised place that keeps aural or visual connection with the outside world to a minimum, a "neutral" space that prevents anything that may distract from the music. To help prevent the merging of inside and outside spaces, visitors must first traverse a foyer, a "transitional space through which we pass in the progression from the outer everyday world to the inner world of the performance."[40] Once inside, the listener, immobile and hushed, is physically separated from the performance, a segregation that re-enforces the timelessness of the proceedings to produce a ritual feeling rather like Wagner's "mystic gulf" (Small goes so far as to compare concerts to a Catholic Mass in "Performance as Ritual").[41] Requiring an audience to sit in silence in a space removed from that of the performers, such a venue seems at first to negate two of Schechner's three "primary transactions": the modern auditorium's design, Small argues, not only "discourages communication among members of the audience," it is also planned "on the assumption that a musical performance is a system of one-way communication, from composer to listener through the medium of the performers."[42]

However, it is important to note that the rigid sectionalisation identified by Small does, in practice, rarely occur in any form of music performance. Physically, performer and audience may be kept apart: but in terms of immersion and emotion, this is not the case. Schechner insists that the root of theatre lies in the "exchange of stimuli" rather than in the difference between passive and active.[43] Such an exchange is immediately obvious in popular music performance, where an audience is free to sing along, talk, move about, and even interact with the musicians: it is also visible in some art music concerts, such as the Last Night of the Proms at the Royal Albert Hall, London. Yet sound's ability to go "around corners, through walls, or totally immerse, even penetrate the observer" (Viola) reduces the spatial "chasm" of the concert hall to ensure that performers and audience are always connected. Picking up on this point, Michel Chion has pointed out the fragility of separate "performing" and "listening" spaces in film. Despite the use of framing and perspective to take the eye away from the diegetic border in mainstream cinema, an audience can always see the edge of the screen. Sound, on the other hand, experiences no such edge as there is no "auditory container"; instead, sound is free to move into the space of the audience, to immerse them entirely, an ability praised by Viola above (3D cinema performs the same function by enabling the image to leap from the screen and press into the viewer's space).[44]

The immersive qualities of sound draw together the bifurcated "special spaces" of the concert hall. After his primary transactions, Schechner suggests four secondary connections, the last of which lies between "the total production and the space in which it takes place."[45] For many, this last transaction is the most important: Polish director Tadeusz Kantor, for instance, has described space as the "urmatter" of theatre, alive and independent of the artist: "Space is not a passive receptacle in which objects and forms are posited" he claims; "SPACE itself is an OBJECT [of creation], And the main one!"[46] In a way reminiscent of Moholy-Nagy, Kantor points out that the apparently neutral area between creator and receiver is in fact always active.

Music and Space

While the sounds produced from the stage can immerse an audience seated in a traditional concert hall, however, listeners are rarely allowed to enter into an audible dialogue with the music. Blesser and Salter believe that this entrenched way of experiencing music has encouraged a relationship between place and compositional style that is not as fluid as the music-architecture symbiosis that informed the Venetian Polychoral School. According to the authors, the nature of the "mythologised" concert hall has had a direct impact on the stylistic trajectories taken by more recent composers:

> The two-way relationship between music and space is actually a pair of one-way relationships. Just as the designs of modern spaces are constrained by the need to host the historical musical repertoire, which is

taken as an inflexible requirement, so composers write their music for immutable spaces that already exist, perhaps having been built a century earlier.... Most often, however, composers assume a fixed aural architecture... because music and its spaces are rarely created at the same time, the two-way relationship between music and its spaces seldom exists in practice.[47]

But while the nineteenth century saw a move towards a more engaged listening practice and an accompanying "mythologisation" of the performing space, the twentieth saw a move towards less sanctified listening strategies. Although examples of an interactive, equal "two-way relationship" between performer and audience are rare in the Western art music tradition, challenges to the "immutable spaces that already exist" began to emerge during the second half of the twentieth century. This happened in several ways. On the one hand, composers experimented with locating performers within the place of reception in order physically to mix up the segregated space of the concert hall. For *Terretektorh* (1966), for instance, Xenakis scattered his orchestra through the audience members, who were seated in a circle around the conductor. For the first three minutes, the audience were engulfed by a single note, an E that rolled around the orchestra providing each listener with a unique auditory point of view, as the composer explains: "It puts the sound and the music all around the listener and close up to him. It tears down the psychological and auditive curtain that separates him from the players when positioned far off on a pedestal."[48] A similar process is at work in his *Persephassa* (1969), in which six percussionists, seated in a hexagonal formation, surround the audience. The performers envelop their listeners within layers of superimposed rhythms that are passed around the hexagon at different speeds and in several directions. In his theoretical writing, Xenakis identified two possible versions of "stereophony." The first was instigated when the sound arose from a fixed place: this form he called "static stereophony." By contrast, the second form—"cinematic stereophony"—was born from what he describes as "an acoustic line with the help of movement, a sound which displaces itself in a line of loudspeakers. The notions of acoustic speed and acceleration are introduced here. All the geometric curves and all the surfaces can be transposed cinematically with the help of the definition of the sound point."[49] Xanakis's forays into surround sound were not alone. Rather than aurally envelop his listeners in his opera *Le Grand Macabre* (1974–1977), Ligeti asked his performers to join them, for instance: disguised as part of the audience, several members of the choir sat in the stalls until their time came to perform, a gesture that refreshed the "inflexible" customs of performance tradition. Kurtág stepped across the "mystic gulf" in a similar way by placing several harmonica players throughout the auditorium in his *Quasi una Fantasia* (1988).[50]

On the other hand, a refreshed understanding of "SPACE" during the middle of the twentieth century enabled sounds from beyond the "special space" occupied by the performers to be included as valid compositional material, an inclusion that opened up a two-way flow of creative influence rarely encountered before. There developed, alongside and in direct opposition to traditional concert practice, a counterculture that ran through Satie to the radical aesthetic promoted by Cage and the small body of American experimental composers that collected around him to form the "New York School"—Morton Feldman, Earle Brown, Christian Wolff, David Tudor, and others—in the aftermath of World War II.[51] The School, heavily influenced by Fluxus (in particular its motto "Art Is Life, and Life Is Art"), launched a sustained attack on the traditional barriers between composer, performer, and listener in an attempt to rejuvenate the space in which they interacted.[52]

While interest in performance space is nothing fundamentally new, as we have seen, for composers associated with both the New York School and the Fluxus aesthetic, context became one of the most important factors. The first step towards a refreshed music/space interaction was the creation of works that avoided fixed and determined sequences of sounds, leaving instead many decisions to the performer: Morton Feldman's four *Intersections* (1951–1953), for example, and Terry Riley's *In C* (1964) give creative command to the performer, ensuring a different interpretation at every recital.[53] Cage's principle of "indeterminacy," however, not only removed music further from the composer's control, but also loosened that of the performer: decisions were no longer in the hands of the musician, but were the result of chance—of a flipped coin or a thrown yarrow stick.[54] Nonmusical processes could include social, biological, and gamelike rules, or be produced by structure generators as in his live *Imaginary Landscape #4* (1951) for twelve radios. Music, Cage proposed, is not something a musician produces, but rather something a listener perceives: as we saw in chapter 1, any sounds can be music, provided that they are heard as such, an aesthetic famously illustrated in *4'33"* (1952), where incidental, "environmental sounds" from the performance space become part of the experience.[55] In 1964, one critic described Cage's *Variations IV* (1963), "for any number of players, any sounds produced by any means with or without other activities" for an "indeterminate duration," as "the kitchen-sink sonata, the everything piece, the minestrone masterpiece of modern music."[56] Whereas works such as Satie's *Furniture Music* (*musique d'ameublement*) from earlier in the century were intended to blend with the environmental sounds of their performance spaces, Cage considered his music to be those noises themselves.[57] Part of the composition, audiences were given an indeterminate space in which to find or negotiate their own concept of music. Once placed in the hands of the audience, music became disengaged from the ritualistic, segregated performance procedures identified by Small, creating instead a new set of relations that was to prove a fundamental stepping stone towards the rise of video art-music (the influence of Cage can be traced, for instance, in the work of Paik, who produced a 29-minute *Tribute to John Cage* in 1973, which he re-edited in 1976).

But this expanded notion of instrumental performance was not simply conceptual: during the 1950s, ten years before the rise of video, it became also physical. Stockhausen, one of the first to explore the implications of spatialised sound, created several works that could not easily be performed from a traditional proscenium stage. In *Gruppen* (1955–1957), a piece of "controlled pandemonium" (Alex Ross) for three orchestras each with a separate conductor, the composer sends a brass chord around each ensemble to create a moving wall of sound.[58] As we saw in chapter 1, the total serialism of *Gesang der Jünglinge* (1955–1956) took this physical awareness a step further. Composed for a boy's voice and electronically generated tones, the piece was the first electronic composition to serialise the distribution of music in space: the sounds were projected via five channels located around the performance space (at the time, a five-track playback machine did not exist, so the fifth channel was presented from a loudspeaker on the stage).[59]

A more recent example of spatial composition is *Virtual Abbey* by John Hobbs and David Hykes (1995), a work that articulates the core principles of sound art laid out in the previous chapter through "the activation of the existing relation between sound and space" (Brandon LaBelle).[60] *Virtual Abbey* was performed in two places simultaneously. The sounds of Hykes singing with the Harmonic Choir in the Kitchen, New York City, were digitally encoded and transmitted via ISDN telephone lines to a French audience situated in Le Thoronet Abbey in Provence. Relayed live, the voices of the Harmonic Choir became instantly awash with the resonant acoustics of the abbey. The reverberant version was then sent back to New York. Here, sound was liberated from its space by a process of acoustic transportation.

As we have seen, composers often write for the acoustics of a certain type of space, whether it be a cathedral or a concert hall. But moving outside the traditional hall with its frontal orientation and fixed seating could encourage an audience to move and respond physically to sound in order to give a performance a fluid and acoustically diverse resonance. Although there are instances of music being written for and performed outside church or concert hall, such as Handel's *Water Music* (1717: first performed on a barge floating down the River Thames), most works, as Blesser and Salter point out above, are conceived for the traditional performance layout. But in a 1958 lecture entitled "Music in Space," Stockhausen imagined a new type of concert hall that would be "suited to the requirements of spatial music. ...a spherical chamber, fitted all around with loudspeakers...a platform, transparent to both light and sound, would be hung for the listeners. They could hear music coming from above, from below and from all directions."[61] The Philips Pavilion, designed for the Expo '58 in Brussels, is an excellent example of a concert hall created with the principle "relation, instead of mass" in mind (fig. 3.2). The structure, conceived by Le Corbusier according to a design by Xenakis, explored the possibility of "cinematic stereophony." Le Corbusier was one of the first to strive for a sonic architectural model, speaking of "an acoustic intervention in the domain of forms....One starts with the acoustics of the landscape, taking into account the four horizons....One then creates forms to respond to these horizons, to greet

Figure 3.2 Le Corbusier, Philips Pavilion, Brussels (1958).

them."[62] Louis Kalff, artistic director of Philips, asked Le Corbusier to create "not a hall, but a platter on which to serve the products of contemporary technology to an international audience."[63] In response, the architect imagined a multimedia collage designed specifically for the space, a *Poème électronique* that, beginning with the "acoustics of the landscape," would form a synthesis of music and architecture: "I will not make you a pavilion façade but an electronic poem which will be enclosed inside a 'bottle'," he wrote.[64] The asymmetric Pavilion was formed from nine concrete hyperbolic paraboloids to resemble a "stomach." As visitors were led through its intestinal contours they received a barrage of multimedia: heard first was Xenakis's interlude *Concret PH* (created from the sound of burning charcoal and spread over around three hundred speakers); further inside, they became enveloped by an electronic piece by Varèse, which was also distributed amongst multi speakers. Like environmental theatre where "the space is organically defined by the action," (Schechner) Varèse's sounds were synthesised with a film projection of a sequence of photographs, ambient lighting, and a female mannequin and a cuboid *Objet mathematique* that hung from the ceiling (see video 3.1▶).[65] Of the final space Xenakis wrote: "I believe that on this occasion music and architecture found an intimate connection."[66]

Stockhausen received the opportunity to realise his own ideas several years later when the West German government invited him to work on a multimedia project that would be presented at the 1970 World Fair in Osaka. Working with German architect Fritz Bornemann, the composer conceptualised a spherical concert hall with a raised platform for listeners in the centre. Around the space, fifty loudspeakers were grouped into seven rings that surrounded the listener's platform (three of the circles were underneath the platform). Preexisting music by Bach, Beethoven, and others could be sent around the speakers either via a system that used a spherical sensor, or via Stockhausen's self-designed ten-channel rotation mill. However, with the help of around twenty performers, Stockhausen also provided live five-and-a-half-hour programs of his own music throughout the exhibition every day, reaching almost a million listeners by the end of the 183-day duration.[67]

Both the Phillips Pavilion and Stockhausen's project recall Giedion's promotion of architectural form, whose "character changes with the point from which it is viewed." Such spatial concert installation calls for listeners to become active, physical participants able to experience multiple sonic viewpoints, or what Schechner calls "multi-focus":

> A performance using multi-focus will not reach every spectator in the same way. Reactions may be affectively incompatible with one another because one spectator will put events together in a different way than the man sitting next to him. In multi-focus, the director's role of presenting coherence is largely turned over to the audience. The performers and technicians control the sensory input (and one works painstakingly on this), but the mix of elements is left to the audience.[68]

Music performance, then, always requires a spatial interaction between player and listener. But as the twentieth century progressed, composers began to rearticulate the space—or "mystic gulf"—that traditionally lay between the producers and consumers of music in the opera house and concert hall. Listeners have been surrounded by performers, invited to contribute to the composition, and asked to travel through a sonic environment in order to construct their own "coherence". As a result, the traditional concert space with its "one-way flow of communication" has been rearticulated from within, or re-imagined entirely. In each case, music has flowed across the standard bifurcated space of the concert venue to encourage listeners into a more active mode of engagement.

The Sanctity of the Art Space

As music moved into the space of the listener, similar spatial shifts began to occur in art exhibition and it is possible to chart for the art gallery an almost simultaneous transition from physically neutral space to interactive environment. Like the bifurcated spaces of the music venue, a dialectical tension has been operational between the social and physical spaces for viewing art from the outset, a tension that Helen Searing has described as "architecture's dual nature as functional craft and expressive art."[69] Sacred art first resided in the church, where it enjoyed a social, narrative function, operating as part of everyday life in a way akin to Bach's cantatas. The public art institute as we know it today only emerged during the late eighteenth century as an alternative to the private collection or religious display (David Carrier argues that the modern institute was born in 1793 when the Louvre in Paris, a royal residence dating from 1190, opened its doors as a public *Musée*).[70] Histories of purpose-built public gallery design often begin in the early 1800s with the visions of Jean-Nicolas-Louis Durand, a French teacher and architect who proposed a design modelled on Rationalist Enlightenment sensibilities, a style based on geometric forms such as the cube separated into four wings, which meet to form a central, domed rotunda. Durand's prototype included long, vaulted colonnades that promoted easy circulation and plenty of natural light, a classical model that played homage to the techniques identified by Searing as the dominant architectural styles from "ancient Greece, Imperial Rome, and Renaissance Italy."[71] Although agreeing that the style owes much to the neoclassical age in which the gallery first emerged, Ivo Maroević contends that this style was a suitable one as it "suggested eternity and exaltation, a temple of the spirit."[72] Although subsequent architects lent an individual voice to the design, Durand's ideas can be traced through John Soane's Dulwich Picture Gallery, London (1811–1814), Karl Schinkel's *Altes Museum* in Berlin (1823–1830), and Leo von Klenze's *Glypothek* (Sculpture Gallery) in Munich (1816–1830), whose galleries, arranged around a courtyard, mix Greek temple fronts with Renaissance niches and Roman vaulting forms.[73] Although the architectural style diversified during the second half of the nineteenth century, the basic concepts were retained, as Maroević reminds us: "historicism and Neo-Renaissance dominated the Dresden Art Gallery designed by Semper, the Rijksmuseum in Amsterdam was built in the Neo-Gothic style, and the Bavarian National Museum in Munich in a combination of Neo-Romanesque and Neo-Gothic styles."[74]

The early public gallery interior matched the grandeur of the exterior edifice. Elegant staircases and common areas resembled the layout of the Baroque mansion, a fluid space that promoted unencumbered contemplation of the art displayed. Prevalent in the early spaces was the salon style of hanging artwork, where paintings are casually massed together, chattering with and bouncing off one another in a visual cacophony. The style is so named after the annual (and, later, bi-annual) public art exhibition held in the Salon Carré (Square Room) at the Louvre that began (or, rather, was revived) in 1737, a regular exhibition of contemporary work (fig. 3.3). In order to display all the paintings in one room, works were hung from floor to ceiling, with the smallest at the bottom and the largest at the top, angled slightly towards the ground. The separation between each virtual world was reinforced by heavy frames, which defined the edges of paintings

Figure 3.3 E. Forest, *Visitors in the Salon Carré Admire the Entries for the Salon of 1843* (1843).

in order to enhance both their self-containment and their isolation from one another. Still the preferred method of exhibition at the Dulwich Picture Gallery, the multiple frames of the salon hang prevent the paintings from interacting with the space around it. (Enjoying something of a resurgence, this style of hanging was favoured by the 2011 Summer Exhibition at the Royal Academy of Arts, London. But although work was hung from dado rail to picture rail in traditional salon style, many works were presented without a frame, creating a confusion of pictorial interiors that jostled against one another). The practice of viewing art in this way is remarkably similar to the behaviour of the eighteenth-century opera audience identified by Johnson above. Thomas Crow recognises the Salon as marking a pivotal point in the social structure of French cultural history, as it provided an immensely popular arena in which "ceaseless waves" of spectators from all classes could consume and comment on artwork together. Opinion was recorded in pamphlets, initiating a feedback forum that was, suggests Crow, partly responsible for a shift in the subject matter and representation favoured by artists. Like early concert and opera theatres, these galleries, with their neoclassical architecture and palatial interiors, were noisy, communal places where the layers of society were clearly visible and opinions were eagerly expressed and debated.

By contrast, the modern art gallery space has been configured in much the same way as Small's concert hall—as unintrusive as possible, windows are often boarded to keep light and noise from the outside world at bay; artworks are separated from one another by an expanse of white wall; and visitors are required to keep noise to a minimum. To put this another way, the viewing of art followed a similar trajectory to that of music listening, moving from social event to more interiorised behaviour.

Concentrating on American art museums at the turn of twentieth century, Searing points out that although the spaces demonstrated a great diversity of architectural style, they were nevertheless "recognizable chiefly by their blank walls and skylights."[75] The strategies undertaken by architects and curators to keep the empty and unobtrusive gallery environment separate from the world outside have occupied many art theorists. In 1976, for instance, Brian O'Doherty contended that the gallery had acquired "a limbo-like status," an "eternity of display" that parallels that of the works exhibited.[76] Describing the traditional gallery space as a "white cube," he claimed that "[a] gallery is constructed along laws as rigorous as those for building a medieval church":

> Some of the sanctity of the church, the formality of the courtroom, the mystique of the experimental laboratory joins with the chic design to produce a unique chamber of esthetics. So powerful are the perceptual fields of force within this chamber that, once outside it, art can lapse into secular status.[77]

Thomas McEvilley has charted for the "white cube" a lineage of sanctified spaces that extends long beyond the Medieval church to include Egyptian tomb chambers, which also "held paintings and sculptures that were regarded as magically contiguous with eternity and thus able to provide access to it or contact with it."[78] Using language similar to that of Small and Schafer above, McEvilley describes the modern gallery as a space "where access to higher metaphysical realms is made to seem available": as a portal for the metaphysical, these spaces "must be sheltered from the appearance of change and time. This specially segregated space is a kind of non-space, ultra-space, or ideal space where the surrounding matrix of space-time is symbolically annulled. "[79] Arguing along similar lines, Miwon Kwon describes the gallery in a way reminiscent of the reverential behaviour encouraged by the "inner world of the performance" (Small): "The seemingly benign architectural features of a gallery/museum ... were deemed to be coded mechanisms that actively disassociate the space of art from the outer world, furthering the institution's idealist imperative of rendering itself and its hierarchization of values 'objective,' 'disinterested,' and 'true.'"[80]

Viewing Strategies

Like Johnson, Jonathan Crary repositions historical interest from work to receiver, arguing against the core narrative of visuality in the nineteenth century which suggests that with Manet, impressionism, and/or postimpressionism, "a new model of visual representation and perception emerges" as it presupposes an "observer who remains perpetually the same."[81] Crary contends that in order to understand these shifts in representational practice, it is necessary to take into account the "phenomenon of the observer."[82] Nevertheless, despite architectural and social differences between the nineteenth-century methods of displaying and consuming art and more recent customs, the viewing strategies encouraged in these "ideal spaces" has remained remarkably consistent. In his work on British art galleries, for instance, Christopher Whitehead notes that the "display methods intended to allow the art work to become the predominant visual feature of an interior" that emerged in the 1850s "anticipated the modernist 'aesthetic' or 'contemplative' mode in art display."[83] He identifies two possible forms of communication promoted by the gallery interior: the first, a passive, or "functionalist" approach, in which the architecture simply facilitates the viewing of art which is allowed to speak for itself; the second, an active mode in which a continuity between architectural space and artwork is mobilised, a continuity that promotes a historicised architectural frame.[84]

The second approach is easy to identify. During the mid-nineteenth century, the idea that the gallery should replicate the environment in which the painting had been created or had originally resided prevailed: according to this belief, the lighting of Italian religious paintings should evoke that of a Catholic church in order to create an accurate historical harmony. This sensibility is still evident: in the brief for the new Sainsbury Wing at London's National Gallery, which opened in 1991, for instance, the staff recommended an interior that "might be church or basilica like": a "sense of formality and balance appropriate to paintings of the early Renaissance is needed. The character of the Galleries should not dominate the paintings.... The layout should provide a degree of ceremony appropriate to the profound experience of looking at paintings."[85] But it is also possible, as we shall see below, to argue that the modern gallery space represents an extension of contemporary art practice in the same way. As a result of innovations in lighting and other practical issues, some of the structural constraints that informed Durand's designs have been loosened, enabling a series of highly individual art spaces to appear. Many reflect the changing nature of the modern art which they house. With the Centre Pompidou in Paris (Richard Rogers and Renzo Piano 1977) and the Guggenheim Museum, Bilbao (Frank Gehry 1997), the emphasis in the architecture-art dialogue identified by Searing begins to shift towards a self-consciousness that was not always well received: Gehry's building, for instance, was accused of interfering with the viewing of art and even for representing "the annihilation of the museum as we know it."[86] The timber frame and large windows of the Lewis Glucksman Gallery (Sheila O'Donnell and John Tuomey 2004) in Cork, Ireland, on the other hand, renders the inside space invisible by merging it with the wooded parkland area beyond.

While a continuity of work and place can be found, however, Whitehead's first mode of communication is more complicated. At first, it seems straightforward to identify the passive, "functionalist" approach to gallery design. In their study of the ways in which we consume visual art, Mihály Csíkszentmihályi and Rick Emery Robinson questioned a selection of museum professionals about their curatorial style: the answers are reminiscent of Wagner's architectural ideology. When asked about the benefits of a clean blank "aesthetic environment" for displaying art, for instance, the authors summarised that "most respondents felt that such an environment focused attention on the work itself and limited the competing information that a more ornate setting might contain."[87] When invited to consider what helps to reduce the space-time matrix that surrounds the viewing of art, respondents mentioned the need for good lighting and seating, as well as the effective management of overcrowding and noise: the gallery workers "insisted on the importance of eliminating distractions, thereby helping the viewer to see something and benefit from it. Taken together, these suggestions relate to one of the basic conditions of the aesthetic experience: the focusing of attention."[88] One museum worker questioned by Csíkszentmihályi and Robinson articulated the "focusing of attention" in the modern gallery in a way that contrasts sharply with the noisy, social experience of early salon-style exhibitions: "viewing art is 'almost something you have to do privately' or perhaps 'with a friend or with the artist there'. Anything more only detracts from the integrity and intensity of the aesthetic experience."[89] Like Wagner's raked seating that draws attention to the stage, and the "mystic gulf" that separates audience from the "unapproachable world of dreams," the gallery visitor remains silent, at once physically separated from the artwork yet drawn into its pictorial plane.

Attracted by the concept of timelessness, art critics frequently discuss the works displayed in a similar vein, suggesting that, before the twentieth century, the idea that art was concerned with space but not time prevailed in both theory and practice.[90] Largely owing to the type of material available during the eighteenth and nineteenth centuries, artworks offered only a still segment of time, a single moment that distilled the "essence" of the subject: scenes were fixed in static, immobile and unchangeable snapshots. But while temporal stasis led to a preoccupation with composition, a desire to create the illusion of depth or movement within a painting as we saw in the previous chapter, artists were further constrained by the spatial confinement of the canvas. Conventional composition developed various techniques to make these limitations seem less problematic, even planned: creating an internal frame with convenient trees, for instance, in order to bring the eye into the picture and away from its edge (a method frequently found in the horizon paintings of Courbet, Friedrich, and Whistler); or focusing on something within the scene to draw attention away from any suggestion of time, depth, or space beyond, as if the composition were purposefully self-contained.[91] Such use of perspective suggests only one possible viewing position for an audience, an optimum position that promotes a feeling of individualism, as Giedion explains: "[e]very element in a perspective representation is related to the unique point of view of the individual spectator."[92] Like the listening strategies promoted by the bifurcated concert hall, gallery visitors are negotiated into an ideal viewing position from which they are able to feel fully absorbed into the virtual space of the painting. Just as the flow of information between musician and audience is seldom one-way, the art viewer cannot be considered an inactive recipient, although they must remain physically separated from the work.

But if we recall Kantor's observation above, that space can never be a "passive receptacle," it becomes necessary to re-evaluate the physical gap between viewer and artwork. To do this, we must first acknowledge that the gallery walls can never be completely "objective," or "disinterested." As his argument progresses, O'Doherty recognises the impossibility of a non-texted art environment, remarking that it is always an intertextual space defined by commerce, aesthetics, the artists, and their audiences: "The white wall's apparent neutrality is an illusion. It stands for a community with common ideas and assumptions."[93] As we shall see below, there have been many successful attempts to deconstruct the illusionary neutrality of the white cube by encouraging the artworks to engage with the walls on which they were hung. The abstract nature of Howard Hodgkin's work, which frequently escapes from the canvas and reaches out across the frame towards the wall, has created particular curatorial debate. Commenting on a touring exhibition of the artist's small paintings in 1990, Richard Calvocoressi, Director of the Scottish National Gallery of Modern Art, explained that the works did not hang obviously together: his response, in the 2002 exhibition of Hodgkin's large works, was to give each painting its own, darkly painted wall in order to create a space that was "more amorphous, less immediately defined."[94] Returning to Blesser's contention that musical composition has been restricted by the performance spaces available, a constraint that encourages composers to "assume a fixed aural architecture," it is possible to identify a similar tendency at play here. Although trying to emerge from the confines of frame, Hodgkin's works were nevertheless situated on blank walls, "less immediately defined," but still existing in an "eternity of display" that hinders "the two-way relationship" between music, art, and their spaces (Blesser).

However, a travelling retrospective of Hodgkin's work four years later at the Irish Museum of Modern Art, Kilmainham, Dublin (February to May 2006) and Tate Britain, London (June to September), demonstrates a reconceptualisation of the traditional exhibition wall akin to the expansions from the stage by Xenakis and Ligeti. Curators Nicholas Serota and Enrique Juncosa worked with the artist to produce a more architecturally holistic approach to display; spread through several rooms, the paintings were placed on walls whose colours modulated from dull grey to luminous green, uneven white to dreary beige, before coming finally to rest in a room vibrating with distressed and streaky gold. The reviews were mixed: putting him in mind of a "gallery makeover," Adrian Searle's review of the exhibition in *The Guardian* concludes that "[t]he effect all this has on Hodgkin's paintings is disturbing. His Bloomsbury studio is top-lit and white-walled, the distractions kept to a minimum. Why add all this extra-textured atmosphere? It doesn't help the paintings."[95] Others disagreed. Andrew Graham-Dixon's reaction in the *Sunday Telegraph*, for instance, was completely different: the coloured walls, he writes;

> make the whole display feel as though it is not set in an art gallery at all, but in some imaginary Renaissance or Baroque palace. The effect is brilliant, giving the satisfying arc of a trajectory to the whole of the artist's life in paint—making it into a single book, so to speak, albeit one with different chapters, and bringing out the inner coherence of Hodgkin's pictures, which in the context come to seem almost like a single, unified decorative scheme.[96]

While, for Searle, the holistic approach to hanging art hindered an easy appreciation of the paintings, Graham-Dixon applauded the "unified decorative scheme" for allowing Hodgkin's splattered edges to echo with the congruent-coloured walls. As the exhibition space became active, each painting struck up a dialogue with its neighbour: and as the viewer's attention was refocused on the spaces between works, the gallery became an interactive, social space, rather than a passive "white cube."

From Object to Process

In the previous chapter, we noted that the containment of painting began to break apart in the twentieth century as visual artists attempted to encapsulate time—and musicalised time in particular—into their work. However, the inclusion of time was not only manifest within the frame: it also began to renegotiate the space between artwork and viewer. Modern art, for the "first time since the Renaissance," explains Giedion, demonstrates a new and self-consciously enlarged "conception of space."[97] As the gallery interior came to favour unobtrusive presentation in order to "focus" attention on the artwork, there can be found a corresponding move to re-activate the exhibition space, a move that mirrored the incorporation of space as primary material by Ligeti, Xenakis, and others mentioned above. And, just as in compositional history, the first attempts at spatial expansion came from within the confines of traditional environments.

O'Doherty understands the history of artistic practice during the twentieth century as operating in direct response to the spaces in which it resides: "The history of modernism is intimately framed by that space; or rather the history of modern art can be correlated with changes in that space and in the way we see it."[98] Once alert to it, O'Doherty's spatial history is clear to see. Towards the end of the nineteenth century, some painters in Europe began to abandon established conventions of realistic representation for a more abstract approach, placing emphasis on the creative process of painting rather than on the subject matter. Accompanying this attack on realism (expressed succinctly by Maurice Denis in his famous 1890 dictum that, before a picture is subject matter, it is a surface coloured with "lines and colours") came a move towards the "literalisation" and "lateralisation" of the picture plane as both space and time became common artistic material.[99]

Although many artistic styles were involved in the move from realism, the process has been discussed most prominently with reference to Impressionist artists (initially a satirical term coined in 1874 by French art critic Louis Leroy) Monet, Pissarro, and Sisley in particular. These artists treated the canvas as an plane with length and breadth but not depth, a horizontal surface in which the subject matter seemed "casually chosen" (O'Doherty): "The edge eclipsing the subject seems a somewhat haphazard decision that could just as well have been made a few feet left or right."[100] As the content of painting became increasingly shallow, the hermetic seal of the frame came under attack as composition and subject matter began to overflow the edge, expanding laterally into the gallery space. Works such as Monet's impressions of water lilies at his Giverny home, painted around the turn of the twentieth century, not only depict a new, flattened spatial representation; they also require a refreshed spatial relationship between work and audience. If the viewer approaches the painting for a closer look, the image begins to fragment, a dissolution that demands an ideal viewing position in order for the illusion successfully to operate (although a similar preoccupation with surface matter and temporality can be found in the later "flatness" of what Clement Greenberg called Jackson Pollock's "American-Type" painting, their abstraction issued fewer orders to the viewer).[101] At first, though, the formal innovations of the Impressionist painters did not influence curatorial habit and, however radical the artwork, the exhibition style remained very traditional. O'Doherty reminds us that the group of painters, having been rejected by the Salon, set up their own exhibition in Paris. But during this 1874 show (that prompted Leroy's use of the term "impressionism"), the revolutionary works were contained within thick frames and conventionally hung: in fact, it wasn't until 1960 that the frames were removed for the Monet exhibition at MoMA.

Cubist artists worked in a more explicit way. Early examples of analytic cubism are infused with transparent geometric planes that emphasise the flatness of the canvas by unfolding the painted space into a linear, two-dimensional surface on which everything is visible at once. Such simultaneity was likened by Giedion to the understanding of space in modern physics, which is "conceived of as relative to a moving point of reference, not as the absolute and static entity of the baroque system of Newton."[102] The inclusion of time onto the canvas as a structuring principle added a fourth dimension to the work, breaking from Renaissance perspective to offer a relative view of an object in which multiple angles are given the same visual weight. Although the process, visible in works such as Picasso's *Le*

Guitariste (1910), is understood by Gene Youngblood as the transference of "exterior reality for interior reality," it nevertheless took the eye from the middle of the picture and sent it back out to the space of the viewer.[103]

The simultaneism articulated by the Italian Futurists represents a different confusion of spatial and temporal dimensions yet again: rather than create a "lateralisation" by sending the painting out into the spectator's arena, Umberto Boccioni called for context to be brought into the represented space. In "The Technical Manifesto of Futurist Sculpture" (1912), the artist called for the simultaneity of the movement and speed existing between an object and its surroundings, a process that directed his pencil drawing of a sculpture, *Table + Bottle + Block of Houses* (1912) in which objects and environment interpenetrate: "LET'S SPLIT OPEN OUR FIGURES AND PLACE THE ENVIRONMENT WITHIN THEM."[104] Such an *"interpenetration of the planes"* (Boccioni) brought the surrounding space into the picture, in order to better dissolve the distinction between work and life: "henceforth the spectator will be placed in the heart of the picture."[105] The result, writes David Ohana, is:

> a synthesis of what a man remembers and what a man sees—a communication of all unseen but existing elements like feelings, smells, and noises, and a simultaneity of movement, space and time. The aim of the futurists was the immersion of the viewer in a total experience.[106]

The moment a dimension beyond the frame is entered, or suggested, the gallery space is powerfully activated, becoming more than a functional "white cube" or a neutral display case. Placing the environment within the picture activated the gallery space in a different way by emphasising the *process* of viewing. The immersion identified by Ohana, however, was not always a pleasant experience. Focusing on the interaction between work and viewer, Futurist manifestos encouraged painters to antagonise their audiences in order to wrench them from their polite viewing habits: writing on the "Pleasure of Being Booed," Marinetti asked that performers infuriate their audiences, suggesting various tricks such as the double-booking of exhibition or performance venues and covering seats with glue.[107] Artists, urged the Futurist manifestos, must "go out into the street, launch assaults from theatres and introduce the fisticuff into the artistic battle."[108] Such sabotage ran along lines similar to the later gestures unleashed by Cage and Xenakis in their attacks on the conventional way of listening to live music.

Just as musical practices during the early twentieth century acquired a growing sense of spatial freedom as composers and musicians began to remove the single focus prevalent in traditional theatre and music performance, Monet, Picasso, and Boccioni began to break from the confines of the frame and the two-dimensionality of the canvas in various different ways. But while early Impressionist and Cubist techniques explicitly displayed their two-dimensionality, several artists extended their work into the space directly in front of the painting. At first, this process was relatively subtle. In 1912, Picasso (in his move towards synthetic cubism) stuck a piece of oilcloth printed with chair caning on a canvas (*Still Life With Chair Caning*), an action that allowed the diegetic consciousness to slide out of its frame into the space beyond: by the '50s, Rauschenberg was combining found objects, such as a chair, with his painted surfaces (*Pilgrim*, 1960), additions that moved the work physically into the spectator's space in order to blur the boundaries between painting and context even further.

As the twentieth century progressed, the architectural configuration of displaying art began to take centre stage with the emergence of installation art: what the work looked like and what it meant became dependent to a large extent on the configuration of the space in which it is realised. A landmark statement was made by Duchamp in 1938 when he hung twelve hundred (empty) coal sacks from the ceiling of the Galerie Beaux-Arts, as part of the International Exhibition of Surrealism. O'Doherty describes Duchamp's inversion of expectation as a gesture "unobtrusive physically but totally obtrusive psychologically."[109] Several years later, during the surrealist exhibition in New York (1942), the artist moved into the physically intrusive with his *Mile of String*, a length of rope positioned with the primary intention of impeding viewing. Experiencing this work was not possible without clear awareness of the exhibition environment.

By the 1960s, and coinciding with the availability of video, gestures that drew the environment into their physical and aesthetic core appeared with increasing frequency. These pieces began to take context as their primary material, mirroring the concurrent expansion of musical material of Cage, Stockhausen, and the sound- and noise-music artists discussed in the previous chapter. Sitespecific, such work was reactive to its location and thus "exposed this space as a material entity" (James Meyer).[110] Hans Haacke's *Condensation Cube* (1963–65), for instance, was physically responsive to its environment: water, enclosed in a Perspex cube, underwent a process of evaporation and condensation in response to the changing light and heat in the gallery; in so doing, the relationship between art and space became entirely codependent. Before he became involved with video work, conceptual artist William Anastasi demonstrated the changing function of the gallery in an exhibition at the Dwan Gallery, New York City (1965). Having photographed the walls of the empty gallery, he then silk-screened the images on to a canvas slightly smaller than the walls themselves, before hanging the work back in its own photographed area: a demonstration of the gallery's transformation from uninflected space to artistic subject, from context to content. A similar emphasis, this time on external space, was enacted by Richard Hamilton in *The Solomon R. Guggenheim* (1965–1966). Based on the recently completed design for the building by Frank Lloyd Wright, the piece consisted of six fibreglass copies of the building, each finished in different colours. When exhibited, the physical places of art consumption were thrown into relief, an action understood by Kynaston McShine as one that will "divorce us from that institution and its content and reduce it to a decorative object."[111]

The process of converting architectural space into a "decorative object" underpinned another conceptual event that took place four years later. In *Wrapped Museum of Contemporary Art, and Wrapped Floor and Stairway, Chicago, 1968–69*, Christo and Jeanne-Claude enveloped the gallery in 10,000 square feet (930 square meters) of heavy tarpaulin, tied up with 4,000 feet (1,219 meters) of manila rope: inside, the lower gallery was buried beneath 2,800 square feet (260 square meters) of cloth, secured with ropes, to form *Wrapped Floor and Stairway* (fig. 3.4).[112] Subverting the traditional gallery function, they managed to contain the container, turning the objectifying cube into the object of interest, a demonstration that suggested that gallery space is not art, in the traditional sense, but has an "artlike" quality, a "meta-life around and about art" (O'Doherty).[113] Dennis Oppenheim demonstrated a similar anti-art action in 1969 in his *Gallery Transplant*: here, the artist used the imprint of the gallery as his primary material by tracing the floor plan of gallery 4 from the then-named Andrew Dickson White Museum of Art (Cornell University) in the snow near Ithaca, New York. The result was a silent, dematerialised objectification of the sanctified museum space and a refusal to produce a collectible artefact.

But whether or not the artwork took specific gallery architecture as its primary material, installation art used space as a compositional medium that could inform form and structure in a way similar to the spatial strategies of Stockhausen. The result required viewing behaviour very different to that identified by Whitehead in the nineteenth-century British art gallery, in which "display methods intended to allow the art work to become the predominant visual feature of an interior." As mentioned, because many video artist-composers came not from filmmaking,

Figure 3.4 Cristo and Jeanne-Claude, *Wrapped Museum of Contemporary Art*, Chicago, 1968–69. Photo Harry Shunk. © Cristo, 1969.

but from the art world, video has been closely aligned with, and even identified as a strand of, installation art. Erika Suderburg defines installation art in terms of spatial activation:

> *Installation* is the noun form of the verb *to install*, the functional move-ment of placing the work of art in the "neutral" void of the gallery or museum. Unlike earthworks, it initially focused on institutional art spaces and public spaces that could be altered through "installation" as an action. "To install" is a process that must take place each time an exhi-bition is mounted; "installation" is the art form that takes note of the perimeters of that space and reconfigures it.[114]

The idea of spatial reconfiguration and impermanence distinguishes installation from other types of art that are transported, already completed, into the exhibi-tion space. Rather, installation works often occupy, and therefore activate, the entire "neutral void" of the gallery space. Such expansion requires a rethink of traditional gallery organisation, in which artworks, sometimes by many differ-ent authors, are separated from one another by frames or, at least, by wall space. Defined by its physical properties, installation art is, as Adam Gopnik points out, "unified more by a common ideology than by a common set of forms—unified more by what it is trying to accomplish than by the way it looks."[115] Beneath the umbrella heading, in other words, are styles too numerous and eclectic to consti-tute a "movement." In support of Gopnik's comment is the difference between two of the earliest examples of installation art, in the historically precise sense of the term: Yves Klein's *Le Vide* ("The Void," Galerie Iris Clert, Paris 1958), was simply a whitewashed, empty gallery space, an absence of content intended to evoke "an ecstatic and immediately communicable emotion" (*Le Vide* Invitation, 1958); two years later, Arman (Armand Pierre Fernandez), responded to Klein's statement with *Le Plein* ("The Full-Up"), in which the same space was crammed so full of found objects, that visitors were forced to view the room from the outside window.[116]

As with the nomenclature of many schools and concepts, the term "installation art" emerged years after the first works to which it is now attached. Instead, dur-ing its early evolution, installation works came under many headings. In 1958, for instance—a time when "installation" referred simply to the way in which an exhi-bition was hung—Allan Kaprow coined the term "Environment" to describe his room-sized multimedia explorations, a designation intended to separate his work from the discrete sculptural object. For a long while, "environment" and "instal-lation" were used interchangeably and, when "Installation" appeared for the first time in *The Art Index* (in its twenty-seventh volume, November 1978–79), there was no description but merely a reroute to the section entitled "Environment": in fact, it was not until fifteen years later (volume 42, October 1993–94) that a list of articles appeared under "Installation." Before the terminological transformation from "Environment" to "Installation", nuanced designations such as "assemblage," "project art," "site-specific art," and "temporary art" emerged as complementary ways of articulating a physical and temporal space.[117] Although subtle differences were implied by each term, the defining feature of each was the spatial, locational, and/or contextual element of the work.

Latent in installation, site-specific and temporary art's combination of disparate disciplines and methods of display was a changing attitude towards the viewer. The recognition that a change in conception was afoot was clearly articulated in 1969 by Jennifer Licht, curator of *Spaces*, the first exhibition of installation art to be held at MoMA:

> [Space] is now being considered as an active ingredient, not simply to be represented but to be shaped and characterized by the artist, and capable of involving and merging the viewer and art in a situation of greater scope and scale. In effect, one now enters the interior space of the work of art…and is presented with a set of conditions rather than a finite object. Working within the almost unlimited potential of these enlarged, more spatially complex circumstances, the artist is now free to influence and determine, even govern, the sensations of the viewer. The human presence and perception of the spatial context have become materials of art.[118]

In her announcement, Licht indicates the institutional recognition of a physically and conceptually expanded art form that listed amongst its tangible ingredients situation and reception. This latter consideration was to have a profound effect on art and its exhibition. In her historical analysis of installation art, Claire Bishop identifies in the genre three main features. One is the inclusion of found objects and materials that, like expanded sculpture, deconstruct the notion of the precious and unique work of art, a technique employed in Arman's *Le Plein*. Her other two points, however, refer to the implications of the spatial expansion of installation works into the viewing area of the gallery, an extension that not only initiates a direct connection between art and observer, but also requires an "activation" of viewers who, confronted with assembled fragments, must mentally assemble and interpret the piece.[119]

Theorist Julie H. Reiss has seized on these last two points, going so far as to claim that the "essence of installation art is spectator participation…the viewer is required to complete the piece; the meaning evolves from the interaction between the two."[120] Like music, the philosophical changes in art aesthetic in the late 1960s prompted a fundamental shift in focus from the fixed object to the viewer. Kwon articulates this change in emphasis in terms of process:

> Going against the grain of institutional habits and desires, and continuing to resist the commodification of art in/for the marketplace,

site-specific art adopts strategies that are either aggressively antivi-
sual—informational, textural, expositional, didactic—or immaterial
altogether—gestures, events, or performances bracketed by temporal
boundaries.[121]

Viewer completion was already a self-conscious component of paintings such
as Rauschenberg's all-black-and-white canvases and the minimal sculpture of
Donald Judd, Jasper Johns, and Dan Flavin in the 1960s, which, much like Klein's
Le Vide, left a space for the viewer to fill. But the idea was ardently embraced by
proponents of early installation works and environments such as Kaprow, who
explored its possibilities in both his art pieces and theoretical texts. Over eleven
years before MoMA's *Spaces* exhibition, the architect of the Happening wrote that
visitors to his show at the Hansa Gallery, New York, did not "come to look *at*
things" but rather found themselves a dynamic part of the surrounding exhibit,
the degree of their passivity or interaction determined, as in the performance
of Cage's work, by their "talents for 'engagement'."[122] An experience rather than
an artwork imbued with prior meaning, Kaprow's environment moved attention
away from the "finite object" and placed it instead on what Licht was later to refer
to as "a set of conditions." Required to "complete the piece," the visitor was given
an increased responsibility over the success or failure of his work, a responsibility that, with one gesture, reduced the autonomy of the artist-as-creator and
increased the fragility and impermanence of the piece. "We ourselves are shapes,"
explains Kaprow:

> We have differently colored clothing; can move, feel, speak, and observe
> others variously; and will constantly change the "meaning" of the work
> by so doing. There is, therefore, a never-ending play of changing condi-
> tions between the relatively fixed or "scored" parts of my work and the
> "unexpected" or undetermined parts.... [it is] possible to experience the
> whole exhibit differently at different times. These have been composed
> in such a way as to offset any desire to see them in the light of the tradi-
> tional, closed, clear forms of art as we have known them.[123]

The possibility of an exhibit that embraces and encourages an ever-morphing
dialogue between its "scored" sections and the "undetermined" part performed
by its visitors recalls the notion of music-as-performance, or Carolyn Abbate's
"drastic" experience of opera, whereby "music" is the result of a dialogue
between work and its performance.[124] As we have seen, visual art, unlike music,
does not traditionally require realisation through performance: the principle of
performativity introduced by early installation artists and the orchestrators of
Happenings, then, initiated a shift between art-as-object and art-as-process,
or what art historian Lucy Lippard calls the "the dematerialisation of the art
object."[125]

RoseLee Goldberg suggests that live performance and theatricality became a tool that enabled artists to draw together more closely the interrelationship between gallery space and exhibit while devaluing the commodity value of art: like the Futurists, Goldberg explains that "performance was the surest means of disrupting a complacent public."[126] While the examples above brought the space of display into sharp relief, Vito Acconci's work highlighted the refreshed role of the visitor that such spatial activation entailed, explaining that his work operated "*in* a public rather than *in front of* a public."[127] In *Service Area*, first enacted in 1970 at MoMA, the artist had his mail forwarded to the museum, explaining that he was treating the space "not as a display (exhibition) area but as a place that provides services: since I've been granted a space in the show, I should be able to use that space for my own purposes, make that space part of my normal life."[128] Acconci's desire to include the public in his work by making the gallery space part of "normal life" was a sentiment that lay at the heart of early video work: "As a medium that is economically accessible and requires minimal technical skills to master, video is ideally suited as a vehicle for the close integration of art and life," explains Christine Tamblyn.[129] In *Proximity Piece* (1970), Acconci moved art and life even closer together (fig. 3.5): the work involved "standing near a person and intruding on his/her personal space" during the exhibition, a transgression that ruptured the institution's aura as a "rarefied-space/isolation box/home-for-museum-pieces."[130]

But while the examples above either drew attention to the gallery space or attempted to sabotage its traditions, other works ventured from its walls entirely, a move embraced by the first video artist-musicians discussed in the next chapter. Kurt Schwitters's *Merzbau* (1923–43) is one of the earliest examples of the evolution from object to environment. *Merzbau* was a work of art situated in the artist's house in Hannover, a collage which gradually evolved into a sculptural environment that extended through six or more rooms until Schwitters was forced to move the tenants from his upper rooms in order to continue. The work not only combined domesticity with artwork; it also suggested a less formal and more organic process of experiencing and collecting art (the house was destroyed in an air raid in 1943).

Gathering pace towards the rise of video art-music, art that was created and situated outside the institutional framework of the museum began to flourish in the form of performance art, Happenings, land art, body art, and mail art. Happenings, actions, and performances, for instance, could take place in any location, such as the courtyard of a derelict hotel in Greenwich Village (Kaprow: *Courtyard*, 1962), while events such as Charlotte Moorman's avant-garde Festival appropriated a different New York City environment each year (from Central Park to the Staten Island Ferry). Land art, on the other hand, was often located beyond the city environment: Michael Heizer's *Double Negative* (1969) was created in the Nevada desert; and Robert Smithson's *Spiral Jetty* (1970) was created in Great Salt Lake, Utah. Although arising from a different aesthetic, the earthworks of

Figure 3.5 Vito Acconci, performance of *Proximity Piece* at the Jewish Museum, New York (1970). © Vito Acconci.

Walter De Maria, Heizer, and Smithson in the late 1960s were also predicated on an avoidance of institutional validity, artefice, and commercialism. De Maria, for example, also the drummer for The Primitives (an early incarnation of The Velvet Underground) in the early 1960s, created land art spectacles that responded directly to environmental factors. *The Lightning Field* (1977) is an ongoing project that consists of four hundred steel poles set out in a large grid (one mile by one kilometre) in the desert of New Mexico. Although created with the intention of attracting lightning, its occurrence is not necessary for the success of the work, and visitors are encouraged to spend the night in purpose-built accommodation in order that they should have as much time as possible to walk in, and experience, the field.

Expanded Cinema

Many artists and composers strove to subvert the environments of art exhibition and music performance from within the establishment by including as creative material the "human presence" of the audience and the "perception of the spatial context." As art became site-specific and context-driven and music began to reach physically into the audiences' space, the role of performance assumed great importance. But as we have also seen, others decided to forge new performance and exhibition arenas in the form of specially designed pavilions or desert terrain. It is in both the refreshed spaces of gallery and concert hall, and the newly created or appropriated environments, that music and art began their collision. However, the communal, interactive environments forged by experimental filmmakers during the 1960s added an element of intermediality to the development. In the previous chapters, the films of experimental artists were placed within an audiovisual lineage; if this trajectory is reframed spatially, it becomes clear how the journey towards intermediality necessitated drastic changes in performance and reception styles. Youngblood, who produced the seminal text on expanded cinema as it was emerging in 1970, explained that the genre could not be defined in terms of its material qualities. The expansion, he suggests, cannot be located in "computer films, video phosphors, atomic light, or spherical projections," but rather in "life's process of becoming, man's ongoing historical drive to manifest his consciousness outside of his mind, in front of his eyes."[131] Bruce Jenkins phrases Youngblood's definition in a more sober way, describing expanded cinema in terms of the spatialisation it fostered: "These films activated the space of projection and by emptying the content of the image focused attention on the presentational rather than the representational."[132]

Interest on the "presentational" can be seen in the earliest examples of expanded cinema. The audiovisual environment created by Jordan Belson and Henry Jacobs for their Vortex concerts (1957 to 1959), for instance, was located at the California Academy of Science's Morrison Planetarium in San Francisco. Making use of the planetarium's multiprojection possibilities and the numerous speakers that surrounded the dome, Belson and Jacobs created an immersive multimedia environment in which visual work was combined with multichannelled sound that mixed Afro-Cuban and Balinese music with excerpts from Stockhausen and Berio. Belson explains that his visual feast included "strobes, star projectors, rotational sky projectors, kaleidoscope projectors, and four special dome-projectors for interference patterns. We were able to project images over the entire dome, so that things would come pouring down from the center, sliding along the walls. At times the whole place would seem to reel."[133]

A similar desire to create audiovisual immersion was behind sculptor Milton Cohen's Space Theatre (from 1957), a loft environment in Ann Arbor that the artist intended "to free film from its flat and frontal orientation and to present it within an ambience of total space."[134] Within the domelike "total space," designed by architect Harold Borkin, film and slides were projected at a rotating mirrored core to create a kaleidoscopic lightshow that entered into a dialogue with the amplified sound of the machinery and the electronic vocal and instrumental music, largely composed by Robert Ashley and Gordon Mumma. The mixture of tape music and live performance was passed between various speakers: the result, explains Cohen, was "one of sound in flight; sound seeking target."[135]

In 1963, Stan VanDerBeek created a large hemispheric dome from an old grain silo located at an artists' colony in Stony Point, New York. Visitors lay on the floor of this "Movie Drome," where they were subject to a "visual velocity" (VanDerBeek) that erupted from several projectors simultaneously. Images from handmade slides, video collages and stop-motion animation were spread, with corresponding sounds, across both hemispheric screen and audience (he later abandoned the project due to technical problems).[136] Several years later, Aldo Tambellini constructed the Black Gate Electromedia Theatre in New York City, the space in which he staged his infamous *Black Zero* in 1965, one of the first "electromedia" environments.[137] This large-scale production included variations of tiny black shapes projected via hundreds of hand-painted films and slides onto a large balloon that increased in size until it exploded: the visual crescendo was accompanied by an aural one in the form of electronic-tape music, the words of poet Calvin C. Herton, and live, amplified cello. Of particular importance to the emergence of video art-music was *HPSCHD* (the computer abbreviation for harpsichord), a collaboration between Cage and intermedia-artist Ronald Nameth that has been described by Salter as "a prototypal and monumental event in the history of live image/sound performance."[138] The event, which took place at the University of Illinois in May, 1969, involved five hours of computer music, programmed by Cage with Lejaren Hiller, that was spread throughout the hall via a circle of over fifty loudspeakers. The compositions, stated Cage, could be used "in whole or in part, in any combination with or without interruptions, to make an indeterminate concert of any agreed-upon length."[139] Seven harpsichordists, sitting at amplified instruments in the middle of the hall, were instructed to play their own, individual solo, but could also choose to play any of the others. The sounds entered into a dialogue with a plethora of Nameth's slides and films depicting "qualities of space", which were projected simultaneously onto large screens.[140] Iles describes the results as "a kind of communal dream space, or metaphor of expanded consciousness."[141]

Significantly, these artists and composers were not operating in isolation. Other examples of "communal dream space" include the expanded cinema actions of Peter Weibel and VALIE EXPORT; the moving light compositions of Jackie Cassen and Rudi Stern; the filmstage performances of Carolee Schneemann, such as *Night Crawlers* (1967) in which live actors interacted with projected film (we'll come back to this in chapter 5); the expanded cinema performances based on inflatable projection surfaces by Jeffrey Shaw and Theo Botschuijver, like *Movie Movie* (1967); and the intermedia performances of Jud Yalkut, such as *Dream Reel* (1969). Salter points out that simultaneous events, such as the Newport Jazz and Monterey Pop festivals, can be considered as "equivalent mass culture centers for a similarly themed exploration of expanded consciousness through audiovisual means."[142] Events such as Andy Warhol's *Exploding Plastic Inevitable* (1966), a combination of film, performance by the Velvet Underground, and live action, or the Grateful Dead's multiscreen projection environments created by John Whitney Jr. and his brother Michael (1966–1967), operated in a similar way (see video 3.2▶).

If we return to Giedion's call for an architecture that emphasised its "many-sidedness," a desire equally apparent in the Cubist search for simultaneity and the Futurists' "*interpenetration of the planes,*" the "expanded consciousness" promoted by expanded cinema can be seen as a clear development of art experimentation from Monet to Kaprow. But by bringing music and sound into the mix, expanded cinema also linked in to a lineage of sonic expansion articulated in various ways from Xenakis to Cage. Although multi-authored, these multimedia spaces enabled sound and image to collide, bringing the spectator into the centre of the work and providing them with an interactive, creative, audiovisual role.

The Audiovisual Space

These multimedia spaces were of great importance to the audiovisual arenas of early video. But just as the audiovisuality of video can be traced back through centuries of creative practice, the increasing spatialisation of music and art that preceded the technology's "integrating birth" (Spielmann) was a long process. The expansion of creative spaces experienced a quickened pace during the twentieth century, in which, to recall Moholy-Nagy, "The principle means of creation is the space itself." At the same time as art began to break viewers from conventional viewing habits, murmurs of discontent were voiced in music circles concerning the ritualistic nature of performance. In the same way as art began to break free from its frame, the performance situation became an important component of music. The "relation" between elements became increasingly important, a refocus that enabled context to become content. As music attempted to break its spatial bonds and art its temporal ones, it was not long before the two converged: no longer contained within a frame or by the stage, art and music began to come together in a newly formed, audience-based performative space.

As we shall see in the next chapter, this space became the hunting ground for audiovisual video artists, who surrounded their viewers with music and images that transcended both the immobility of gallery exhibition and the segregation of performer/listener in the concert hall. Video's ability to resculpt the gallery space in real time links it to the spatial expansions of both music and art and the multimedia spaces of expanded cinema. If we decentre the discussion of video from object to the environment in which video pieces reside, it is possible to trace for it an assortment of ancestries that enhance its intermedial qualities. On closer inspection, then, it is possible to revoice the assertion in my introduction to suggest that video art-music represents the culmination of both intermedial and spatial experimentation. In fact, the two histories are inextricably intertwined and although they are here presented in separate chapters, it must be remembered that neither expansion would have been as groundbreaking without the other. The material expansions of art and music outlined in the previous chapter can therefore be framed in terms of a parallel *spatial* expansion in both disciplines.

4

The Rise of Video Art-Music

1963–1970

The hybrid or the meeting of two media is a moment of truth
and revelation from which new form is born. For the parallel
between two media holds us on the frontiers between forms
that snap us out of the Narcissus-narcosis. The moment of the
meeting of media is a moment of freedom and release from the
ordinary trance and numbness imposed by them on our senses.
(Marshall McLuhan)[1]

As music performance spread from its stage and visual art from its frame, a new, intermedial space was formed that provided the perfect environment for video artist-composers. Today, audiovisual video pieces are collected and commissioned by the main art galleries, museums, and concert halls worldwide, with audiovisual pieces found in both permanent and touring art collections and appearing on some of the world's largest opera stages. It is commonly believed that this accept-ance of video art-music into the museum and gallery world was signalled by two of the major retrospectives of video artists: in 1982, the Whitney Museum of American Art held a retrospective of Nam June Paik's sculptural video work, including his *TV Garden* (1974–78) and *TV Clock* (1963–81); five years later, the Museum of Modern Art (MoMA) presented a large-scale video exhibition with a Bill Viola retrospective. But evidence of institutional acceptance can be found much earlier. During the early to mid-1970s, for instance, the Everson Museum of Art hired the world's first curator of video, David A. Ross; MoMA established a video art gallery; and the Whitney Museum began its film and video gallery.[2] By 1976, most of the major galleries and museums in America had exhibited video pieces and both the Rockefeller Foundation and the New York State Council on the Arts (NYSCA) had begun to support the format financially. When compared with the length of time it took for photography to be accepted as an artistic dis-cipline (as the most recent example of a "new" mode of expression), video's rapid success is rather astonishing.

And yet, the relationship between video and the institutional space was not always a congenial one. While the intermedial qualities of video create a

double-channelled being—the artist-composer—these same qualities pose significant problems for its exhibition, or performance. The creation of music to
be watched as well as heard, and artwork that was audible as well as visual,
made the boundaries between exhibition and performance fragile: if the genre
represents the convergence of music and art histories, where should these
works be housed? Hans-Peter Schwarz, director of the Zentrum für Kunst
und Medientechnologie, Karlsruhe (ZKM, Germany), described media art as
an "explosive charge" at the gates of traditional art establishments, a charge
which, led by video artist-composers, was not at first successful.[3] Before the
major art institution became a "convenient outlet" (Marita Sturken) for video
pieces in the mid-1970s, the format occupied alternative exhibition and performance spaces, locations that were not devoted to either music or art and
could thus be more easily appropriated: the small, privately owned gallery;
people's houses or lofts; public spaces.[4] In this sense, video art-music was not
alone. Intermedial environments have always had a problematic relationship to
existing institutions. While the mass appeal and considerable economic opportunities of film had enabled the creation of a whole new environment—the
cinema—other twentieth-century multiauthored works had requirements that
a traditional gallery or concert hall space could not fulfil. Their realisation, as
we have seen, often demanded a new space. On the one hand, buildings and
theatres were purpose-built to accommodate the multimedia environments,
as we saw in the previous chapter—Wagner chose to build his own theatre in
Bayreuth for his self-styled operatic creations, for example, while the mixed
media, gestural dance performances at the Bauhaus were performed on multiple stages housed in specially designed buildings; similarly, the Black Mountain
College collaborations between John Cage, David Tudor, Robert Rauschenberg,
Merce Cunningham, and Charles Olsen were initiated at Lake Eden. On the
other hand, locations previously used for other purposes were occupied—
Jordan Belson's avant-garde music and visual "Vortex Concerts" of the late
1950s, for instance, took place in a planetarium; during the early 1960s, Allan
Kaprow staged his Happenings in old churches, lofts, and courtyards (fig. 4.1);
the expanded cinema performances of Andy Warhol, in which multiscreen film
and slide projections accompanied live music, were held in huge, derelict warehouses; and Fluxus performances took place in the Café-au-Go-Go, Yoko Ono's
Chambers Street loft, and Larry Poons's Epitome Café. Disciplinary hybridity
during the twentieth century, then, encouraged art and music to move away
from established and specialised spaces. Many of those working with video
during its early years came from experimental backgrounds and had already
engaged with music, film, installation, dance, and live performance before they
turned their attentions to the new format.

    While multidisciplinary performances and "Vortex Concerts" required spaces
larger than those available in the gallery or music venue, audiovisual video
work encouraged listening and viewing strategies at odds with conventional

Figure 4.1 Allan Kaprow, Happening 1962, New York. Photo © Lawrence Shustak. Courtesy the Estate of L. N. Shustak.

modes of behaviour. Initially, the resultant "explosive charge" was blocked by traditional institutions: but inclusion within these spaces was also rejected by those working with the format (and we shall come to this shortly). The similarity of video's communicative strategies to the easily consumed domesticity of television, combined with the format's technological and spatial requirements, challenged the aesthetic (and ideological), financial, and physical operations of institutional exhibition. Although all three challenges are interlinked, the ideological concerns were voiced most strongly by curators, concert promoters, and, significantly, artists themselves. Ten or so years after the first use of video as artistic material, for instance, Kaprow assessed the form, arriving at a less than encouraging conclusion. Video environments, he claimed, were little more than "a lavish form of kitsch" that resemble "world's fair 'futurama' displays with their familiar nineteenth-century push-button optimism and didacticism."[5] Kaprow argued that the inclusion of video into environmental art bred complacency in the viewer, who remained little more than "wowed" by the new technology:

> Intriguing as these [video] works are, they are also discouraging. The level of critical thought in them, their built-in assumptions about people, the indifference to the spaces into which the hardware is put, and the constant reliance on the glitter of the machines to carry the fantasy strike me as simpleminded and sentimental.[6]

Despite video's move into the gallery several years later, Kaprow's scathing assessment remained a common one. In an article for *The New Yorker* in 1991, for example, Adam Gopnik complained that video works "claim the world, but most of them certainly don't *feel* like the world. Instead, they have a rote, self-satisfied peppiness and slickness. What one senses just beneath the contentious surface of the new installations is the complacency of the privileged."[7] Gopnik's sentiment was echoed in the *New York Times* two years later by Roberta Smith, who grumbled that "a lot of artists are spending too much time with sophisticated equipment in darkened rooms" and that contemporary installation has been marred by "[d]elusions of High Tech."[8] According to such assessments, the "glitter of machines" promoted artistic "complacency": those working with video, in other words, were more interested in "simple-minded" technological experimentation than with the creation of a viable audiovisual aesthetic.

While Kaprow, Gopnik, and Smith bemoaned the aesthetic denigration threatened by video's technology, the audiovisual capacity of the "sophisticated equipment" also challenged well-established concert hall and art gallery procedures. As we saw in the previous chapter, the gradual "mythologisation" of art music's performance spaces as listening behaviours changed from the noisy, rowdy audiences of eighteenth-century opera to the attentive public of today resulted in stringent concert-going rituals that have proved remarkably difficult to shake, despite the efforts of Cage and others in the 1950s. Even though interest in the spatialisation of music has been apparent for centuries, Christopher Small's description of the concert venue is one based on rigorous sectionalisation: aural or visual connection with the outside world is kept to a minimum; the listener, motionless and silent, is physically separated from the performance. This is also the case in the cinema (although initially video artists were eager to distance themselves from the commercialisation of this moving image genre). Moreover, music venues are not set up for the display of moving images: to install up to one hundred TV monitors and complicated, interactive surround-sound systems would require substantial financial backing and the occupation of that space for a long duration to make it worthwhile; but both requirements are contrary to the transient nature of the concert hall performance schedule.

The gallery space is often configured in much the same way—natural light is blocked and walls and floors are painted in neutral tones: artwork, in other words, is isolated from everything beyond the gallery walls. Like Small's concert hall, the gallery—or what Brian O'Doherty calls "the white cube"—is also a ritualistic space in which the "sanctity of the church" and the "formality of the courtroom" combine to create a rather formidable environment to attack.[9] Viewers must stand at a selected distance from the work, unable to move around without losing the "best view"; they must contemplate but not touch. Because video works often take over an entire room, the viewer-listener can be immersed entirely, required to cross the normally forbidden threshold in a gallery or concert hall to become part of the work's interior space: to become, in other words, the material of the piece. Early on, in particular, video works, created especially for the site, would not be seen by the curator(s) before arrival. Site-specific artwork, such as the minimalist light sculptures of Dan Flavin and the floor sculptures of Carl André, explains Erika Suderburg, "must be reactive to its site, informed by the contents and materials of its actual location, whether they be industrially, 'naturally' or conceptually produced."[10] The use of closed-circuit video systems in the early pieces of Nam June Paik, Steina and Woody Vasulka, Bruce Nauman, Frank Gillette, Gary Hill, and Peter Campus produced work that was "reactive to its site" at a fundamental level. But as a result, the commissioning of video pieces was both difficult and worrying for the curator. In the catalogue to the Whitney Museum's exhibition, *Anti-Illusion: Procedures / Materials* in 1969, which included a Nauman video corridor, curators Marcia Tucker and James Monte explained that:

> During its organization, we discovered that the normal curatorial procedures of seeing and then selecting or rejecting works to be included could not be followed. After visiting numerous studios and galleries, as well as viewing slides and photographs, we discovered that the bulk of the exhibition would be comprised of painting and sculpture which we had not seen and would not see until perhaps one week before the opening date of the show. That this method of putting together an exhibition is risky for the artist as well as the Museum goes without saying.[11]

Apart from the "risky" business of collecting together unseen pieces, gallery staff also had to get to grips with the technological and practical aspects of video equipment. Large and noisy, many early video pieces occupied entire rooms. This, together with the darkness often required for successful video projection, demanded a method of organisation at odds with the multipiece display of the traditional gallery. So, while the concert hall was the wrong shape for interactive video pieces—a seated arena facing a stage does not allow for easy, spatial mobility—the gallery was hindered by its strict viewing habits: "[t]he spotless gallery wall" standing as it does for "a community with common ideas and assumptions" (O'Doherty) was extremely difficult to shake.[12]

These spatial problems, however, were not caused by the installation element of video alone: they also resulted from video's introduction of sound into the gallery, a place often so silent that viewers are forced to whisper to one another. Artist Lynn Hershman Leeson recalls that "in 1972, the University Art Museum in Berkeley closed an exhibition of mine because I used audio tape and sound in a sculpture entitled *Self Portrait as Another Person*. The museum curators claimed that electronic media was not art and most certainly did not belong in a museum."[13] Unlike image, sound cannot be contained by a frame. Free to move around corners and through walls, it creates problems of confinement and curators have to find inventive ways to prevent the noise from one installation bleeding into other rooms. But not only do sound and music enlarge the sphere of influence of an artwork, they also introduce into the gallery a temporal element. Existing in Stravinsky's "psychological" dimension, audiovisual installation art is at odds with what Margaret Morse has described as "the dominant mode of perceiving in museums and galleries" and required refreshed modes of engagement.[14] Static artwork allows viewers to decide how long to stand in front of a picture: with video, they are required to stay for the duration of a predetermined, or live, sequence of events. Some video works have a specific running time with a narrative that takes a set amount of time to unfold: others, such as Paik's broadcast television works which run continually, can be experienced for any duration. Nevertheless, as images and sound move through time, a mode of perception fundamentally at odds with the traditional type of gallery experience is activated. Viewing in a gallery, in other words, becomes akin to listening; it is temporally determined and involves an aural immersion in the work presented. In the '60s, the transformation required of O'Doherty's timeless white cube was radical. Today, video and the "notion of transgressive, anti-art" may have been accepted into the gallery, but the changes it demanded when it began to appear as part of several large-scale exhibitions in the 1970s, were, and remain, revolutionary ones.

Nevertheless, it is important to note that the initial rejection of video by the major galleries was mirrored by an equally strong rejection of the galleries by video artist-composers. The use of unusual spaces was not simply down to the institutional dismissal of the technological, multidisciplinary and interactive quality of video art-music; it was also the result of an ideological incompatibility between artist-musicians and traditional methods of funding and exhibition. Video emerged during a time of great political and social upheaval. The race riots in American cities from 1964–1968, the assassinations of Martin Luther King and Robert Kennedy in 1968, the Stonewall Bar raid in 1969, combined with civil rights issues, feminism, the gay liberation movement, and anti-war demonstrations led artist-musicians to question their relationship with, and to, their audiences and exhibitors. This was particularly true of the gallery. The revelation that many major art institutions were funded from undesirable sources had a direct impact on artistic direction. The presence of the Rockefeller family on MoMA's Board of Trustees was disapproved of by those who believed the family to be supporting and profiting from the Vietnam War, for instance.[15] Gregory Battcock revealed that:

> The trustees of the museums direct NBC and CBS, the *New York Times* and the Associated Press, and the greatest cultural travesty of modern times—The Lincoln Center. They own AT&T, Ford, General Motors, the great multi-billion dollar foundations, Columbia University, Alcoa, Minnesota Mining, United Fruit and AMK, besides sitting on the boards of each others' museums. The implications of these facts are enormous. Do you realise that it is those art-loving, culturally committed trustees of the Metropolitan and Modern museums who are waging the war in Vietnam?[16]

For many, these "implications" resulted in avoidance of the major gallery and its mechanisms. Art that benefited from such money was frowned upon, while the autonomous "timeless" display procedures of the traditional gallery space, which dissociated art from the outside world and its political and social problems (including the perceived corruption of the galleries themselves), had to be rejected. Alternative spaces began to emerge in New York's SoHo neighbourhood, such as 112 Greene Street, an old industrial space with rough walls and floors where artists could work in "a really free way" (Alice Aycock).[17] Such avoidance of institutional inclusion was loudly voiced in 1969 by the Art Workers' coalition:

> In general, the art object is inadequate to the artist as a means of barter for the necessities of life, irrelevant to the people in a world of hunger, war and racial injustice and precious only to the rich who use it to increase their wealth and maintain their position. To resolve the conflict, artists must develop art that is real for our time, and that is meaningful to those not in on the making of it, that reaches the people and that does not reinforce the horrible sanctity of private property.[18]

While certain antiestablishment ideas can be found as early as the International Exhibition of Surrealism at the Galerie Beaux-Arts in Paris (1938), which made use of many found and intangible objects, such as coal sacks, plants, sound, and odour, the late 1950s and 1960s saw the development of work with little possible (or at least highly problematic) market value, such as land art, process art, conceptual art and performance. Dennis Oppenheim made shapes in wheatfields while Michael Heizer dug holes in the Nevada desert, for instance; Richard Long took and recorded long walks; and On Kawara sent and received postcards. In a similar vein, and as we saw in the previous chapter, George Maciunas, writing in 1964, attempted to explain the aesthetic drive behind the Fluxus group by describing it as "definitely against art-object as non-functional commodity—to be sold and to make [a] livelihood for an artist. It could temporarily have the pedagogical function of teaching people the needlessness of art including the eventual need-lessness of itself. It should not therefore be permanent."[19]

Although the knee-jerk reaction of major galleries against video work was an aesthetic one, the format's resistance to commodification and the "ideological conditions" of viewing required, posed yet another point of conflict. By the time Paik shot his first video on the streets of New York City in 1965, artists and writers had begun to experiment with and theorise the idea that art was not a fixed object that demanded a single interpretation, but was, rather, something that encouraged a continually shifting engagement between itself, other objects, and the subjective recipient: an "art that is real for our time." As we saw in chapter 1, early video work (as defined by its period of "constitution") was less something on display, and more a performance, something that includes as valid art materials space, time, and the audience: what Fredric Jameson referred to as "material occasions for the viewing process."[20] The immediacy of video, derived from its basis in the magnetic technology of sound recording, further enhanced this relationship through its ability to simultaneously record and transmit sound and image: to remain continually "in the process of coming into being" (Belton).[21] By drawing together the processes of videoing and experiencing, creator and receiver, video existed in, and moved through, the time and space of the visitor. Site-specific, interactive, and imbued with a sense of both the immediate and the transient, early video rejected this easy commodification of art: it repelled the notion of a collectable art object through its ability for reproduction. In theory, it is possible to create multiple copies of each video piece although, in practice, the site-specificity of many early works, together with their use of closed-circuit television and audience participation, made this difficult. One can even go so far as to say that video's situation ensured its uniqueness (the same argument can be made for Warhol's works). Even so, the threat of reproducibility made it difficult to place value on early works, and initially the marketability of creative video seemed poor. How do you sell something that is either infinitely reproducible (video) or site-specific (installation); something, moreover, created by artists, not yet known, who were working with a low-art medium associated with the popular cultures of commercial TV and mainstream cinema?

The embrace of the unrepeatable—the single event—in certain music circles had similar goals: Cage's chance-determined performances, Ligeti's graphically notated works, and Riley's fragment-controlled improvisations led to music heavily reliant on circumstance for its execution. The result was music that could be vastly different in each performance. Such performances and process-based artworks contributed to the devaluation of the commodity side of the art or musical (imaginary or not) object. "The 'work' no longer seeks to be a noun/object but a verb/process," explains Miwon Kwon, a process that provokes "the viewer's critical (not just physical) acuity regarding the ideological conditions of that viewing."[22]

For many video artist-composers, then, the use of alternative spaces was a protest against institutionalised exhibition as much as a practical necessity, a gesture along the same lines as Duchamp's metaphorical urination on the gallery. So where were video pieces found and what led to their eventual acceptance into the art world? From a vantage point some fifty years later, the "whole new story" that Scott Bartlett prophesied "our new technologies" would enable is a difficult one to recount.[23] Works from video's young period are difficult to find, with early pieces badly preserved, catalogued exhibitions few, and Events and Happenings unreliably recounted. Early videotape was of poor quality, and much evidence of video art-music's exploratory uses have since degenerated beyond any viable viewing condition, a deterioration that has made the genre's beginnings almost impossible to trace. Left only with a small array of eyewitness accounts, published reviews, interviews, and photographs, the reconstruction of an exact timeline, or the assessment of public reaction to early video art-music and its installation (or performance) is problematic. The difficulties of unearthing an accurate timeline have been compounded by the insatiable desire of early video artists and musicians to narrativise their field: "The need for history increased when information begins to erode and become irretrievable," writes Sturken; "[a]s the *electronic* history of video fades, its *written* history gains importance."[24] According to her, the accelerated development of video, when compared with other media such as photography, provokes the perception that it "must be quickly historicized."[25] As discussed in chapter 1, those working with video were irresistibly drawn by what they perceived to be its *lack* of a past, while simultaneously (and somewhat paradoxically) gripped by the prospect of constructing a brand-new history. Viola recalls that, by 1974, "people were already talking about history, and had been for a few years.... 'Video may be the only art form ever to have a history before it had a history.' Video was being invented, and simultaneously so were its myths and cultural heroes."[26]

This "invention" was not only the product of video's "cultural heroes" however. Sturken bemoans the false narrative that video exhibitions, such as the 1982 and 1987 retrospectives, have imposed on the genre's history.[27] These two exhibitions, she speculates:

> presented a major history...that was selective in its presentation and produced a particular historical narrative....It is paradoxical that institutions are the primary historical interpreters of a medium that initially developed outside of and in opposition to the established art world and still considers itself not to have gained full acceptance in that world.[28]

The quick historicisation of video art-music was achieved through a mixture of contemporary mythologisation and the subsequent reimagining through modes of exhibition. But the tangle of history is complicated further by the multidisciplinary tendencies of those working with video technology. All of the early practitioners came to video from another discipline and used the format to enrich or progress existing experimentation. Gene Youngblood contextualised the medium within the context of "expanded cinema," situating it amongst the disciplines of film, performance, and various other contemporary fields.[29] While it is important to remember that many filmmakers rejected video as being a poor-quality alternative to filmstock, an alternative, moreover, developed by US military and used in Vietnam, the two moving-image formats were often used for similar investigations (the multiscreen work of Stan VanDerBeek and Malcolm Le Grice that required live performers for instance) and were frequently presented in the same spaces. Indeed, despite the differences in their articulations, many filmmakers also turned their hands to video. Warhol was what Jud Yalkut called "a dabbler in video," while VanDerBeek, David Hall, Joan Jonas, Richard Serra, Bartlett, Ed Emshwiller, Tom DeWitt, and Nauman used both video and television in their work.[30] It follows that, while Expanded Cinema is a definable genre, "expanded cinema" (in lower case) is a much more general term applicable to many different audiovisual environments including video.[31] Along similar lines, television, during the earliest years, was aesthetically (and sometimes practically) intertwined with video works and consequently constitutes an important part of this narrative. A survey of video art-music's rise to popularity, then, requires a survey as multidisciplinary as its form. And it is therefore with two instances of innovative and artistic uses of television that we shall begin.

1963–1965: Pre-video "TIME art"

Exposition of Music—Electronic Television was Paik's first solo exhibition. Held from the 11–20 March 1963 at the Galerie Parnass in Wuppertal, Germany, the show represents the first appearance of a television screen in a gallery: "this exhibition's twenty hours...made 1963 into zero hour for the history of video art," argues Dieter Daniels; "and that is true even though no video equipment was used here."[32] Conceived as a total Event, rather than as an exhibition of isolated works, *Exposition of Music* included four "prepared" pianos, mechanical sound objects, several record and tape installations, twelve modified TV sets, and the head of a freshly slaughtered bull (fig. 4.2). Not only did the use of television as artistic material and the inclusion of audio elements mark the beginnings of a video aesthetic several years before the format became widely available, but Paik's methods of presentation also offered a possible answer to the spatial problems of gallery exhibition, while at the same time maintaining a connection to the aesthetic of the alternative space. The Galerie Parnass consisted of a few rooms in the private home of architect and curator Rolf Jährling. Paik, however, did not limit himself to these few rooms but distributed his pieces over Jährling's house, including his bathroom and bedroom. In so doing, the demarcation lines between family home, gallery, and concert hall were destroyed, and the "white cube" traditions of segregation, timeless display, and silence were demonstrably removed. Paik's

Figure 4.2 Nam June Paik: *TV 8* with Tomas Schmit assisting at setup.
Exposition of Music-Electronic Television, Galerie Parnass, Wuppertal (1963).
Photo © Manfred Montwé. © Nam June Paik Estate.

first environment, then, created a new arena for its emerging audiovisual pieces, manipulating the space to suit its needs.

The desire to merge art and life—to move beyond the confinement of place—was also apparent in the television pieces. Rather than create his television work from scratch, Paik placed magnets in or on monitors, distributed randomly in the space, that were tuned to receive live broadcast television, manipulating the sound and images to produce kaleidoscopic shapes, luminous colours, and electronic noises, a process described by Cage, who had experimented with composing for radio sets, as "antique sets used not as junk but required to come alive not as they did formerly but, poor things, according to a new trick."[33] Altering, and so drawing attention to, a familiar object, the process foregrounded the mechanics of reproduction, an exposure that Paik hoped would demystify the "invisible" nature of broadcast technology: "[t]elevision has been attacking us all our lives," he said, "now we can attack it back."[34] Such demystification can be seen in *Zen for TV*, where the broadcast picture was concentrated into a single line which, when the monitor was placed on its side, resulted in a vertical column of light: similarly, the monitor receiving live transmission in *Rembrandt Automatic* was placed face down on the floor. As discussed in chapter 1, Les Levine has argued that television can be considered "neither an object nor a 'content'": rather, it is a process that enables communication. By highlighting and distorting this process, Paik produced content from this communication.[35] Both *Zen for TV* and *Rembrandt Automatic* preempted Paik's subsequent video work, in which technology and its processes were foregrounded and the "immediacy and presentness" of images "always in the process of coming into being" were embraced.[36] However, there was a downside to Paik's use of live television. The single fledging German television channel (German public service television) broadcast only between 7:30 and 9:30 each evening (it was not until later that year that ZDF, the second German television channel, was introduced), which drastically limited the exhibition's opening hours.

Speaking of his early moving-image work in a letter to Jährling (1962), Paik declared that "it must be stressed that it's not painting, not sculpture, but rather a TIME art, or: I love no particular genre."[37] As though to counter the optical emphasis of his moving-image pieces (and before video enabled audiovisual synthesis), Paik also included several examples of audio "TIME art." According to another letter to the curator in the same year, Paik explained further that his "TIME art" consisted of *Objets Sonores* and *Instruments for Zen Exercise*.[38] Although the inclusion of four of his *Klavier Integral* instruments (1958–1963) in the exhibition could be seen as a voicing of frustration towards the enforced technological audiovisual separation (fig. 1.4)—a piano is rendered unplayable by being covered with, amongst other things, barbed wire, dolls, and smashed eggs (Joseph Beuys, in an apparently impromptu frenzy during a visit to the exhibition, destroyed one of the instruments with an axe)—many of his other *Objets Sonores* pointed towards an imminent coexistence. *Random Access*, for instance, worked along similar lines to his visual improvisations by noting the materiality of sound production (fig. 4.3). Consisting of records suspended on a string, a record player, a radio, and strips of audiotape stuck to the walls, the interactive *Object Sonore* allowed visitors to choose and arrange sound fragments and their volume.

Another "TIME art" piece, *Participation TV*, went one step further, to produce an extraordinarily close pre-video audiovisual interaction. Although many of the monitors that made up this piece showed Paik's processed television images, several were also responsive to external manipulations, some of which were sound-based. *Participation TV* was hooked up to a microphone which, when spoken into, produced flashes of coloured light on the screen in a direct translation of sound into image: another (*Kuba TV*) was connected to a tape recorder whose recorded music determined the parameters of corresponding shapes through its dynamics; and the size of a single bright light on *One Point TV* was determined by the volume of a radio linked into the monitor. In these participatory examples, the audiovisual space was activated, enabling music and art to take a step closer to each other. Present in this "zero hour" of video, then, was a preoccupation with art as an explicit two-way communication process: the desire, in other words, to abolish the segregation between performer and receiver.

The fusion of life with art was also at the centre of Wolf Vostell's 1964 exhibitions. Like Paik, Vostell used his first one-man show to distort the relationship between television monitor and receiver in order to create "a disturbance in reflection in the audience's awareness" (Rudolf Frieling).[39] *TV Dé-coll/age* took place two months after Paik's exhibition, running from 22 May to 8 June in New York's

Figure 4.3 Nam June Paik: *Random Access. Exposition of Music-Electronic Television*, Galerie Parnass, Wuppertal (1963). Photo © Manfred Montwé. © Nam June Paik Estate.

Smolin Gallery, a small, privately owned, noncommercial space. Although this was not Vostell's first investigation into the moving image (on 19 May of the same year, he had performed *TV Burying* at the YAM Festival, New Brunswick, a piece that involved throwing cream cakes at a broadcasting monitor before wrapping it in barbed wire and burying it), it was his first immersive environment. The show highlighted his concept of *décollage*, an idea that operated in direct opposition to the material and semantic accumulation of collage: instead of building meaning, layers of information were peeled away. This process involved smudging or defacing pictures found in magazines and on television, or tearing down posters. Vostell explained his activities with reference to his *TV Dé-coll/age* exhibition:

> 6 television sets with various programs / the picture is decollaged— 6 fusions / pots with plastic airplanes that melt in the heat—6 grilled chickens on a canvas / to be eaten by the public from the picture— 6 chicken incubators / on canvas / the chicken should hatch on the day of the exhibition—everyone receives an ampoule of liquid he can use to smudge magazines.[40]

Although one of Vostell's reasons for joining forces with the Fluxus group had been to explore his musical interests more thoroughly, *TV Dé-coll/age* was less musically focused than *Exposition of Music—Electronic Television*. Instead, Vostell was more concerned with pushing at the limitations of traditional performance spaces, a "charge" clearly evident in his next two Events. Although organised by the Galerie Parnass (which by this time was establishing itself as an important centre for moving audio-art experimentation), *Neun Nein Dé-coll/agen* was an expansive Happening spread across nine locations (visitors were driven to each *décollage* piece in a bus: for one Event, they were asked to lie on the floor to experience his film, *Sun in Your Head*, while sprayed with perfume and bathed in lights; another Event took place in a train yard [see video 4.1▶]). Moving from the specialised space into a communal, "real life" arena, Vostell attempted to fuse art and life; an ideal that resonated with the concurrent activities of Kaprow. "Marcel Duchamp has declared readymade objects as art, and the futurists declared noises as art," explained Vostell: "it is an important characteristic of my efforts and those of my colleagues to declare as art the total event, comprising noise/object/movement/color/and psychology—a merging of elements, so that life (man) can be art."[41]

Although less geographically diverse, Vostell's next "total event," *You*, was held on 19 April 1964 at the home of Robert and Rhett Delford-Brown in Great Neck, Long Island. Again, visitors were asked to move from one area to the next, passing through a small forest where TV monitors placed on hospital beds replayed baseball games and speakers emitted the word "you," to arrive at a tennis court and swimming pool where actors performed wearing gas masks and throwing smoke bombs. Situated outside and requiring movement between various audio and visual pieces, Vostell's second and third exhibitions rejected the physical and behavioural restraints of both traditional gallery and concert hall. Such spatial expansion and the performative nature of the Event undermined methods of curation and preservation central to many art endeavours. Rather, operating as a "verb/process" in order to avoid the "horrible sanctity of private property," Vostell's work falls in line with the anticommodity tendencies of land art and process art.

By 1965, the expansion of music and moving image spaces had begun to gather momentum. Several filmmakers were including the area surrounding the cinematic screen in their experimentation, an exploration clearly apparent in Robert Morris's *Waterman Switch*, in which Muybridge's slides of a nude man lifting a stone were projected on a screen, while a live performer stood in front of the images, mimicking every action. A similar preoccupation with the space of projection can be found in Stan VanDerBeek's *Movie Drome*, a venue in which visitors lay on their backs to experience multiple films projected (often in random sequences) on the dome's ceiling and walls, as we saw in chapter 3. Such heightened sense of spatialisation can also be found in a number of music events during this year. Cage's *Variations V*, performed at the Lincoln Center, New York on

23 July of the same year, for instance, was "an environment in which the active elements interpenetrate…so that the distinction between dance and music may be somewhat less clear than usual."[42] The space, conceived in collaboration with Cunningham, Barbara Lloyd, Tudor, and Gordon Mumma, contained a lattice of photoelectric cells that translated the movement of the dancers into light and sound: Paik's distorted television images, VanDerBeek's films, and sounds controlled by Robert Moog amongst others, were also included to produce a clear example of Youngblood's contextualised understanding of expanded cinema.

The Expanded Cinema Festival, held by the Filmmakers' Cinematheque, New York, from November to December 1965, is another example of a spatial audiovisual convergence. Organised by John Brockman, the festival included image, sound, and light projections. Brockman described the Cinematheque as the "home for underground cinema" and explained his curatorial method: "I commissioned thirty performance pieces by world class artists, dancers, poets, dramatists, and musicians. They were free to do anything they wanted, the only stipulation being that their piece incorporate cinema."[43] These "world class" contributors included Paik (who displayed his manipulated television images on twelve old TV sets), Charlotte Moorman, Rauschenberg, Claes Oldenburg, La Monte Young, and Warhol: their work included multiple screen presentations, work with multiple and handheld projectors, moving slide projections, kinetic sculptures, and balloon screens; all, in other words, instances of "TIME art." Rauschenberg's filmic expansion in Map Room 11 was particularly musical: not only did his piece combine film with live dance; he also asked performers, their feet in old tyres, to bash into a bedspring wired to create electronic sounds. As a result, the spaceless darkness of the cinema, in which the spectator is encouraged to feel disembodied (or rather, re-embodied) was replaced with an activated site. Although focused primarily on the film medium, the show—illustrating Paik's dictum, "I love no particular genre"—marked an important step towards audio moving-image experimentation and received major media attention. (As Brockman noted, "within a year there were two Life covers and a New York Times Magazine cover on derivative works.")[44]

It is clear to see that those working with and manipulating television monitors were not operating in isolation, but were adding to the already expanding dialogues of music, moving-image, and art. At least initially, Paik was content to find ways in which his audiovisual explorations could be housed in less radical spaces than those chosen by Vostell and less specialised than VanDerBeek's architectural Movie Drome. Shortly after moving to New York City in 1965—"I came to the US only because of Cage," he announced—and having undertaken his mythical journey with the video recorder, Paik staged two exhibitions in the city.[45] Nam June Paik: Cybernetics, Art and Music was held at the New School for Social Research and built upon his earlier notions of Objets Sonores and moving image "TIME art." The show included several spectator-controlled television pieces such as Magnet TV, in which the workings of the cathode ray tubes inside the monitors could be manipulated by powerful magnets, and an opera performed by robots, including the remote-controlled *Robot K-456*, which delivered taped speeches by John F. Kennedy as it walked. Performance rather than exhibition, *Cybernetics* asked audience members to control the works themselves in order to create unrepeatable "events." The next show, *Nam June Paik: Electronic Art* was held at Galeria Bonino, a small, privately owned space, from 23 November to 11 December and marked the first of several one-man shows that Paik held between 1965 and 1971. Yalkut filmed the exhibition and, using Paik's distorted television pieces as primary visual material, produced a series of filmic *Paikpieces*. First in the series was *Turn, Turn, Turn*, a film based upon a sampled and adapted version of the song of the same name by the Byrds. Although the synergistic spaces of *Variations V* and *The Expanded Cinema Festival*, and the interactive audiovisual work of Paik and Vostell did not yet include video, then, by 1965, there were already emergent audiovisual environments in which "TIME" was the key element.

1966: Multimedia Environments and Terry Riley's Turtle Tank

The success of *The Expanded Cinema Festival*, together with an invigorated investigation into performance space in Happenings and Events, led to an increasing number of spatial and technological experiments during the following year. Warhol's multimedia *Exploding Plastic Inevitable*, for instance, created an immersive environment in which live music from The Velvet Underground was combined with screenings of Warhol's films and dance performances by regulars from the Factory. Other groups to strive for a disciplinary synthesis included *The Company of Us* (USCO), a multimedia troupe which held the McLuhan-like view that technology was a means of uniting people within a sophisticated "tribalism." USCO's unity of intent pointed towards the single-authored possibilities of video that would soon be available: "[t]he work (USCO) did together was anonymous" explains Yalkut, one of the first filmmakers who would later embrace video technology; "You did not know who did any particular thing. We had a poet, a painter, an electronics engineer—and I was the filmmaker."[46] Their unified vision was presented in *US Down by the Riverside: The USCO Show*, an exhibition curated by Gerd Stern and USCO at The Riverside Museum, New York in the summer of 1966. The exhibition included a light garden and a tie-dyed meditation environment: of audiovisual importance was *The Tabernacle*, a hexagonal space hung with a series of paintings that faced into an internally lit, turning metal lingam and a fountain with multichannelled speakers placed on either side.

By 1966, then, the combination of sound and the moving image within expanded spaces was becoming an increasingly popular pursuit. Paik had placed musical objects and distorted television pieces within a single environment: Vostell had dotted his Happenings with sound installations and televised images; Rauschenberg had invited dancers and noise producers to interact with a projected film; Warhol had bathed The Velvet Underground's live performances in his movies; and USCO had created multiauthored audiovisual situations. By this time, in other words, the video aesthetic was already apparent in the confluence of other media. As a result, the inclusion of video in *Nine Evenings: Theater and Engineering* at the large, empty, 69th Regiment Armory, New York from 13–23 October can be viewed as part of a natural evolution. The series of Events is significant for two reasons: its inclusion of video technology; and the audiovisual nature of most of its pieces. *Nine Evenings* was organised by Billy Klüver, an electrical engineer who, driven by a desire to initiate collaboration between engineers and artists, had previously helped to realise the ideas of Cage, Rauschenberg, Warhol, and Jasper Johns. Described by Michael Kirby in *The Art of Time* as "probably the most elaborate and expensive presentation of avant-garde performance ever attempted in this country," *Nine Evenings* was the culmination of ten months of collaborative work between ten New York artists, including Rauschenberg, Cage, Tudor, Robert Whitman, and Cunningham, and thirty engineers from the Bell Telephone Laboratories.[47] The results included both the innovative use of existing technologies and the development of new systems to create audiovisual works that involved video, wireless sound transmission, closed-circuit television, Doppler sonar devices that could translate movement into sound, and infrared television cameras.

Rauschenberg's piece *Open Score*, first performed on 14 October, involved a tennis game between Frank Stella and Mimi Kanarek (fig. 4.4): each time the ball

Figure 4.4 Robert Rauschenberg, *Open Score*. Nine Evenings: *Theatre & Engineering* (1966). Photo courtesy of Experiments in Art and Technology.

was hit, a contact microphone transmitted the sound to an FM radio receiver which then fed an amplified version to speakers (the technology was devised by Bill Kaminski from Bell Laboratories). Each resultant sound caused one of the tennis court lights to switch off until the space was in darkness. At this point, three large screens hanging from the ceiling came to life, showing infrared footage of the 500 audience members who had, until that point, felt safe and unobserved in the darkness (see video 4.2 ▶). Although no video was used, sound was given the power to reduce visibility to nothing.

As with many of his other works and true to his dictum that "we find noise fascinating," Cage's piece, *Variations VII*, made use only of the sounds existing at the moment of performance (fig.1.6). Unlike his earlier work 4'33", however, these sounds were not taken solely from the performance space, but were, rather, picked up from anywhere, so long as the sounds were live. This required inclusion of a technological aspect that was already present in the work of several other contemporary composers, such as Stockhausen and Varèse. With the help of engineer Cecil Coker, ten telephone calls were made to locations around New York City, including restaurants, an aviary, Cunningham's studio, and the turtle tank in Terry Riley's house: at these locations, the receivers, attached to magnetic pickups, were left off their hooks and the ambient noises they picked up fed into a sound modulation system created by Tudor. These sounds were then combined with those from contact microphones situated within the performance space and attached to various household appliances. Finally, the sound of electrodes capturing the brainwaves of a performer, the noise from twenty radio bands, two television bands, and two Geiger counters, oscillators and pulse generators were added to the mix. Each time a visitor passed through a light beam placed at ankle height, the resultant aural mélange erupted from various speakers (see video 4.3 ▶). Like Vostell before him, Cage produced an interactive, multidisciplinary work that straddled many locations: performers, spread far beyond the confines of the Armory, created a porous and expansive space; and the visitors, situated within its walls, were an integral part of the work's composition. Fundamental to both Rauschenberg's and Cage's work, then, was the use of sound as a means to construct and control a visual environment.

But it was Whitman's *Two Holes of Water—3* that used video to pull together hitherto separate audio and visual elements. Whitman made use of a new miniature fibreoptic video camera, alongside film and live performance relayed via closed-circuit feed to create a theatrical piece that was simultaneously film, video, dance, and music. With technological design by Robby Robinson and lighting by Jennifer Tipton, the performance was extravagant, involving seven cars (to evoke the feeling of a drive-in movie theatre), three equipped with 16mm projectors, three with video equipment, and several performers—two slowly moving in front of a curved mirror, one typing, another pouring water. Real-time images of the performances filmed by the fibreoptic video camera inside the coat pocket of Levine and relayed through a closed-circuit system and seven video cameras were sent to Whitman, who created a live montage that was projected onto multiple screens hanging around the armoury. Other live images were taken from broadcast television and included news bulletins and commercials. Accompanying these were film clips, including footage from Whitman's own work. The live and filmed images were projected via the equipment attached to the cars: at the same time, films were shown on a white screen that lay on the floor.

Alongside this array of technological mediations was a soundtrack of localised noises: the sound recorded from contact microphones attached to the exhaust pipe of one of the cars, which emerged from a freight elevator during the performance and on the typewriter, as well as the occasional sound of a car horn. These live noises were combined with the sound of crickets and the voice of Bertrand Russell (see video 4.4⊙).

Two Holes of Water—3, then, is one of the first examples of an integrated audiovisual, performative piece involving video. Allowing the performers to be recorded and projected live, while sounds from the space were similarly manipulated and combined, this piece represents an important step towards the audiovisual synchronicity, interactivity, and performative possibilities explored by later video artist-composers and demonstrates the ability of the medium to synergistically unite many other disciplines. Moreover, existing only in real time, Whitman's site-specific piece rejected the notions of permanence and display, producing instead a transitory and improvisatory audiovisual space. Here, the visitor was activated, becoming integral to both the sounds and the moving images generated. Like Eisenstein montage, the merging of several elements to form an intermedial space created a new and "emergent" (Cook) form.[48]

Although some critics, such as Lucy Lippard, complained about the technological difficulties encountered during the series, *Nine Evenings*, like the USCO exhibition, was an immediate success: not only was it attended by thousands of people, but its legacy is demonstrated by the recent release of a ten-DVD set documenting the performances.[49] Such success led to the foundation of an organisation designed to explore further the possibilities of artistic and technological fusion. *Experiments in Art and Technology* (E.A.T.) was set up in 1967 by Klüver, Rauschenberg, Whitman, and Fred Waldhauer and was founded on the belief "that an industrially sponsored, effective working relationship between artists and engineers will lead to new possibilities which will benefit society as a whole."[50] Their hope that further exploration of art and technology interchanges would be explored was first realised through an exhibition (*Some More Beginnings*, at the Brooklyn Museum, New York, 25 November 1968 to 5 January 1969, which included Aldo Tambellini's *Black Video 2*), resulting in an invitation to design an immersive dome for Expo '70 at Osaka, Japan.

It is clear to see that 1966 marked an important step towards audiovisual video art. Not only was video used as a live, creative tool, but the spaces of intermedial work continued to expand: old warehouses and a simulated tennis court were enlarged through live links to domestic homes and restaurants, spaces which were, in turn, increased through combination with broadcast TV, radio and closed-circuit video. Moreover, these "elaborate and expensive" performances led to the establishment of several groups dedicated to intermedial, technology-based practices.

1967–1968: "We haven't the faintest idea these days what art is for or about"

During the next two years, the use of video by artists and musicians continued to proliferate. In 1967, Paik's musically centered aesthetic led him to several collaborations with avant-garde cellist Moorman, including an infamous performance of *Opera Sextronique* at the Filmmakers' Cinematheque on 9 February, in which Moorman performed a sort of striptease as she played: Aria Two had to be played topless; Aria Three bottomless; and Aria Four in the nude. Moorman only got to Aria Two before she was arrested. Although perhaps prompted by Paik's playful desire to shock, the striptease also commented on the servile nature of concert performance attire and the nature of the traditional art music recital, a gesture that provoked, "the viewer's critical (not just physical) acuity regarding the ideological conditions of that viewing" (Kwon): according to *The Village Voice*, Moorman "was escorted from her interrupted cello concert to the station house by the police."[51]

Over the next decade, these collaborations became more technologically based, resulting in audiovisual video pieces that fundamentally critiqued the nature of music performance and reception (one of these, the *TV Cello*, is explored in chapter 5). Moorman's engagement with the moving image began soon after *Opera Sextronique*, when she included one of Paik's earliest video works in the New York Annual Avant-Garde Festival, an inclusion that represented the festival's first engagement with the technology. Curated by the cellist, the festival had begun in 1963 at the Judson Hall (now the CAMI Hall) on 57th Street, New York. Featuring the work of Cage, Edgar Varèse, Morton Feldman, David Behrman, Earle Brown, and others, this first event was particularly musical. By 1967—the fifth festival— the events had become more diverse. Held on the John F. Kennedy Staten Island Ferry Boat over the twenty-four hours beginning 29 September, the fifth festival included pieces by Carole Schneemann, performances by Jim McWilliams, and films by Stan Brakhage and Michael Snow. Paik's collaborative contribution with Yalkut played at the interface between film and video: *Videotape Study No 3* was a short, black-and-white filmed performance with a soundtrack by Behrman and Kenneth Warner and edited by Yalkut, in which Paik distorted footage from news conferences by US President Lyndon B. Johnson and New York Mayor John Lindsay (see video 4.5⊙).

By 1968, the spaces of video work began to diversify. Small galleries with viewing conditions less well-established than those of the major institutions continued to embrace video's "explosive charge" at the conventional art experience. From 17 April to 11 May of that year, for instance, the Galeria Bonino hosted a second Paik show. *Nam June Paik: Electronic Art II* was a small exhibition of work that Paik had created in collaboration with other artists. One room was well-lit and included an array of Paik's decorated TV monitors, including *Untitled*, a television set displaying a diagonal line, which German avant-garde artist Otto Piene then covered with painted silver plastic pearls. The other room was dark and housed eight sets and a wall of colour TV monitors. This second room required a transformation of O'Doherty's bright and timeless gallery space: in the darkened area were placed moving-image portals that introduced both the outside world and time into the previously autonomous white cube.

But while Galeria Bonino continued to establish itself as an important outlet for moving-image experimentation in 1968, other spaces started to become active. On the one hand, the array of unusual performance locations continued to grow; on the other, and somewhat paradoxically, video practitioners found that major institutions were becoming increasingly receptive to their work, a receptivity that complicated the alternative ideologies of many audiovisual artists. The change in thinking was marked by two 1968 exhibitions held in "conventional" spaces. *Cybernetic Serendipity: The Computer and the Arts* was a travelling show curated by Jasia Reichardt and selected by James Harithas (who later, while at the Everson, became the first museum director to initiate a regular program of video exhibitions, with the help of video curator Ross). Although the focus was on computer-generated art, *Cybernetic Serendipity*, like *Nine Evenings*, marked an important step towards integrating art with technology. The exhibition began in London at the Institute of Contemporary Arts (2 August to 20 October) before moving to the Corcoran Gallery, Washington D.C., although the tour was here cut short (Michelle Henning speculates that the exhibition, although sponsored by companies such as IBM, Boeing, General Motors, Westinghouse, Calcomp, Bell Telephone Labs, and the US Air Force research labs, was too expensive to sustain).[52] Reichardt remembers that "130 contributors, of whom 43 were composers, artists and poets, and 87 ... engineers, doctors, computer scientists and philosophers" were involved in creating a reactionary environment that transgressed disciplinary borders.[53] Cage, Bruce Lacey, Wen Ying Tsai, Jean Tinguely, Lowell Nesbitt, and others created pieces that explored the claim asserted in the accompanying catalogue, that "the computer demonstrates a radical extension in art media and techniques."[54] This radical extension was explored through computer-aided art, music, poetry, dance, film, sculpture, robotics, installation, and animation to produce what one newspaper review described as "a veritable Luna Park of slideshows, display booths, and fun houses."[55]

There were many kinetic environments and moving-image pieces, including Paik's *Robot K-456* and some of his distorted TVs. Other works were concerned primarily with the creation of musical effects and sounds: Edward Ihnatowicz presented a sound-activated sculpture that turned towards noises made by the visitor; composer Peter Zinovieff installed equipment that would improvise on a musical snippet sung or whistled into a microphone. As was so often the case for multidisciplinary exhibitions dealing with "TIME art," there were major curatorial problems: the lack of sound insulation in the gallery meant that the audio pieces leaked into the space of other works, while the interactive computer systems interfered with each other.

Despite these technical problems, however, *Cybernetic Serendipity* was a great success, drawing in approximately forty thousand visitors (as reported in *Time* magazine).[56] As a result, the exhibition received a good deal of "extremely favourable" media attention (Rainer Usselmann), with many reviews giving particular commendation to the promotion of audience inclusivity: the show was, according to Michael Shepard, writing in the *Sunday Telegraph*, "guaranteed to fascinate anyone from toddling age to the grave" and was "the most important exhibition in the world at the moment."[57] This idea of accessibility represented an important change in the nature of contemporary art, which could often result in a degree of alienation. That the newly emerging art-technology fusion was conjuring forth an artistic space that promoted a "sophisticated amusement arcade," "fun-house"-like appeal thus places the exhibition more in line with the Happenings of Kaprow than with gallery-bound complexity of other contemporary art forms.[58] As new media infiltrated the institutional space, then, it brought with it some of the anti-establishment traits—audience participation, rejection of art as a marketable "noun/object," embrace of the unrepeatable—which were being promoted beyond the gallery walls.

Evidence of this uncomfortable fit can also be found in the reviews which, although favourable, nevertheless voiced a note of concern. What was this new form of emergent art? "The winking lights, the flickering television screens and the squawks from the music machines" wrote Robert Melville in the *New Statesman*, "are signalling the end of abstract art; when machines can do it, it will not be worth doing."[59] Shepard goes further—for him, the exhibition represents not so much an "end" to abstract art, but rather illuminates the sense of "desolation" that he perceives to surround it: "we haven't the faintest idea these days what art is for or about."[60] Perceived less as art than as an entertaining "amusement arcade," the "winking," "flickering," and "squawks" of *Cybernetic Serendipity* were at once fun and yet, for many, perplexing.

But despite its technological basis and exploration of audiovisual fusion (criteria that informed the video aesthetic), the exhibition did not include actual video work. As a result, it was not until the arrival of *The Machine: As Seen at the End of the Mechanical Age* (25 November 1968 to 9 February 1969), curated by Pontus Hultén at MoMA (before travelling to Houston and San Francisco), that video pieces were first included in a major gallery setting. As part of its journey through the technological and machine art of almost one hundred artists, Paik's videocassette works, *Nixon Tape, McLuhan Caged,* and *Lindsay Tape* were presented. This initial inclusion of video work in MoMA signals the beginning of a radical change in thinking about the electronic moving image.

However, the increasingly manifold nature of the unconventional exhibition/ performance space during 1968 suggests that many of those working with video still preferred to work outside the institutional art world, as though the experimental nature of their medium required a similarly fresh physical and ideological site. Levine, for instance, preferred to present work in his private, personal space. *Iris*, a sculpture with six television monitors and three video cameras, was installed in his own studio. When the visitor stood in front of the eight-foot-high stack of monitors, her image, as in Whitman's Event, was relayed simultaneously via a closed-circuit system to the screens in close-up, middle-distance, and wide-angle. These three views were then juxtaposed with distorted images. During this year, Tambellini inverted Levine's preference for the private site: rather than locate his work in his own space, he moved into that of the receiver. Collaborating with Piene, Tambellini created *Black Gate Cologne* (1968), a piece broadcast by Westdeutsche Rundfunk (WDR-TV) in Cologne. An interactive, multimedia, live-action piece, *Black Gate Cologne* involved Piene projecting Tambellini's films onto inflated polyethylene tubing while the audience moved around the space. The Event was recorded and the images from five television cameras were mixed and superimposed. The result was then broadcast to television viewers, who could experience the piece from their own homes. Here, audio and visual arenas converged in the domestic space.

But while Levine and Tambellini presented work in the domestic arena, the collaborative nature of many video pieces encouraged the creation of brand-new audiovisual sites. In 1968, there began to develop small communities of artists and composers devoted almost exclusively to the medium of video: as a result, several collectives emerged that created new locations for the presentation of video work. One of the first communities was *Commediation* in New York City, a collection of video artists including Gillette, Harvey Simon, David Cort, Ken Marsh, Howard Gutstadt, and, on occasion, Paik, who aimed to document political events and so use video as a tool for political change (in effect, the group acted more as a nucleus for discussion than as an activist group). Around the same time, similar groups formed in the Bay Area: *Ant Farm*, a media-architecture collective located in San Francisco, whose members (including Chip Lord and Doug Michels) used video to critique and satirise the mass media; *Land Truth Circus*, founded by Hall, Diane Hall, and Jody Proctor, was an experimental video collective; and *The Electric Eye* was a San Francisco-based video performance group. Although the equipment was still heavy and bulky, work produced by these collectives was explicitly social and video and was embraced for its ability to document events on the street. Other specialised spaces for video projection were less focused on social activism. The Black Gate Theatre in New York, for instance, was opened in March 1967 by Tambellini and Piene. Their intention was to host "electromedia" performances and, by 1968, these events included Tambellini's own work with video tape.

While the rise of video collectives and the development of specialised locations (both private and public) for video presentation is evidence of the format's increasing popularity in 1968, the use of the technology by several composers reinforced its hybrid nature. Terry Riley, for instance, was involved in collaborative work that included video. *Music with Balls* was commissioned by KQED (an experimental workshop) and the Dilexi Foundation (San Francisco) and resulted in what Youngblood described as a "synaesthetic alloy."[61] In a way similar to that of film construction, Riley's desire to combine four elements—music, sculpture, cinema, and video—required collaborative input from sculptor Arlo Acton and video-mixer John Coney, in order to produce a half-hour transmedial video for broadcast. The composer's interest in spatialised sound led him again into contact with video when, on 22 March, he presented a live, six-hour performance of *Poppy Nogood and the Phantom Band: All Night Flight* for organ, time-lag accumulator (the phantom band), soprano saxophone, and multiple loudspeakers at SUNY Buffalo as part of the *Intermedia '68* tour. This tour, produced by Brockman, involved a series of late-night concerts, many involving video, held in colleges and galleries around New York, before finally ending up at the Brooklyn Academy of Music.[62] The works performed included work by Riley, Yalkut, and members of USCO: video pieces were created by Ken Dewey with Jerry Walker, Levine with George Fan, Tambellini, and Schneemann. Tambellini presented the last performance of his *Black Zero* (1965) at the Brooklyn Academy, an audiovisual work that included hand-painted films and slides, a giant black balloon, electronic-tape compositions, and the sounds from a live, amplified cello, a multimedia extravaganza that, to quote Vostell, seemed "to declare as art the total event." Tambellini shared the night with Schneemann, who presented *Illinois Central Transposed* (1968), a silent, 16mm film on video of her anti-Vietnam War group performances. The projected film was accompanied by sound, slides, light beams, performance, and invited audience interaction.

Although its single-authored potential was not yet realised, by 1968, video's "synaesthetic alloy" was regularly included in audiovisual environments situated in a diverse array of both art and music spaces: the private; the noncommercial; the reappropriated; the domestic; and the institutional. But it was inclusion in the latter that caused the biggest stir (although it must be recognised that a large-scale exhibition such as this would necessarily receive greater media attention than Events in more unusual settings). While it is true that the concepts of installation, viewer participation, and the audiovisual artwork were no longer radical ones in the culture at large, in the gallery—the neutral "white cube"—they still represented a significant divergence from long-established aesthetic values.

1969: Living Sculpture and the Silence of Seeing

By 1969, various aspects of the artistic and musical counterculture from earlier in the decade were finding their way into major creative spaces and the nature of exhibition was beginning to change. As we saw in the previous chapter, although it included no video work, MoMA's *Spaces* exhibition invited artists to create installational work in situ for the first time. Curator Jennifer Licht explained that "[s]ome of the aims of the recent artists' protests have been directed toward dissociating art from the marketing system, and demands were made of museums to accept some direct responsibility. The works for this exhibition will be created especially, and dismantled afterwards. Here we can assume a role that belongs uniquely to the public institution and lies outside the domain of the art dealer."[63]

By assuming "direct responsibility," however, numerous problems were created (the piece by Roger Morris, for instance, included Norwegian spruce trees, which required watering and a certain degree of humidity to flourish). Of equal importance to the innovations outlined by Licht, was the inclusion of several sound pieces, such as a noise- and motion-activated sculpture garden created by artist-group Pulsa. Conversely, Michael Asher's anti-noise installation involved lining a room with acoustic panelling to absorb sound. This absorption turned the experience of viewing art into what Brandon LaBelle described as "an acoustical absence."[64] Asher explained that he wanted to "control and articulate sensory space" in order to prevent any sort of objectification: this, he hoped, would contrast with "phenomenologically determined works that attempted to fabricate a highly controlled area of visual perception."[65] The use of sound, or rather nonsound, to regulate the visual experience was again explored by Asher in another sound installation the same year. Using an audio oscillator, an amplifier, and a loudspeaker to investigate the opposite end of the sound spectrum, Asher constructed a series of extra walls in the Museum of Contemporary Art, San Diego. In this new space, the "the vertical surfaces responded to the sound frequency, which caused them to resonate as if they were tuned, while the horizontal surfaces, due to their sound-dampening effect [a carpet], reduced the frequency" (Asher).[66]

While galleries were opening their doors to sound art and redefining their modes of exhibition, moving images were making a more frequent appearance in music events. Cage's mixed-media Event *HPSCHD*, discussed in chapter 3, was held in the circular assembly hall at the University of Illinois in May 1969. Created in conjunction with composer and computer programmer Lejaren Hiller, the piece required "7 harpsichordists, 208 tapes, 84 slide projectors, 52 tape recorders, 52 speakers, 12 movie projectors, a 340-foot circular plastic screen, as well as amplifiers, additional plastic screens, slides, films, posters and other materials" to produce what James Pritchett has described as a "circus approach" to performance.[67] Through means at the other extreme from those of Asher's, *HPSCHD* produced "control" over its "sensory space" by moving music explicitly into the audiovisual.

As art was embracing the audio, video began to be represented at an increasing number of organised events. Nauman's first corridor installation, *Performance Corridor* (fig. 4.5), in which the visitor is required to pass down a narrow passageway, thus assuming "the position of the performer as soon as he or she enters" (Nauman) in order to view a video showing the back of the artist ambling

Figure 4.5 Bruce Nauman, *Live-Taped Video Corridor* (1970). Photo by Paul Rocheleau, courtesy of The Soloman R. Guggenheim Museum, New York, Panza Collection, Gift, 1992 (92.4165). © Bruce Nauman.

down the same space, for instance, was included in *Anti-Illusion: Procedures / Materials* at the Whitney Museum (19 May to 6 July 1969).[68] During the same year, Nauman's *Corridor* became the first video work to be exhibited in a gallery on the West Coast when it was presented at the Nicholas Wilder Gallery, Los Angeles. Nevertheless, Daniels has pointed out that, even as late as 1970, an electronic image still meant, for most people, a TV image.[69] This is demonstrated most clearly by the titles of many of the major moving-image events of 1969–70: *TV as a Creative Medium* (Howard Wise Gallery, New York); a special issue of *Art in America* called "TV—The Next Medium" (1969); and *Vision and Television* (Rose Art Museum, Waltham, MA, 1970). But, despite this, the video medium lay at the heart of both exhibition and discussion. Curated by Wise, *TV as a Creative Medium* included work by Paik, Gillette, Ira Schneider, Tambellini, and others and has often been recognised as the first American exhibition given entirely to television and video work. With a history of exhibiting kinetic- and light-art, the Howard Wise Gallery seemed the obvious space to devote to the newly emerging, if eclectic, moving-image genre. Like the Galeria Bonino, the privately-owned space had long engaged with nontraditional art forms, particularly multimedia and kinetic work. To some extent, Wise's personal wealth (he had acquired his fortune elsewhere and took no salary from the gallery) gave him the freedom to create an experimental, nonprofit-orientated space in which he could curate radical shows. Two exhibitions in 1967 clearly illustrate this: embracing the "risky" business of site-specific work in February, *Lights in Orbit* and its enhanced version, *Light/Motion/Space*, at the Walker Art Center, Minneapolis (which one visitor described as like "being inside a kaleidoscope") included light pieces by USCO amongst others, while the *Festival of Lights*, December-January, incorporated television pieces by Tambellini, and Serge Boutourline.[70] Wise viewed video as a natural extension of light- and kinetic-art and became one of the first curators and patrons to support and promote creative video work: he was "a central figure in the visibility, production, and acceptance" of the medium, explained Sturken; "[f]or almost 20 years, he has been one of the few patrons of video art."[71] Interestingly, however, Wise later concluded that a gallery setting was not an ideal one for video pieces and, after closing the gallery, he founded a tape editing and distribution facility called the *Electronic Arts Intermix* (EAI).[72]

The May exhibition in 1969 assumed seminal importance to the "invention" of video's "myths and cultural heroes" by acting, according to Sturken, "like an indicator of the diversity of concerns in early video—the legacy of machine art and kinetic sculpture, issues of mass media and information, as well as explorations of the aesthetics, technology, and time-based aspects of the medium."[73] Despite this diversity, however, the exhibition represents an early attempt to identify (or form) a cohesive video community. Davidson Gigliotti explains further:

> TV as a Creative Medium was a catalytic event around which a video art community began to coalesce. New names and faces had appeared on the scene every year since 1965, but until the Spring of '69 there had been no center, no real cohesion, no sense of a community of purpose. After the show at the Howard Wise Gallery, it was possible to identify oneself as a video artist, and to recognize other video artists.[74]

Wipe Cycle by Schneider and Gillette, for instance, was an important example of early interactive video work (fig. 4.6). Situated in front of the lift into the gallery space, nine monitors, stacked three-by-three, presented a mixture of closed-circuit images and prerecorded video footage. A camera focused on the lift videoed visitors as they entered, instantly projecting a grainy black-and-white image of each person onto the middle monitor to create, in a way similar to Levine's *Iris*, an immediate interaction between work and audience: "[t]he most important function" wrote Schneider, "was to integrate the audience into the information."[75] After eight seconds, the newly recorded image appeared on two screens and, after sixteen, on two others before the delayed images switched axes. The outer four

Figure 4.6 Frank Gillette and Ira Schneider, *Wipe Cycle*, Howard Wise Gallery, New York City (1969). Photo courtesy of Ira Schneider.

screens showed prerecorded images and, according to a predetermined cycle, the monitors were intermittently wiped blank. In a way similar to *Wipe Cycle*, Paik's teledynamic environment *Participation TV 2* involved four colour television sets whose signals were manipulated by acoustic signals until they showed, in Paik's words, "multi-color echoes, or fog, or clouds, which are electronically produced. Sometimes you can see yourself floating in air, dissolving in deep water."[76] A review in *Time* magazine explains that "visitors are urged to perform in front of four video cameras" in order that their image would undergo electromagnetic distortion.[77]

However, as is so often the case, Sturken's understanding of the "diversity of concerns" fails to include the sound-based nature of many of the works included. And yet it was this audio component that represented one of the more radical aspects of Wise's exhibition. Paik's and Moorman's *TV Bra for Living Sculpture* premiered at the exhibition and took Schneider's desire for audience integration one step further. Described by one reviewer as "the show-stopper of this quite dazzling exhibition," *TV Bra for Living Sculpture* was an example of early audiovisual composition.[78] Created in the same year as Gilbert and George's first "singing sculpture," *Underneath the Arches*, and embodying a similar aesthetic, the piece involved Moorman playing her cello with two small Plexiglas cases housing television tubes strapped across her front. In a review for *Arts Magazine*, Yalkut described the performance in some detail:

> Sound modulations, hand clapping, singing, screeching, yelling, whispers, the ringing of a bell, all activate the neon tangles of fluorescent tracers, expanding and contracting the frequency modulations within involuted vortexes of color. Three TV cameras, red, green, and blue eyes survey the infinity of movements possible to the spectator-performer. Color-separated ghost shadows mirror and re-echo one's gestures, one's dance with light, with visual toys, with silence. In total feedback loop, a color monitor facets and fragments the closed circuit images of Charlotte Moorman's cello improvisations.[79]

Quashing any possible accusation of Adornian pseudomorphosis, Paik here embraced video at its most basic; as a device able simultaneously to record and play back music and image.[80] But this is not all: unlike his earlier, more formalist approach to video, Paik here attempted not only to demystify the technology, but also to personalise it. "The real issue implied in 'Art and Technology' is not to make another scientific toy, but how to *humanize* the technology and the electronic medium, which is progressing rapidly" he writes:

> By using TV as bra...the most intimate belonging of human being, we will demonstrate the human use of technology, and also stimulate viewers NOT for something mean but stimulate their phantasy to look for the new, imaginative and humanistic ways of using our technology.[81]

The "humanised" *TV Bra for Living Sculpture* integrated both sound and image, and performer and audience, condensing the Howard Wise Gallery into an intermedial, interactive space.

Although less spatially aware, several other sound pieces reinforced the audiovisual direction in which video work was heading. Paik offered for sale a rewired television set that showed a moving knot of coloured lines: the set was linked to two microphones. When receiving low sounds, one mic would reduce the width of the lines; high sounds, filtered through the second mic, controlled the height of the kinetic cluster. The holistic results were similar to those of a colour-organ; more technologically based, perhaps, but not fundamentally different. Joe Weintraub's *AC/TV (Audio-Controlled Television)* worked along similar lines. The piece "[t]ranslates music into a complex kinetic image on the screen of any color TV" explains Weintraub:

> The brightness is controlled by the volume of the music. The colors are controlled by the pitch. The patterns are dependent on both,...As soon as I became aware of the Color Cathode Ray Tube, I realized that the red,

blue and green guns in the CRT were ideally suited for audio control by the low, middle and high frequencies of music.[82]

Significantly, sound and the moving image were here being created *simultaneously* by a single medium, rather than by various media as in previous audiovisual work, an act that destroyed the space-time divide that segregated Gotthold Lessing's *Nacheinander* and *Nebeneinander* arts discussed in chapter 2. Although *TV Bra* was more of a "show-stopper," the TV monitors which could translate sound into image were the more radical offering of the exhibition.

In 1969, then, many aspects of video—from its place of exhibition/performance to its audiovisual capabilities—were developing. But two other important innovations from 1968 were also expanded during this year: the video collective, initiated by Gillette and Tambellini; and the increasing presence of video pieces on broadcast television, also instigated by Tambellini. The founding of two of the most influential video collectives during 1969 represents an important step in video art's "history," as it signals the desire to both create with and theorise about the format in a more systematic way. The Videofreex, a group that encouraged communal video production, began when Parry Teasdale and Cort met at the Woodstock Music Festival. With an emphasis on accumulation, those involved, including Gigliotti and Mary Curtis Ratcliff, were concerned with documenting countercultural activities in order to produce an alternative history to that offered through the television medium. This desire to record that which was not ordinarily shown on broadcast television, through a medium which could record and transmit live, was the impetus behind many of their projects. Later that year, Don West, network executive at CBS, proposed a "counterculture" television programme, *The New Project: Subject to Change*, which, shot and edited by the Videofreex, would address various edgy topics.[83] Although the broadcast was not a success, the Videofreex began to teach video to those interested in recording alternative lifestyles in New York and aired the results in regular Friday-night sessions. In 1971, the collective moved to the Catskill Mountains in upstate New York, where they lived and worked together. A year later, they founded one of the first pirate TV stations, *Lanesville TV*, in which they invited a two-way flow of communication through listener participation; and in 1973, they published *The Spaghetti City Video Manual: A Guide to Use, Repair and Maintenance* to encourage others to grasp the potential for social and creative video. Global Village, on the other hand, cofounded by John Reilly and Rudi Stern and later including Schneider, focused primarily on teaching video production. Situated on Broome Street in SoHo, New York, Global Village established the first closed-circuit video theatre dedicated to underground and experimental work (Broome Street was later to become an important centre for video dissemination: in 1970, The Kitchen opened on the street, providing a video library available for anyone to use, and a space in which video and alternative news coverage could be presented).

Video collectives, forming at the same time as major galleries and museums were becoming interested in video work, were a reminder that the format represented not just an aesthetic revolt, but also a social one. Video could record things "as they were" and offer unmediated documentation of public events (at least, this was the ideal), which could be easily disseminated. With an emphasis on communality, accessibility, and communication, "a merging of elements, so that life (man) can be art" (Vostell) was promoted which ensured that much video work remained socially active.

So while certain anti-art gestures began to reach major institutions, video artist-composers began to push the boundaries of their work still further, with many preferring to remain beyond the realm of the public institution. In 1969, the nature of the museum was again called in question when Boston's WGBH-TV (where Paik was later to become artist in residence) became one of the first stations to embrace the inclusivity and transient quality of audiovisual video pieces by launching a series of six television shows entitled *The Medium is the Medium*. Produced by Fred Barzyk, the collection of thirty-minute programmes, made by Paik, Kaprow, Tambellini, James Seawright, Piene, and Thomas Tadlock, explored unconventional approaches to production (see video 4.6▶). "We adopted some of John Cage's theories" explained Barzyk: "many times we'd have as many as thirty video sources available at once; there would be twenty people in the control room—whenever anyone got bored they'd just switch to something else without rhyme or reason." [84] For his piece, *Electronic Opera No 1*, Paik used a combination of images from various sources. Processed through tape delays and positive-negative image reversals, the movement of dancers was manipulated into various levels of slow motion. These images were then combined with images of hippies and familiar faces such as that of Richard Nixon. In keeping with the visual montages, the music was several times interrupted by a yawning Paik, who, complaining about the monotony of life, told the television audience to "turn off your TV set". Here, the combination of music and image was not along the metaphorical lines promulgated by Klee in his concept of "polyphonic painting"; nor did it translate—or pseudomorphosise—sound into pictorial space as Kandinsky had attempted to do upon hearing Schoenberg's music. Instead, a temporal visual rendition was enabled by the moving-image technology and the enlarged space of the work's execution. Paik was able directly to instruct his audience, who were no longer contained within a museum or gallery room, but, dispersed across Boston, were sitting in their own homes. TV, originally used by Paik as artistic material, here became the museum itself; both artistic content and the means of its own dissemination—The Medium is the Medium.

This enlarged sphere of influence was also at the heart of Kaprow's piece, *Hello*. While Paik played around with images and sounds from various prerecorded events, Kaprow opted for a multilocational dialogue. Linking direct closed-circuit systems in various sites around Boston (M.I.T, a hospital, and the airport were among the venues) to five TV cameras and multiple monitors, Kaprow created a two-way communication piece capable of breaking both the spatial confinement of the gallery and the silent objectification of its exhibits. Initiating an interplay between art and the mass media, with video and broadcast television the enabling strand, Kaprow continued the aesthetic promulgated in his Happenings: to dissolve the boundaries between art and life. Here, as in many installation pieces, the audience, now greatly enlarged, was the central focus. This exploration of the broadcast gallery/concert venue was investigated in the same year in Germany, Sweden, England, and on several other US networks. When German film-maker Gerry Schum began his broadcast of *Fernsehgalerie* ("Television Gallery") on Sender Freies, Berlin, he announced that "[t]he circle of people that can be reached by galleries and museums is minimal."[85] Articulating the same anti-art ideal that was behind many early video works, Schum continued that "[o]ne of our ideas is communication of art instead of possession of art objects.... The 'TV Gallery' is more or less a mental institution, which comes only into real existence in the moment of transmission by TV."[86] Schum's "Television Gallery" recalls both Levine's understanding of television (discussed in the Introduction), as an art form in which the dialogue between sender and receiver is more important than the message, and John Belton's association of video with "immediacy and presentness."[87] Continually in the "process of coming into being" (Belton), video evoked the transitory nature of live music performance, an evocation particularly apparent in Paik's intermedial television opera.

The 1970s: Video's Global Groove

As a result of video art's appearance on various television networks during 1969, a belief began to emerge that broadcasting channels were not impervious to change for the better. By 1970, Paik had aligned himself almost entirely with the video medium and, in an essay entitled *Global Groove and the Video Common Market*, he set out something of a manifesto, which was to become the theoretical backdrop to his major piece of 1973, *Global Groove*. Paik felt that many world issues were created by prejudiced television coverage of events, such as the Vietnam War. According to his belief, Asian society was incorrectly depicted on Western television, resulting in a negativity that could lead to prejudice and hostility. In anticipation of the world wide web, Paik maintained that a free video market should be established, in which television companies from all over the world could share programmes in order that the "circle of people that can be reached by galleries and museums" would be enlarged. This would allow consumers multiple perspectives, mutual understanding, and increased tolerance.

As we have seen, the Videofreex worked according to similar, socially orientated beliefs. During 1970, two new and influential video collectives were established. The *People's Video Theater* (PVT) was founded by Ken Marsh and Elliot Glass. Like the *Videofreex*, PVT members were interested in community video and aimed to record instances of social importance—marches, protests, and so on—that occurred on the streets of New York and yet were often sanitised when covered by network television: in recognition of video's "immediacy and presence," these videos were played back in the evenings in the PVT space, and were followed by discussion with participants and audience. Raindance provided a similar community for artists and composers working with video (Viola was one such hybrid involved with the group). Members Gillette, Schneider, Ryan, Beryl Korot, Michael Shamberg, Megan Williams, and Louis Jaffé compiled databanks of alternative footage (although the bulky one-inch tapes and heat-sensitive reel-to-reel videotapes were incredibly difficult to store and preserve).

Raindance, however, signalled another important transition period within the history of video art-music. Those involved attempted to situate video work within the cultural and cybernetic ideas being discussed by Marshall McLuhan, Buckminster Fuller, and others (in the early 1970s, Korot and Phyllis Gershuny began a magazine called *Radical Software*, in which the video process and its ideologies were considered).[88] Such structured critical thinking about video was significant and prompted, in the Spring of 1970, the first academic event to focus on video work. The *Alternative Media Conference*, held at Goddard College, Plainfield, Vermont was attended by around three hundred delegates. Although several installations were presented (the Videofreex brought their *Blue Calzone*, a giant inflatable TV set), there were also panels and papers discussing the theoretical implications of the video format.

Now supported by discussion groups and the activities of various communes, video activity flourished in 1970. The exhibition/performance of video in New York City during this year included *A.I.R*, a multi-monitor video installation by Levine that was part of *Software* (curated by Jack Burnham) at the Jewish Museum; the inclusion of several video pieces from America and Latin America and Europe in *Information* (curated by Kynaston McShine) at MoMA; and a video installation by Keith Sonnier at the *Warehouse Show* at the Leo Castelli Gallery. There was also a significant extension of interest in video beyond New York. Curated by Russell Connor, *Vision and Television* was held at the Rose Art Museum, and the catalogue, written by Connor, included what is considered to be the first reference to "video art." Many artists already encountered contributed to the exhibition: the work of Paik, Moorman, Gillette, Schneider, Tambellini, members of the Videofreex, Yalkut, Stern, Levine, Weintraub, and USCO was presented alongside video pieces by Paul Ryan, Eric Siegel, Ted Kraynik, John Reilly, and Eugene Grayson Mattingly. Also during this year, *Body Works*, curated by Willoughby Sharp (who became an important driving force in the development of video work), was presented at the Museum of Conceptual Art, San Francisco. Amongst the pieces shown in this first video exhibition on the West Coast was work by Nauman, Acconci, Oppenheim, and Sonnier.

The presence of video collectives and the increasing number of entire gallery spaces given to video work demonstrates the extent to which, by 1970, the audiovisual format was recognised as an important form of artistic expression.

There followed numerous private and public exhibitions which included, or focused entirely on, video. And, as we saw at the beginning of the chapter, the next few years saw a burst of activity and exhibition/performance of this "TIME art" within major art institutions (something Sturken attributes to the significant increase in state support during this time, particularly from the NYSCA). The *First Annual National Video Festival* was held in 1972 at the Minneapolis College of Art and Design and included works by Paik, Schneider, Campus, Emshwiller, and Tambellini amongst others. Significantly, it also included panel discussions by theorists and historians, such as Youngblood and Barbara Rose. Not only present in various private and public spaces, video was also initiating organised discourse and critical thinking. The festival was followed, in 1974, by two large conferences on television and video in New York: *Open Circuits: The Future of Television* at MoMA; and *Video and the Museum* at the Everson Museum. At work, then, was the theorisation of video art-music while the genre was still in its infancy. Artists in the early sixties had embraced video as a brand-new material with little historical baggage, a genre with "no formal burdens at all" (Ross).[89] And yet, only a decade later, "people were already talking about history" as that history was itself forming; to return to Viola, "[v]ideo was being invented, and simultaneously so were its myths and cultural heroes."[90]

While artists and composers in the early 1960s considered video work a brand-new form, and while those in the 1970s tried to invent its "myths and cultural heroes," it was in fact the spaces of these constructions that were most significant. Early video art-music represented the coming together of two histories and the radical redefinition of performance and exhibition procedures that this entailed. The resultant audiovisual video pieces launched an "explosive charge" (Schwarz) at the gallery's fundamental system of beliefs, namely the visual primacy of "art." As video artists and composers would have it, art could now involve sound, it could be combinative—literally art-music: the gallery environment was no longer a place merely for visual contemplation, but was, rather, one for audiovisual immersion. In the end, it was not a matter of solving the problems presented to the gallery by the audiovisual art form, but rather the ability of the art institution to evolve with its technologically advancing content, and its ability to open its doors to another discipline: music.

5

Interactivity, Mirrored Spaces, and the Closed-Circuit Feed

Performing Video

Today at the tip of so many and perplexing
Wandering years under the varying moon,
I ask myself what whim of fate
Made me so fearful of a glancing mirror.
(Jorge Luis Borges)[1]

The combination of image and sound within a "total event, comprising noise / object / movement / color / and psychology" (Wolf Vostell) is one of the most arresting characteristics of early video work.[2] Able to unite disciplines within an expanded space, video art-music pressed at the rituals identified as operational in the white cube (Brian O'Doherty) and the sacred and segregated spaces of the concert hall (Christopher Small), both of which are predicated on the belief that art and music are "systems of one-way communication."[3] As we saw in chapter 3, the desire to transgress such a physically sectionalised practice links video work with the experimental creative ideas that informed architecture, music, and art during the early twentieth century. As music and image moved towards one another within the emergent "liquid architecture" (John Whitney), the possibilities of audiovisual immersion moved towards realisation, bringing forth refreshed forms of identification and engagement.[4] Within these new environments, visitors were invited across the threshold and into the performance in a move that dissolved the physical, as well as aesthetic, boundaries between author (composer/artist), performer, and audience.

At the level of reception, this was not a new phenomenon. Although many of the intermedial traits found in video work have been traced back to Wagner's desire to immerse the audience within his "world of dreams," the composer's emphasis on the "mystic gulf" between work and receiver flows more easily into the procedures of mainstream film, in which nondiegetic music, combined with a darkened auditorium, helps to focus attention on screen and fiction.[5] Frances Dyson points out that the immersive qualities of audio have always been present in cinema, where the close syncing of sound and image can create the illusion of full dimensionality, or realism.[6] Until recently contained within a two-dimensional screen (3D films now give the illusion of expansion), the visual track of mainstream films, like the pre-twentieth-century painted image, was framed by the four sides of a movie screen: "*Onscreen* refers to space perceived within the rectangular bounds of the image," explains Claudia Gorbman. Underpinned by aesthetic strategies very different to those of video art-music, mainstream fiction films aim to construct "fabula" (story) according to certain narrative structures.[7] Engagement with these structures can be enhanced by making the film world seem as spatially familiar—or realistic—as possible: "*Offscreen*," continues Gorbman, "refers to inferred space, space that the diegesis gives us to believe exists, but which is not perceived because it lies outside the rectangular bounds of the image."[8] To preserve the illusion that a film's world is fully dimensional, the single-point perspective of cinema can be cleverly disguised. Pans, shot-reverse-shot sequences, and diachronic montage can help render the *offscreen*—or what Noël Burch refers to as the "imaginary"—film space "concrete."[9] As a result, the "imaginary" area is perceived by viewers to be a "continuum of the real" (André Bazin).[10] The existence of this "continuum" is supported by three-dimensional sound—the footsteps of a recently departed character receding into the distance, for instance, or the sound of a car roaring into the space behind an audience help to conceal the limits of the image, and so convince the viewer that the diegesis extends in every direction. As Michel Chion points out, there is no "auditory container" for film sound in the same way as there is a "visual container" for the image: as discussed in chapter 3, sound is not confined to the flat screen and the limits of a camera lens, but can travel into the audience's space.[11]

It has commonly been asserted that nondiegetic music—music not from the film's world—operates in much the same way as off-screen sound, its three-dimensional property adding depth and dimension to the screen. But nondiegetic music is different from off-screen sound as it does not emanate directly from the film's world. Rather, it operates from beyond both the visual container and Burch's "concrete" space altogether: its source never revealed; its sounds never referred to by the film's characters. If the source is exposed (through *acousmêtre*), the result is often humorous (think of Count Basie and his orchestra performing "April in Paris" in the middle of the desert in *Blazing Saddles*, 1974), or disempowering (the revelation of the little old "humbug" behind the curtain in *The Wizard of Oz*, 1939, as we have seen) (see video 5.1 ▶).

Gorbman locates the power of music for film in its ability to "signif[y] in relation to the story": although often running "parallel" to the image, the composed film score rarely denotes a concrete relationship between image and sound, but rather fleshes out important moments of characterisation and plot via a more abstract signifying vocabulary.[12] Acting as a kind of aural close-up to the visual narrative, music in film is able to create leitmotivic prophecies, subvert an audience's narrative expectations, and encourage an emphatic response to the unfolding drama. It is Gorbman's belief that the general tendency of the image/ music interaction is to provide a sequence of symbols to be read in a single way in order to provide a unified reading of the film. And yet, although music (particularly orchestral scores) can enhance a film's emotional depth, illusorily realism, or narrative drive, many have noticed a peculiar "inaudibility," by which the filmgoer can fail entirely to hear the score.[13] By evading the conscious awareness of the audience to appeal directly to their sensory backgrounds—"that area least susceptible to rigorous judgement and most susceptible to effective manipulation" (Gorbman)—"inaudible" music is able to secure together spectators and fiction.[14] Musical perception, in other words, becomes an unconscious process that conceals awareness of the physical, material heterogeneities of film, thus drawing the audience "further into the diegetic illusion."[15]

Caryl Flinn has used psychoanalytical structures to theorise the workings of these "inaudible" sounds further, stressing that it is not that the music is literally "unheard," but rather at what level the perception of it takes place.[16] By appealing to the unconscious mind, music is able to encompass the spectator, causing the boundaries between active and passive, body and environment, self and other to dissolve: Mary Ann Doane, for instance, understands film and its music as a "fantasmatic" body held together by the illusion of organic unity, a perceptual cohesion within the film text.[17] With the help of surround sound and dark cinemas, this fantasmatic body initiates, argues Flinn (after Guy Rosolato and Didier Anzieu), a state of "regression" in spectators, inducing in them a return to a pre-linguistic state.[18] Because a child enters the auditory realm before it develops its visual sensors, sound can trigger reminiscence of maternal fusion and "conjur[e] forth the lost qualities of aesthetic wholeness" (Flinn) thought forever lost.[19]

Operating within this unconscious level of perception, however, music can activate an audience, just as the listener in a concert can become mentally agile and functional, as we saw in chapter 3. The sense of wholeness is manifested differently within each filmgoer, as the ways in which sound and image can combine cognitively are determined by the individual's connection with the language of film music and her previous history with certain musics.[20] In *Narration in the Fiction Film*, David Bordwell explores the ways in which film requires completion by the spectator: according to him, there is no need for the "narrator" to play an overt role, because spectators construct narrative for themselves during the process of viewing.[21] So it is not simply a matter of creating "rapport" with an audience: rather, the audience is a necessary component of a film's narrative, the extra ingredient required to interpret cues embedded in the action in order to make sense of an otherwise incomplete audiovisual progression.

Although subconscious hearing, or what Wittgenstein may have referred to as hearing in the realm of the "inarticulate conscious" (the domain that hovers between the conscious and subconscious mind), gives the score great importance to the reading of a film, moments of audibility can also be extremely powerful.[22]

When the narrative folds into Aimee Mann's "Wise Up" in the middle of PT Anderson's *Magnolia* (1999), for instance, the result is devastating: not only does the action stall for the length of the entire song, but each of the ensemble cast sing along to a section of the melody, thus ensuring that the music is not just consciously heard; it also explicitly controls all elements of the rapidly disintegrating plot. Similar moments of audibility occur in many of David Lynch's films, including *Inland Empire* (2006), in which the songs (some of them written and recorded by the director), batter and disarm the audience with their abrasive and nightmarish sounds.

And yet, despite the ability of real-world sounds to break from film's "visual container," and the capability of music to emotionally and psychologically enhance the aesthetic parameters of film, the visual continuum is nevertheless curtailed by the edges of the screen: any extension into the "imaginary" space remains illusory, as viewers are not free to experience the full 360-degree surround of the film world at will. Two experimental films from the year in which video art-music was born successfully deconstructed the two-dimensionality of the cinematic image. But they had to employ live performers to do so. For his Happening *Moviehouse* (1965), Claes Oldenburg encouraged attention to move from cinema screen to the audience by dotting sneezing and popcorn-eating actors throughout the stalls.

In a similarly expansive gesture, Robert Whitman's *Prune Flat* (1965) reimagined the space in front of the cinema screen by combining live performance with filmed images to create what Gene Youngblood later referred to as a "higher ordering principle of intermedia, or what might be called 'filmstage'."[23] Unlike the expanded cinema Events discussed in chapter 3, this Happening took place in a traditional film theatre. Dressed in white, two female actors moved across the stage, performing various actions: at the same time, their filmed images, performing the same gestures as well as alternative movements, were projected onto the cinema screen behind them. Ultraviolet lighting "kept the people flat, but also made them come away from the screen a little bit" so that they appeared "strange and fantastic" (Whitman). Also onstage was a third girl: her filmed image, which slowly undressed, was projected onto her real, fully clothed body until she appeared both naked and covered at the same time. But despite leaking into the cinema's space, Whitman's work sought to accentuate the "mystic gulf" between performer and receiver, which, explains the artist, "I tried to keep and make even stronger."[24] Carolee Schneemann created similar moments of contained "filmstage" in her theatre performances: "I do a lot of performing just in the light of film projectors. So that it's a very compacted image and there are no peripheral distractions. It becomes central to the environment without your really having the sense of film, because the bodies or forms of people are quite embedded in it."[25] But although the combination of performance and pre-existent film created events fuelled by live energy and aleatoric actions, the difficulties of creating and projecting filmed images in real time meant that at least one part of the piece was prerecorded and unable to change.[26]

The initial similarities between "filmstage" and video performances provided an easy avenue of critique for the detractors of video art-music. Speaking of the performance videos by Vito Acconci, Joan Jonas, and Wolfgang Stoerchle, Allan Kaprow raged that "most of them are just more or less adequate recordings of the performances or are compositions of 'special effects' which could simply have been done just as well or better as film. Videotape is simply cheaper and faster."[27] But this is not the case. *Movie House* and *Prune Flat* brought the filmed images into the spectators' space and yet, like the "one-way flow of communication" (Small) of mainstream film and television, remained removed from visitors at the discursive level: audience members could not alter events; nor were they physically engulfed by them.[28] By contrast, video art-music encouraged a different form of spatialisation, or "acoustic architecture" (Bill Viola).[29] In the first chapter, the video signal was discussed in terms of its "immediacy and presentness" (John Belton), an irreversibility and decay that can place image within the temporal domain of music.[30] This technological characteristic, combined with the difficulties of editing early video, encouraged artists and musicians to use the format for live recording, thus enabling video image and sound to be responsive, performative, and spontaneous. Able to record and transmit immediately, early video could take images and sounds from the performance space and use them as compositional material in real time: image was able to break from the "visual container" of film, in other words, and move into the nondiegetic space of music to create what Paik referred to as "a TIME art."[31] Like expanded cinema and "filmstage," early video often included performance; but the continually scanning video signal, which ensures that "[v]ideo images are always in the process of their own realization" (Belton), meant that the videoed sounds and images could also be performative.[32] The difference between film performance and video events, then, can be rearticulated in terms of immersive interactivity.

Immersion, Immediacy and Hypermediacy

Dyson understands immersion as:

> a process or condition whereby the viewer becomes totally enveloped within and transformed by the "virtual environment". Space acts as a pivotal element in this rhetorical architecture, since it provides a bridge between real and mythic spaces, such as the space of the screen, the space of the imagination, cosmic space, and literal, three-dimensional physical space.[33]

Although speaking in relation to new media, Dyson's understanding of immersion is useful here. She speaks of "'being in', rather than 'looking at', virtual environments," a perceptual change that encourages a passage across the threshold from gallery into work to enable the visitor "to occupy the space and time, the here and now, the virtual present of a separate but ontologically real space."[34]

The immersive environment operates in a variety of ways when video technology is involved: ways that can loosely be categorised in terms of video's "first birth" and its later period of *"constitution"* (André Gaudreault and Philippe Marion).[35] At first glance, it is easier to apply Dyson's notion of immersion to the high degree of media specificity found in recent video art-music. Referring to its "technology-dependent relationship," Chris Meigh-Andrews understands the evolution of video and its methods of projection as one predicated on technological advancement.[36] This advancement has created, suggests Catherine Elwes, "contrasting spatial dynamics" between early and more recent video work.[37] Whereas Nam June Paik and Vostell placed great emphasis on video equipment and its mode of display, sculpting with the television set to form shapes such as a *TV Chair* (1968) or a *TV Bed* (1972), more recent work has been characterised by "[t]he emergence of the video image from its cuboid container" (Elwes).[38] Artist-musicians such as Viola repositioned interest from the object of display onto, or rather into, the flat screen. Often occupying darkened rooms, the "aesthetically independent genre" (Yvonne Spielmann) has been marked by a more cinematic, less sculptural style than that found during video's "first birth."

In their theory of Remediation, Jay David Bolter and Richard Grusin distinguish between immediacy and hypermediacy in order to understand the "double logic" at play in new media.[39] Drawing our attention to the literal meaning of perspective—"seeing through"—the authors formulate a theory of media immediacy as fundamentally erasive in nature. Following Norman Bryson's suggestion that the Western oil paint tradition has been "treated primarily as an erasive medium" that focuses our awareness on the scene depicted and away from "the surface of the picture-plain," Bolter and Grusin use point-of-view television, webcams, and period dramas as examples of genres that make us think we are "'really' there."[40] In such instances, "the logic of immediacy dictates that the medium itself should disappear and leave us in the presence of the thing represented."[41]

The logic of immediacy can be found at play in the more cinematic, self-contained and representational style of recent video work. In *Five Angels for the Millennium* (2001), for instance, Viola creates an immersive environment that is spatially separated from the rest of the gallery space (fig. 5.1). Installed in London's Tate Modern, the piece requires visitors to undergo a form of "mimetic engulfment" (Claire Bishop) when they enter the pitch-dark room to find five images projected directly onto the gallery walls (or, at least, this is the illusion created).[42] Each screen shows a man diving into, or re-emerging from water in extreme slow motion, his watery sounds elongated into a distorted, reverberant echo. Just as the electroacoustic, organised sounds (John Cage) lap around the audience, the borders of each projection melt into the darkened room, making the spaces of projection and reception indistinguishable from one another. Visitors frequently sit on the floor of this audiovisual simulacrum, thoroughly sutured

Figure 5.1 Bill Viola, *Five Angels for the Millennium* (2001). © Bill Viola.

into the slow temporal trajectory so different from the hectic London streets outside. By thus drawing attention away from context and into the diegesis that spreads out into the space of nondiegetic music, Viola's five audiovisual glimpses of ascension operate through a process described by Liz Kotz as a "seductive immateriality" compatible with the illusory modes of discourse commonly found in cinema.[43]

But not all contemporary video work relies on absolute "immateriality." For her audiovisual installation, *Administrating Eternity* (2011) created for the Hayward Gallery, London, Pipilotti Rist invites visitors into an immersive sensorium in which the flat screen is replaced by a forest of gauze strips that hang from the ceiling. As visitors navigate through the work to the sound of slow ambient music, they come across scenes projected onto the strips at various depths, perspectives, and speeds, ranging from a field of sheep to slowly opening flowers (fig. 5.2). Whereas visitors to *Five Angels* tend to sit on the floor, or stand with their backs against the wall, *Administrating Eternity* encourages people to walk through its softly billowing maze of material until a pleasing perspective is achieved, at which point floor cushions in the shape of legs, arms, and torsos provide a comfortable (if rather unsettling) place to rest. Although in the foreground, Rist's materiality is transitory and ethereal, disappearing in the breeze as you draw near to each imagined landscape.

Figure 5.2 Pipilotti Rist, *Administrating Eternity*, 2011 Hayward Gallery.
Photo by Linda Nylind. © Pipilotti Rist.

Inclusion

Five Angels and *Administrating Eternity* allow visitors to chose where to sit or
stand, how long to stay for and how "present" to be. Like every performance, both
environments are influenced by the people experiencing them: a room occupied
by one visitor will be experienced differently to one swarming with chattering
school children, for instance. And yet the works are not *performative*: once begun,
the flow of audiovisual information follows a predetermined course. Early video
work often operated differently. Although there were, of course, exceptions, pieces
from video's "first birth" functioned from within two distinctive parameters: first,
a focus on the video equipment; and second, the *inclusion*, not simply the immersion, of the audience.

   If immediacy is a transparent, "present" form of media that emphasises the
content of a work over its presentation (the linear narratives and sutured audiovisuality of mainstream film is an excellent example of this), then hypermediacy
(at its most basic) can be used to describe a work that highlights its materiality.
Bolter and Grusin, however, are careful to point out that the two forms of communication remain densely entangled:

   New digital media oscillate between immediacy and hypermediacy, between transparency and opacity. This oscillation is the key to
   understanding how a medium refashions its predecessors and other

contemporary media. Although each medium promises to reform its predecessors by offering a more immediate or authentic experience, the promise of reform inevitably leads us to become aware of the new medium as a medium.[44]

Although, like Dyson, Bolter and Grusin focus on new media—and in particular the fragmentation of computer interfaces—their emphasis on process and non-linearity can be useful when considering early video work.[45] As we have seen, video was initially used as a component of other creative events, acting as a facilitator for intermedial discourse. As such, the equipment—the video technology; the TV monitors—was often used sculpturally, remaining a highly visible component of multimedia Events, such as Robert Whitman's *Two Holes of Water—3* (1966). In such work, the materiality—or "opacity" (Clement Greenberg)—of display is placed in the foreground through the processes of fragmentation, nonlinearity, and heterogeneity. But the realisation of *Ars est artem demonstrare* (Greenberg) leads to a paradox: early video work at once distances an audience, while also including them as compositional material.[46] Les Levine's *Iris* (1968), discussed in the previous chapter, illustrates this paradox well: three video cameras relayed a closed-circuit feed of both performance space and visitors onto a stack of six television monitors. Like Boccioni's *"interpenetration of the planes,"* the surrounding space was literally brought into the artwork, dissolving the distinction between work and life not just metaphorically, but also physically, as the artist explains:[47]

> I don't tend to think of my work purely in psychological terms, but one must assume some psychological effect of seeing oneself on TV all the time. Through my systems the viewer sees himself as an image, the way other people would see him were he on television. In seeing himself this way he becomes more aware of what he looks like. All of television, even broadcast television, is to some degree showing the human race to itself as a working model. It's a reflection of society, and it shows society what society looks like. It renders the social and psychological condition of the environment visible to that environment.[48]

While viewers became an integral part of the work, able to change how it looked and the speed with which the images progressed, they did not get sucked into a new world, but rather remained aware of the work's materiality (as a stack of monitors). Mediated space and the "real" space of the work (in this instance, Levine's own studio) here coexisted as equals and the success of the work relied on the ability of the visitor to hold together in her consciousness the palpable presence of both worlds. This led to a complicated interplay between representational and emergent modes of communication, an interaction summed up by Chris Salter in terms of separation and variability: "If representational accounts privilege a demarcation between subject and object or self and world, performative ones imply a world in which subjects and objects have not yet come into being and, even if materialized, are always in a constant state of flux and transformation that is unstable and difficult to repeat."[49]

Early video art-music, then, articulated an interactive spatial dynamic very different from that which came to characterise later video work, manifesting a form of hypermediacy that required an "activated spectatorship" (Bishop) at odds with Small's understanding of performance as "one-way communication."[50] As we have seen, video became available during an era of great experimentation understood by Andrew Ross as a "cultural crusade" to replace "'passivity' with 'participation'"; and as a result, it developed in close relation to performance art, actions, and Happenings, which were founded on real-time creativity within a set of loosely defined parameters.[51] RoseLee Goldberg has noted that artists have often invited performance into their work "as a way of breaking down categories and indicating new directions" when a line of creative enquiry has "reached an impasse": "Live gestures have constantly been used as a weapon against the conventions of established art."[52] At the time, Acconci claimed that "[w]e hated the word 'performance'" because it "had a place, and that place by tradition was a theatre"; according to him, it suggested an event to be consumed from across a bifurcated space, providing a "point you went toward," an "enclosure" that could provide only "abstractions of the world and not the messy world itself."[53] The "messy" potential of performance was explored by Kaprow and Cage, amongst others, who encouraged spontaneous participation from audience members, explaining that "[t]here are freedoms for the viewer... but they are revealed only within the limits dictated by the art work's immediate as well as underlying themes" (Kaprow).[54]

The combination of performance with video was no surprise as many artists and composers were involved with both disciplines. Performance artists could either collaborate with video artist-musicians (the Charlotte Moorman-Paik partnership is perhaps the most famous example); or combine performance and video themselves (Jonas and Schneemann, for instance, or Ulrike Rosenbach working in Germany and VALIE EXPORT in Austria). Operating within this discourse, early video artists treated the new audiovisual technology as equivalent to a performer, able to improvise and be reactive to its changing environment via a closed-circuit feed rather than exhibit prerecorded and edited footage. Having raged against the low quality, reportage usages of video technology, Kaprow expressed more benevolent feelings towards the ways in which the format could transfigure its immediate context:

> The close-circuit, environmental videographers, in contrast, are trying to make use of what in the medium is *not* like film or other art. The most experimental feature of their work, it seems to me, is its emphasis upon situational process rather than some act canned as a product for later review.[55]

With its emphasis on the "situational process," early video work could collapse the "mystic gulf" (Wagner) between creator, performer, and audience; between the spaces of performance and reception.[56] But the nature of this collapse was highly variable. Despite being "performed" live, some pieces remained relatively self-contained: Tambellini, for instance, opted for "video constructions," in which images and sounds were generated electronically on TV monitors with no information taken from the immediate or broadcast context; Paik's *TV Buddha* (1974), in which a bronze sculpture contemplates its own image as it is fed live onto a small monitor several feet away, on the other hand, was spatial and live, but not interactive.[57] For others, such as Douglas Davis, Juan Downey, Frank Gillette, Bruce Nauman, the Pulsa group, Ira Schneider, and Keith Sonnier, however, the immediacy of the closed-circuit feed encouraged a multilayered transgression of social, psychological, and physical borders. When considering the potential of the early technology, Kaprow explained that "video for these artists is a system of echoes, communications, reflections, and dialogues linking the self with what is outside the self and back again. This hardware linkage proposes to alter positively the behaviour of human and nonhuman participants alike."[58] This alteration of behaviour could be achieved in one of two, often interlinked, ways: artist-composers could turn the camera on themselves; or onto the audience.

"Mirror, Mirror, on the Wall..."

Video pieces that focused on the artist-composer as protagonist clearly stem from practices in performance art. Acconci, for example, combined both arenas by videoing his performances: in *Centers* (1971), the artist points into the camera (it is unclear whether he is gesticulating at us or at his own mirrored image, fig. 5.3); while in *Air Time* (1973), he converses with his own mirrored image.[59] In her influential article of 1976, Rosalind Krauss postulates video as narcissistic, pointing out the conceptual change that such a statement requires: narcissism is a subjective psychological state that is ordinarily associated with the artist; the video medium, on the other hand, is considered objective, an "appurtenance" through which the artist's ideas can be channelled. Krauss, however, considers it "inappropriate to speak of a physical medium in relation to video" because the format's "real medium is a psychological situation, the very terms of which are to withdraw attention from an external object—the Other—and invest it in the Self."[60] The medium as "psychological situation" is most evident in self-reflexive pieces that shattered the barriers between performer and camera via a mirrored image. As video practice moved towards its constitution in the early 1970s, mirrors, reflections, metamorphoses, and fragmented self-images were increasingly used by artists such as Acconci, Hannah Wilke, Dennis Oppenheim, and Martha Rosler in order to represent and critique larger cultural issues, including social structure, feminism, and the nature of art and music and their performance strategies.

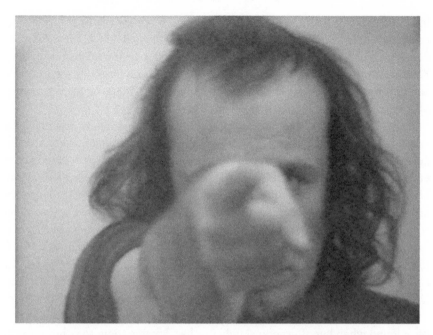

Figure 5.3 Vito Acconci, video still from *Centers* (1971). © Vito Acconci.

At first glance, mirrors suggest truth and self-realisation: the world reflected back at you appears simply a reversed, yet faithful image of the one in which you stand. Yet mirrors have not always been understood in this way and there is a long record of reflection as signifying not merely inert copy, but rather a power-ful transformational device. It is this history that early video artist-composers tapped into. The complex forms of identification set into motion by a glimpsed reflection can be traced back to Greek mythology, in which Echo and Narcissus were punished for their respective disloyalty and vanity by imprisonment in aural and visual replication: the echo, in which a sound (or image) is returned as a literal copy without the ability to change or interpret the original utterance; and the narcissistic, in which a reflected image is misunderstood by the beholder as real-istic and other. Latent in the latter is the belief that a mirrored image holds the power to either provide additional information, or to deceive the viewer.

It is from the magical possibilities of metamorphosis and prophecy that the myths of reflection have sprung. Mentioned in Chaucer's "Squire's Tale," the idea (still alive in modern crystal-ball gazing) that hidden knowledge can be revealed via a magic mirror—"a device for making physically and temporally distant phenom-ena visible to the beholder" (Herbert Grabes)—flourished throughout the Middle Ages and the Renaissance.[61] The magic mirror was a staple of the sixteenth- and seventeenth-century magician, who claimed the ability to conjure forth the vision of spirits into a looking glass with the assistance of an intermediate agent—or scryer. Legend has it, for instance, that in 1605, Dr. John Dee, with the help of his scryer Edward Kelley, used a magic mirror to prophesy the Gun Powder Plot conspiracy to kill King James 1.[62] Stemming from the belief in looking-glass predictions sprung the superstition that to break a mirror invites bad luck. Ruth Kassinger has pointed out that, by the same logic, a mirror could ward off evil, and draws our attention to the English fashion, during the seventeenth century, of sporting hats covered with tiny mirrored tiles.[63]

Other belief systems and fables view the mirror not as a link to other physical or temporal locations, but rather as an entrance into an alternate reality. The disquieting effects of infinite reproducibility is articulated in Borges's "The Library of Babel", in which the "burnished surfaces" of mirrors located in the hallways of his labyrinthine, hexagonal literary universe "are a figuration and promise the infinite."[64] In these instances, the fragmented, mediated self offered by the mirror range from the nightmarish—the evil queen's murderous reaction in the Brothers Grimm's fairy tale to her famous question, "Mirror mirror on the wall: Who's the fairest of them all?"—to the idealistic—the mirror in *Harry Potter and The Philosopher's Stone* that reflects not truth but your greatest desire, for instance. Often, these two extremes are held in an oscillating tension: the world reflected back when one looks in a mirror is at once similar yet recognisably different, as Alice found when her afternoon slumber in her drawing room took her into the reversed arena of her looking glass. However, in Lewis Carroll's world of conundrum and riddles, things are not only physically reversed, they are also conceptually topsy turvy: Alice encounters the Red Knight, who (speculates Tweedledee) is asleep dreaming of Alice; Tweedledum and Tweedledee are the inverted images of each other; inanimate objects in Alice's drawing-room world come alive; and soundless artefacts, such as garden flowers, acquire a voice.[65]

The Fragmented Body

Chrissie Iles points out that the reflective potential of the closed-circuit video feed could be used as a "technological equivalent" to the mirror. Indeed, open structures, inclusivity, and the element of chance were at the heart of closed-circuit video work that promoted as its "central strategy," "the fragmentation of the single temporal and spatial viewpoint." (Iles).[66]

Jonas frequently spoke of the nature of reflection and its ability to deflect the audience's attention from object to process and, by extension, from single to fragmented, communal perspectives:

> From the beginning, the mirror provided me with a metaphor for my reflective investigation. It also provided a device to alter space and to fragment it. By reflecting it, I could break it up. I could mix reflections of performers and audience, thereby bringing all of them into the same time and space of the performance. In addition to creating space, a

mirror also disturbs space, suggesting another reality through the looking glass—to see the reflection of Narcissus, to be a voyeur, to see one's
self as the other.[67]

Even before Jonas acquired her Portapak in 1970, the mirrored environment was
a staple in her performance pieces: during *Mirror Piece I* (1969), performers carried
large, oblong mirrors; at one stage, they lay on the floor with the mirrors rising
vertically from their stomachs so that a visitor situated at their feet saw not their
torsos, but rather four legs; in *Mirror Piece II* (1970), the artist wore a costume covered in small mirrors that chimed together as she moved through an environment
reflected back at her via numerous large mirrors and glass panels held by performers. According to Iles, the choreography of the performers was particularly musical
as it evoked the repetitive structures of La Monte Young and Terry Riley.[68]

The fractured, reflected lower bodies of *Mirror Piece I* and the multiple dis-
placements of *Mirror Piece II* seem to suggest an undoing of the Lacanian "mirror
phase," in which a child between the ages of six and eighteen months acquires a
unified (if troubled) and complete sense of individual self, or ego (although this
moment is also one of radical rupture, as it is the first time the infant experiences
a disconnect with the (M)other: moreover, since he does not *recognise* but precisely *misrecognises* the unified image in the mirror as himself, the misrecognition
(*méconnaissance*) itself speaks of a mere illusion of unity). Before this, the child
is unable to differentiate between the limits of his body and the world beyond.[69]
According to Lacan, the infant is captivated by his own mirrored, and unified
counterpart, as it "anticipates the mastery of the body that the infant has not
yet objectively achieved."[70] This moment, Lacan tells us, is one of triumph and joy
as it anticipates an important passage in the development of ego. Nevertheless,
speaking of the captivation a child experiences when coming face-to-face with
his own image, Lacan refers to the term capitation, which in French, as Dylan
Evans has remarked, can mean at once an alluring and seductive engagement
with the mirrored image; yet also conjures forth a sense of "imprisonment" or
"disabling fixation," as though the image were deceptive; a trap like that waiting
to ensnare Narcissus.[71] The *corps morcelé* (fragmented body, or body in pieces)
in Jonas's *Mirror Pieces* peel away all sense of a coherent self. Lacan would have
it that a person faced with a *corps morcelé* in later life will experience a sense of
intense unease and entrapment, as though a retrograde rite of passage had been
initiated. And yet Jonas's performances embrace the shattering of this unity and
the freedom from the socially constructed, mediated notion of female and femi-
ninity that this entails, by creating "a mobility and multiplicity of perspectives"
(Spielmann).[72]

Notions of fracture and dissonance also informed her spatially expanded performances, such as *Jones Beach Piece* (1970), for which the audience were located
a quarter of a mile away from the action. Similarly, for the performance of *Delay
Delay* in the Hudson River, New York (1972), visitors were positioned on a nearby

roof in order to get a complete view of the performers progressing through the numbered grids of Jonas's score, a form of stylised movement influenced by Noh and Japanese Kabuki theatre, as the artist explains:

> Performers clapped blocks of wood together at different distances from the audience. One saw the gesture of clapping in wide overhead arcs before hearing the sound, the lag depending on the distances and the atmosphere. This separation of action and sound, of sight and hearing, isolated for the audience the relativity of perception. The clapping gesture marked the perimeters of the space, but the sound transmission, the desynchronized delay, was its measure.[73]

Although no mirrors were included in *Delay Delay*, the work was based on an aural echo, a form of "desynchronized delay" caused by the distance between action and reception, a distance that made it impossible, as Douglas Crimp has noted, "to link gesture and sound."[74] As a result, sound, like the image produced by a magic mirror, became fragmented and independent of its original utterance. The same elements were captured in her video work, *Song Delay* (1973), in which the desynchronised sounds of distant performers slapping together pieces of wood above their heads in a river bed competes with the noise of the horns from passing boats (see video 5.2 ▶).

Jonas's work with the video camera continued her process-based experiments with the fragmentation of both image *and* sound by enabling her to construct a "psychologically-charged, subjective, feminine territory" (Iles).[75] In her early video work, the "relativity of perception" was not achieved through increased spatialisation, but rather through a reflected interiority: "My work is often considered personal or private, perhaps because of the presence of the author as performer. Friends have told me that they feel they are looking into a private world. I do try to bring the audience into my space. There is an intimacy."[76] To achieve this, she incorporated many of the mirror's mythical and magical properties into performances, as Iles explains:

> In Semitic and Japanese cultures, the mirror represents a feminine divinity, or sun goddess, and in Christianity, the Virgin Mary. Mexican culture attributes to it both solar and lunar properties, symbols of which occur repeatedly in Jonas's work, from the enigmatic male/female couple in mirrored costumes, to her chalk drawings on blackboards in her video performances, in which she half erases the sun to create a lunar shape. In this sense, although a single reading is never implied, she can be understood to be depicting, in drawing, the same symbolism of duality which appears in other aspects of her video performances, where black and white, light and dark, and positive and negative are continually juxtaposed.[77]

The creation of "intimacy" through reference to the history of reflection is apparent in two of her earliest video performances. Dating from 1972, both works featured Jonas as her alter ego, Organic Honey. Her first video performance, *Organic Honey's Visual Telepathy*, took place at the Lo Giudice Gallery in New York. The complex Event required three performers in addition to Organic Honey, a camera that projected live feed onto a large screen and a monitor whose images oscillated between live and prerecorded footage. Despite the displacement initiated by the multiple viewpoints, Jonas explained that "I am never separated from my own exposure."[78] As we saw in chapter 1, the artist hummed and sang as she tried on different costumes, including a feathered headdress, a mask of a doll's face, and silk robes, in front of a large mirror, in which visitors could also see themselves. This layering of projected and mirrored spaces created a compound interplay between real and other, as Crimp notes: "there is no central self from which the work can be said to be generated or by which it can be received. Both the performer and spectator are shown to be de-centred, split."[79] As the performance progressed, Organic Honey hit the mirror until it broke in a final rejection of the unified, female image.

Organic Honey's Vertical Roll, performed in the Ace Gallery, Los Angeles, amongst other places (the work later became a single-channelled video), operated in much the same way:

> I was interested in the discrepancies between the performed activity and the constant duplicating, changing, and altering of information in the video. The whole is a sequence of missing links as each witness experiences a different series by glancing from monitor to projection to live action. Perception was relative.[80]

The artist performed activities, such as drawing, in front of a camera. But when her movement was relayed as video image, it was not correctly synchronised with the television's frequencies, which resulted in an interrupted electric signal that produced a continual vertical roll (fig. 5.4). Referred to by Jonas as "the out-of-sync dysfunction of the television," the roll moved up the screen, splitting the image in half. Different parts of her body—legs, torso, face—were shown from a variety of angles as a constantly moving *corps morcelé*. Acconci pointed out that "on a TV screen, a close-up face is approximately the same size as an actual face," a coincidence of scale that enabled Organic Honey to interact with her own fragmented image.[81] The camera also picked up a mirror, which the artist hit rhythmically with a metal spoon. The loud, angular, metal beat coincided loosely with the rolling image, as though the insistent sound was causing the image to judder—at one stage Organic Honey herself marches and jumps in time to the beat: "I had begun to dance with the TV," she explained.[82] While the closed-circuit feed included the real, it also negated it through transformation, replacing it with a disturbing grainy, black-and-white image with a shallow depth of field. From here

Figure 5.4 Joan Jonas, video still from *Organic Honey's Vertical Roll* (1972).
© Joan Jonas.

it is possible to return to Krauss's understanding of "the medium of video art" as "the psychological condition of the self split and doubled by the mirror-reflection of synchronous feedback."[83] As "perception" became "relative," the screen suggested another, metaphorical space, where, as Alice experienced in her looking glass, things were not just mirrored, but also alive. Spielmann reads this work as an expression of the transition from reality to mediated duplication in the media, a usually invisible shift exposed by Jonas's appearance "in the space between the video camera and the taped monitor image."[84]

Video technology could also be used to explore reflection and fragmentation in aural terms. In Nauman's *Lip Sync* (1969), the bottom half of the artist's mouth is seen in close-up (see video 5.3▶). The artist wears large headphones and articulates the words "Lip Sync" over and over again: as he does so, he hears an immediate relay in his headphones and attempts to synchronise image and sound. However, after an intermittent delay, the two slowly fall out of time with each other in a way that Nauman compares to the shifting repetitions of minimalist music, a technique that informs works like Steve Reich's looped tape piece *It's Gonna Rain* (1965) and the phasing technique of his *Piano Phase* (1967).[85] A similar idea was explored by Richard Serra, a close friend of Jonas and collaborator with Philip Glass (who worked as his gallery assistant during the early '70s). In 1969, the pair joined forces to produce *Word Location*, a spatialised sound work installed on Long Beach Island, New Jersey. Thirty-two waterproof speakers, running a fifteen-minute tape loop of the word

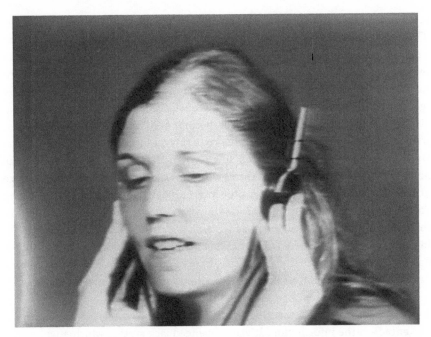

Figure 5.5 Richard Serra, video still from *Boomerang* (1974).

"is" were dotted over a thirty-acre area of marsh and coastland, the distance between each was such that there could be no sound bleed between them. *Boomerang* (1974) demonstrates the influence of Glass on Serra's solo video work (fig. 5.5). The piece involves a close-up of artist Nancy Holt sitting in a recording studio. As she speaks, her words "come back on top" of her "like a mirror reflection" through a pair of large headphones in an extremely close echo. Her monologue focuses on the disorienting experience of being out-of-sync with one's own actions: "I have a feeling that I am not where I am"; of being "removed from reality." Krauss reads this auditory echo as the artist's "great difficulty coinciding with herself as a subject," a fragmentation and dislocation similar to that of Organic Honey's visual mirrored environments.[86]

Solitary Interactivity

Whereas Jonas directed many of her investigations onto herself, many of her contemporaries used the mirrored environment to collapse any physical and psychological distance between author and receiver by allowing "[t]he human presence and perception of the spatial context [to] become materials of art" (Jennifer Licht).[87] Events such as Billy Klüver's *Nine Evenings* (1966), for instance, filled entire rooms, requiring visitors actually to cross the threshold and enter the diegetic heart of the performance. Once they had become an integral component of a piece, audience members could introduce "flexibility, changeability, fluency" (Cage) into the creative formula.[88] Margaret Morse explains that "Inter," derived from the Latin for "among," "suggests a linking or meshing function that connects separate entities": interactivity, she continues "allows associative rather than linear and casual links to be made between heterogeneous elements."[89] As we have seen, early video technology can usefully be considered a facilitator for intermedial discourse when used to "mesh" together disciplines in responsive, process-driven structures. The importance of the audience to this mesh was summed up by Steina and Woody Vasulka, who described The Kitchen Videotape Theatre, which was initially located in the kitchen of the Mercer Arts Center, New York, as "a theatre utilizing an audio, video, and electronic interface between performers (including actors, musicians, composers, and kinetic visual artists) and audience": within this theatre, they promoted video as an "activity" rather than an "art a priori."[90] In chapter 4, we encountered Gillette's and Schneider's *Wipe Cycle* (Howard Wise Gallery, 1969), a work that placed focus almost exclusively on audience members despite being installed in a conventional gallery setting, as Schneider explains:

> The most important function of *Wipe Cycle* was to integrate the audience into the information. It was a live feedback system which enabled the viewer standing within its environment to see himself not only now in time and space, but also eight seconds ago and sixteen seconds ago. In addition he saw standard broadcast images alternating with his own delayed/live image.... It was an attempt to demonstrate that you're as much a piece of information as tomorrow morning's headlines—as a viewer you take a satellite relationship to the information. And the satellite which is you is incorporated into the thing which is being sent back to the satellite. In other words, rearranging one's experience of information reception.[91]

Like the mirrored environment, then, a closed-circuit video feed could present a visitor with their own fictive double through a process of mimesis and transformation.

But the incorporation of audience into work required profound spatial and cognitive reconfigurations. As the audience became a key component of the piece—as both audio and visual material—a psychological fissure emerged that could create feelings of intense interiority or, by contrast, of great inclusivity. Writing about Levine's *Iris*, for example, Youngblood notes that the work makes the viewer uncomfortable and self-conscious because it:

> turns the viewer into information. The viewer has to reconsider what he thought about himself before. He must think about himself in terms of information. You notice people in front of *Iris* begin to adjust their appearance. They adjust their hair, tie, spectacles. They become aware

of aspects of themselves which do not conform to the image they previously had of themselves.[92]

Acconci, Nauman, and Oppenheim were amongst those who constructed solitary spaces that emphasised the physical and psychic spaces of the single viewer. As we also saw in the previous chapter, the possible distance and alienation experienced when encountering your own image lay at the heart of Nauman's *Live-Taped Video Corridor* (1970), a work that Paul Schimmel has described as an "environment of controlled response" (fig. 4.5).[93] Using plywood, Nauman created a narrow walkway inside the Whitney Museum of American Art, New York. Separated from their viewing colleagues, visitors were asked to walk down the claustrophobic passageway towards two monitors placed on top of one another: on the lower screen was played a prerecorded videotape of the empty passage, while the upper monitor displayed a live feed from a wide-angle lens security camera situated at the installation's entrance. However, as visitors moved towards the monitors and away from the camera, they witnessed their own mediated image, from the back, travelling away from them. The result, as described by Morse, was that the body appeared to have become "unglued" from its "own image."[94] But even as their image receded, visitors were made to scrutinise themselves from unfamiliar angles, almost as though they were glancing into a magic mirror: "it's very easy to describe how the piece looks," explains Nauman; "but the experience of walking inside it is something else altogether which can't be described."[95] It is possible to find the transformational possibilities of reflection and the potential for "disabling fixation" at play here. Like many others, Grabes has argued for an understanding of reflection predicated on mimesis, rather than inert reproduction: "If the mirror transforms without one's active participation, or without one's being able to avoid possible transformation, we then have an instance of the magical influence of the mirror or, if the emphasis is on the beholder's personal reaction to the reflected image, of a primarily emotional transformation."[96]

Similar transformational environments were explored by Peter Campus, who, like Nauman, moved towards live, interactive work in the early seventies. In pieces such as *Kiva* (1971), *Stasis* (1973), and *mem* (1975), the audience were enmeshed with the work so that "the retroflection of one's projected image and its accompanying sensations" became as one (Campus).[97] The result was a conversion of static gallery into what the artist describes as "durational space."[98] Both *Live-Taped Video Corridor* and Campus's early video environments demanded from the audience a form of conceptual blending, whereby the visitor must choose certain inputs from both real and mediated world and from them construct a partial match. When combined, these inputs, which are individual to each viewer, form a new and blended mental space.

Like Jonas, Dan Graham created complex refracted environments by combining mirrored reflections with videoed ones; and, like Nauman and Campus, he articulated the concepts of fragmented narcissism by asking his visitors to view themselves. However, Graham added a further temporal dimension to Campus's "durational space" by layering not only locations, but also different time frames in the form of time-lag: "mirrors reflect instantaneous time without duration," explained the artist, "whereas video feedback does just the opposite, it relates the two in a kind of durational time flow."[99] In *Present Continuous Past* (1974), the visitor stands in a mirrored room which appears translucent and immaterial; on one wall is a camera that relays their image onto a screen with an eight-second lag. If the camera caught the monitor's mirrored image in its glance (depending on the position of the viewer), the image projected eight seconds later included the room from sixteen seconds ago, and so on. Here, the viewer ran the risk of not only confronting multiple versions of herself, but also of glimpsing the ghost of a previous visitor long since departed.

Unlike Jonas's mirrored performances, these examples of solitary, participatory video environments did not include music or sound as integral components. While it could be argued that the pieces were installed in conventional gallery spaces at a time when they remained places for quiet contemplation, the radical sensibilities at play suggest a more aesthetic reason. These whole-room works could be profoundly unsettling as they asked the visitor to confront their own fractured image, either walking away (Nauman) or staring back from a distant past (Graham). As we have seen, music, when combined with the moving image in mainstream fiction film, can help an audience to relax, to believe in the story and to disregard the edges of the "visual container." While it is true that many scenes and, in some cases, entire films (such as the Coen Brothers' *No Country for Old Men* (2007)) can function perfectly well with little or no music, absolute silence can be disquieting (think of the calm before the storm in a horror film). Watching your own image acting independently in silence contributed to the ghostly effect of the reflected environment. And yet, silence did not necessarily mean that these works were not musical. If we recall Daniel Albright's belief that there is "a deep concord" operating among artistic media, it is possible to identify certain musical processes resonating in these works.[100] While the interlocking repetitions of *Lip Sync* and *Boomerang* can clearly be linked to the structures of minimalist music, Campus's concept of "durational space" and Graham's attempts to produce "durational time flow" demonstrate an aesthetic not dissimilar to that of the absolute filmmakers in the early twentieth century; but while Richter and Ruttmann created visual music that moved through time, these early video artists employed space as an organisational principle. As the time-lapsed images in *Present Continuous Past* infinitely receded, for instance, the multiple moving versions of the visitor appeared to run in counterpoint to one another, creating a kind of spatial, visual fugue.

The Communal Consciousness

Nauman, Campus, and Graham, then, played with time and space to form metaphorical visual-music structures. Other early video environments included visitors not as solitary figures, but rather as communities, placing emphasis on the social and physical interactions of a viewing, and listening, audience. It is in such works that intermediality really comes into play. As we have seen in previous chapters, Paik was a key protagonist in the rise of video art-music. A composer first, his interest in sounding media informed his entire career and he incorporated many new forms of technology into his work in order to create new modes of audiovisual articulation. The Paik-Abe Video Synthesizer (1969–1970), for example, was a collaborative project between the artist-composer and Shuya Abe (a Japanese electronics engineer). Filmmaker Tom DeWitt saw the synthesizer signal as an opportunity to further remove video work from the representational:

> To free the video artist from the confines of the real camera-recorded world, it is necessary to develop instruments which generate a television compatible signal from raw electronics. A synthesizer is the paint and palette of the video artist, a device which lets the artist construct spaces from the dictates of imagination.[101]

The early Synthesizer operated as a colour organ by creating abstract coloured images when played like a keyboard. Using seven black-and-white surveillance cameras that each ran through a nonlinear processing amplifier and a colouriser, the instrument could alter images in order to "paint with time" (Walther Ruttmann).[102] "The video synthesizer has to be played in real time, like a piano" explained Paik: "From a purely artistic viewpoint that is highly interesting—a truly new thing that has no precedent. You simply play and then see the effect . . . it might end up producing a new fertile genre, called 'electronic opera'."[103] Paik's first "electronic opera" was *9/23/69 Experiment with David Atwood* (1969), a collage created from the manipulation of electronic abstractions, television footage, and prerecorded material through the video and audio synthesiser. Although this work was not transmitted as a whole, sections of it were included in *Video Commune: The Beatles from Beginning to End*, a piece that was broadcast live on Boston's public TV station (WGBH) on 1 August 1970. *Video Commune* was a four-hour visualisation of the Liverpudlian quartet's output, played in chronological order and interspersed with prerecorded footage and clips from Japanese television. During the broadcast, and true to his participatory spirit, Paik encouraged passersby to enter the studio and have a go on the Synthesizer. A year later, the instrument was placed in the Galeria Bonino, New York as an interactive audiovisual installation, an example, according to Paik, "not [of] cybernated art . . . but [of] art for cybernated life."[104]

While the Paik-Abe Video Synthesizer operated on a relatively small scale, *Wrap Around the World* (1988), a global event created to celebrate the forthcoming Seoul Olympic Games, was expansive: as we have seen, it employed satellite technology to create a piece that could be experienced by over 50 million people simultaneously. Live performances by artists and locals located all over the world were placed together, including a "transpacific duet" between Ryuichi Sakamoto in Tokyo and Merce Cunningham in New York City, a car race in Ireland, a Kung Fu demonstration in China, Salsa dancing in Brazil, and an explosion of noise by punk band Die Toten Hosen from outside Beethoven's house in Bonn.

Some of Paik's most intense audiovisual work was created in collaboration with avant-garde cellist Moorman. After attending the Juilliard School of Music for a year, Moorman played with the American Symphony Orchestra (from 1964–66). At the same time, she began devoting her energies to more experimental practices and performance art (she established the annual New York Avant-Garde Festival in 1963). Amongst her collaborators were Cage, Yoko Ono, Otto Piene, Jim McWilliams, and Joseph Beuys, who conceived of a felt-covered cello for her to play in his *Infiltration Homogen für Cello* (1966).

But it was with Paik, whom she met in 1964, that she achieved her notoriety as a performance artist. Describing their working relationship, Moorman explained that "Paik thinks of me as a work of his, he does not think of me as Charlotte Moorman. He can do with me what he pleases, and I'm very honoured about the whole thing."[105] Elsewhere, however, she placed herself in a more involved role: "All these pieces [we did together] are half mine. In performance, these are not Nam June Paik pieces, but Nam June Paik/Charlotte Moorman pieces. They are collaborations."[106] At first, Paik himself became Moorman's *Human Cello* during a 1965 performance (Philadelphia College of Art, 26 February) of Cage's indeterminate *26'1.1499" for a String Player* (1953). Moorman popped balloons, fired a gun, and rubbed the sole of her shoe (which had sandpaper stuck to it) in a pan of sand before putting down her cello to play Paik, who, stripped to his waist, knelt in front of her holding a single string stretched along his back. As we have seen, Paik and Moorman were later arrested for performing a striptease at the 1967 American premiere of *Opera Sextronique* at the Filmmakers' Cinematheque in New York City (although Paik was released without charge, Moorman was convicted for indecent exposure). Moorman again appeared topless for *TV Bra for Living Sculpture* (1969), which, outlined in the previous chapter, premiered at *TV as a Creative Medium* (Howard Wise Gallery, 1969). This time, however, the cellist wore an undergarment made from two small TVs.

On 23 November, 1971, the pair premiered *Concerto for TV Cello* at the Galeria Bonino, an audiovisual, interactive work that deconstructed performance practice, music and the concert space while at the same time remaining firmly linked to the audiovisual lineage outlined in chapter 2. Coming towards the end of video's integrating birth, this work demonstrates everything we have so far been discussing: it was a live performance piece that included the audience; it was both hypermedial and immersive; and, although not explicitly single-authored (in the way that Vasulka's *Violin Power* is), it was intermedial and transformational at the level of its articulation. Three television sets of diminishing size were encased in clear Perspex cases and mounted on top of each other to resemble the body of a cello, which was strung with a single string (the instrument continued to evolve for the next few years to acquire a bridge, tuning pegs,

Figure 5.6 Nam June Paik and Charlotte Moorman, video still from *Concerto for TV Cello* (1971). © Nam June Paik Estate.

and three more strings: fig. 5.6). When Moorman played the instrument, electronic pickups distorted the sounds in real time before feeding the resultant screeches and whines through speakers: "When I play," explained Moorman in a television interview, "I don't make conventional cello sounds, I make TV Cello sounds." The instrument was connected to several video cameras that transmitted a live, closed-circuit feed of the performance onto the cello's monitors. Moorman's actions were relayed immediately onto the screens, her video image appearing as though it were miming, a perfect lip-synch to the live events. Both performer and instrument, she was able simultaneously to play and be played, becoming inextricably linked to the cello and her own image. Occasionally, the video's gaze moved from Moorman to audience members as Paik moved around the space with the video camera, capturing them on the cello as they listened and watched. As their images were relayed onto the screens, they became active participants, with the ability to change the visual display and become an integral part of the performance. At such moments, the *TV Cello* destroyed the traditional gulf between performer and audience, activating the neutral concert space by making it primary material for the concert itself. Not only was the single work replaced with an object and a performer, it also included and mobilised the space in which both were presented (see video 5.4⊙). The installation, then, was not merely played or watched; spreading itself into its surroundings, it became both immersive *and* hypermedial environment.

But Paik's installation did not only use images taken from the performance space; nor did it avoid prerecorded material. Indeed, it remediated video footage of Moorman in previous performances, brief clips of Happenings in which

Paik was involved, snapshots of Janis Joplin, and images of important moments from the twentieth century, all interspersed with magnetically distorted broadcast transmission.[107] A simultaneity of eras, locations, and events, the footage extended the work's frame of reference beyond its immediate surroundings. And yet, the prerecorded images did not remain intact. As Moorman played, the pickups that created these "TV Cello sounds" also transmitted electronic signals (via the Paik-Abe Synthesizer) to the television screens, distorting the images as the installation was played to produce horizontal and vertical flashes of colour. In chapter 1, I suggested that video could act intermedially to enable the synthesis of traditionally separate media and here this is played out: the act of playing not only created sound, but caused a corresponding visual reaction as Moorman became both composer and artist in an immediate, *intermedial* way. Related directly to the ebb and flow of the music, the images were quite literally structured and controlled by sound: both the audio and the visual components of the *Concerto*, in other words, were born simultaneously.

This move into intermediality was the direct result of the work's expanded screen space: its cross-fertilisation of images between live events and the monitors. If we recall that, even in instances of "concrete" off-screen space in film, there is always a temporary frame, an implied nondiegesis that "lies outside the rectangular bounds of the image" (Gorbman) in order to provide both an extension to, and imaginary support for, the visual world, it is clear to see that the nature of video art-music as an intermedial, multidimensional form allows it to expand beyond these diegetic restrictions in ways similar to nondiegetic music. As the "offstage" of each monitor became visible either on another screen, or onstage, or in the audience, offscreen space was rendered impossible. But, in an inversion of film, screen space was expanded laterally not by sound but by image. As we have seen, sound and music in film are not confined to the screen, but are free to go "around corners, through walls, or [to] totally immerse, even penetrate the observer" (Viola): they are able to enlarge the diegetic world in both physical and emotional ways.[108] Able to embody a whole room and beyond within its instrument-shaped diegesis, the *TV Cello* became infinitely extendable, smashing the confines of Chion's "visual container" and destroying the boundaries between video and life, active and passive, body and environment, as reality and image became locked in a two- and three-dimensional interplay.

In bursting from its frame, image moved into the "imaginary" space previously occupied by sound alone: the realm of Flinn's subconscious listening and Wittgenstein's "inarticulate consciousness." Once in this musical space, the *TV Cello*'s images were fully at the mercy of sound, its representations of the world beyond the screens warped and distorted into abstract shapes by Moorman's playing. The spatialisation enabled by the *TV Cello* created the sensation of "wholeness" not unlike that encouraged by the soundtracks to mainstream cinema (as understood by Flinn). In this literal manifestation of Bazin's "continuum of the real," the visitor, unable to identify the boundaries between her body and the world beyond, is returned to a childlike state, but in a way fundamentally different from that created by Jonas: rather than remain a fractured *corps morcelé*, they are here reconfigured within the work's "fantasmic body."

In moving into the immersive, video work such as *Concerto for TV Cello* changed the relationship between work and viewer into one more akin to listening than watching as it expanded into, and interacted with, the space in which it is shown. It did so via processes of simultaneous immediacy and hypermediacy: the work was both highly material and thoroughly immersive. As a receptive, reactive, and intermedial system, video was able "to occupy the space and time, the here and now, the virtual present of a separate but ontologically real space" (Dyson).[109] *Concerto for TV Cello*, then, merged art and music spaces: but it did so by moving into a social space and immersing and activating its audience in a newly blended audiovisual environment. With this in mind, it is possible to return to the inversion of Christian Metz's reading of film space outlined in chapter 1: as a process-based facilitator, early video offered more than an illusory, extendable screen space; it could move both reality and the closed-feed image into a musical space.

Epilogue

Towards the Twenty-First Century

Acting as a facilitator, early video technology enabled performative, intermedial spaces: and by inviting everyone into the realm of the projected image and amplified sound, video art-music collapsed the physical and conceptual segregation between "performing" and "listening" spaces (Barry Blesser and Linda-Ruth Salter).[1] This spatial collapse lay at the heart of work set into motion by many video artist-composers throughout their lives. In Nam June Paik's first major retrospective (at the Whitney Museum of American Art, New York in 1982), for instance, the artist-composer included his earliest robot piece, *Robot K-456* (1964 in collaboration with Shuya Abe), a radio-controlled walking machine named after Mozart's Piano Concerto No.18 that intoned a recording of J. F. Kennedy's inaugural address. During the retrospective, however, the audiovisual robot enacted a rebellion against the commodification of art and its traditional viewing procedures by walking out of its own exhibition. Controlled by Paik, *Robot K-456* travelled towards the intersection of Madison Avenue and 75th Street before crossing the road: at this point a car, driven by artist William Anastasi, hurtled into the machine, knocking it over and destroying it forever. In a TV interview after the event, Paik explained that we must not be controlled by technology but must learn how to use (or control) it creatively. Yet the robot's death also illustrated Paik's belief that artwork should be impermanent; something to be experienced, like music, rather than collected and commodified like the paintings of many of his predecessors. Curator of the retrospective John Hanhardt read the event in a similar way, describing it as "a statement of liberation, demonstrating that the potential for innovation and new possibilities must not be lost, but must be continually reimagined and remade by the artist."[2] Not only did this gesture signal the end of the poor robot and his voice, then: the destruction of one of the exhibition's attractions also signalled the metaphorical end to the institutionalisation of art.

Or did it? The subsequent retrospectives of Paik suggest otherwise. Yvonne Spielmann reminds us that "for a new medium to assert itself implies institutionalization, economy, production, and aesthetics, which means that related and preceding media formats are subordinated and transformed."[3] As we have seen, the radical battle between artists and institutions throughout the twentieth century has had a clear impact on the diversity of exhibition sites available today. Kynaston McShine has pointed out that these days, "the relationship between museum and artist is far less adversarial than it was a few decades ago; occasional disruptions aside, the status quo prevails. Museums are allowed to maintain their lofty functions."[4] But there are still numerous examples of transgression. Chris Burden's *Samson* (1985) is one of the less subtle examples of a continuing adversarial relationship. The artist aimed a 100-ton jack at the walls of the Henry Art Gallery at the University of Washington: linked to a gearbox in a turnstile through which every visitor to the exhibition had to pass, the jack expanded marginally with every turn. This example aside, it appears that artists can now do as they please with the space provided. While the interior of the Pompidou is moveable to allow artists to shape their own space, other institutions built along more traditional lines have fared less well: in 1994, Richard Wilson, in a bid to place the top of a billiard table level with the ground, drilled through the floor of London's Matt's Gallery until he reached the water table; and, in 1999, Michael Elmgreen and Ingar Dragset dismantled sections of wall from the Portikus Gallery in Frankfurt. However, such gestures are now relatively commonplace and do not necessarily endanger the "lofty function of the Museum", as Graham Coulter-Smith explains: "Since the 1990s such radical interventions into the fabric of the art gallery are no longer shocking, or transgressive, they are *what is expected.*"[5]

Initially, video art-music operated in oppositional, antagonistic ways. But once it became a "genre," artist-composers began to receive more substantial financial support and found acceptance within the established art world. While it is true that the inclusion of recent video work into gallery spaces was made viable, in part, by the contemporary cinematic aesthetic and installational presentation (which is immersive but not interactive), older works have also entered into arena of the preserved, despite being created within the spirit of an anticommodity aesthetic. And yet, to place these works into a gallery space can result in an awkward disjunction of values, as such presentation ignores performative gesture and replaces communal modes of articulation—the interest in the connective, tranformational strands—with physical, sculptural objects. As a result, the discourse that thrives in the space between work and audience, author and performer, performer and physically-activated spectator, is often negated.

In 2000, Hanhardt curated *The Worlds of Nam June Paik* (Guggenheim Museum, 11 February to 26 April), explaining in the accompanying catalogue that the artist's early interactive video works, such as *Participation TV* (1963) and *Magnet TV* (1965), were here presented as a one-way flow of information: they were, however, "accompanied by videotape and photographic documentation of original installations" so that visitors could understand the synergistic way in which they originally operated. The exhibition also included "a tribute to Charlotte Moorman with her *TV Cello* (1971), as well as photographic and videotape documentation of her legendary performances."[6] Despite sharing a curator with the Whitney's 1982 Paik retrospective, the Guggenheim chose a style of exhibition that suggested that the ability to reimagine, or recreate Paik's live, performative works was somehow becoming more difficult.

The first major retrospective of Paik's work since his death in 2006, held at Tate Liverpool (cohosted by Museum Kunst Palast, Düsseldorf and Liverpool's FACT: 17 December 2010 to 13 March 2011), faced similar problems. In their introduction to the catalogue, the curators wrote that "we not only wanted to celebrate Paik as the inventor and 'hero' of media art, but also to show his artistic path to that goal and highlight the diverse talents ... of the multifaceted phenomenon 'Paik'."[7] During the opening night, Paik's *TV Robots*—ten-foot high creatures huddled together in family gatherings while their bellies flashed with prerecorded footage—drew the biggest crowd: elsewhere, the *TV Garden*—a room with thirty screens nestling amongst hundreds of plants—provided some respite from the chatting exhibits of the other rooms. But although the retrospective was entitled "Nam June Paik: Video Artist, Performance Artist, Composer and Visionary," the very notion of "exhibition" jostled uneasily with the artist-composer's original intentions. In fact, lurking beneath Tate Liverpool's elegant display was the niggling feeling that the radical gestures that these works once symbolised had here been pushed to one side. Displayed in one of the most famous galleries in the world, these pieces became artefacts of the kind that Paik rejected with the death of his Kennedy-intoning robot. In an accompanying symposium, curator Sook-Kyung Lee was questioned about Paik's original hope that his video pieces would enable unrepeatable events (either because the circumstances were unique, or the work—like *Robot K-456*—had been destroyed). Her reply was quite simple: the artist was no longer here "to make a different copy"; with Paik's death, in other words, his video structures had entered into the canon as unrepeatable, highly collectable historical artefacts.[8]

The silencing of aesthetic intent was most clear in Tate Liverpool's presentation of *TV Cello*. Situated on a plinth and separated from the viewer by a bold white line, the instrument was presented as object rather than process. Immobile and unplayed, the cello's only sign of life was the flickering prerecorded footage on its belly. But, as we have seen, early video acted as an intermedial adhesive that drew together music and art practices: at this stage, it was not a stand-alone genre. Furthermore, early practitioners were clear in their belief that art should function as an extension rather than a replication of everyday life, and should thus be receptive and malleable, existing only at the minute of its articulation. The manipulation of live broadcast TV and the actions of the visitors meant that life from both within the performance space and beyond were included and transformed during the event: as such, early video operated not only as a "chord, vibrating between media" (Daniel Albright), but also as a pulse between composer-artist and audience.[9] To present the *TV Cello* as an enduring object, then, transgressed its fundamental aesthetic existence as a living, immersive work. More importantly, it denied the significance of music in the development of video intermediality.

But what if the *TV Cello* had been performed at Tate Liverpool? If we return to Spielmann's understanding of intermediality as born from "the exchange and transformation of elements that come from different media" and Paik's hope that video would act like the nervous system of audiovisual and social discourse, then it is clear that a new performance of *Concerto for TV Cello*, with excerpts from *Family Guy* and live footage from the Iraq War morphed with the images of a contemporary audience, would form a fresh and energised intervention.[10] After all, at the heart of Paik's work was the question (and concern) of how television and broadcast media would effect private spaces, democratic decisions, and interpersonal connections in the future.

And yet, the material nature of the *Cello*'s radical voice was certainly of its moment: the newness of the video equipment, the closed-circuit feed, the performative gesture, and the intermedial utterance have today become commonplace and ubiquitous. Technology has caught up with the imaginings of the early video practitioners and audiovisual gestures have moved into other, more user friendly media formats. Early artists and composers who have enjoyed longevity continued to develop their ideas in light of newly emerging technologies: as we've seen, Paik's later work incorporated satellite technologies in order to reach as many people as possible, while Steina Vasulka used computer interfaces to move her *Violin Power* into more elegantly articulated realms of intermediality. Now, the current wave of video artist-composers use digital technologies to express their new "spatial dynamics" (Catherine Elwes), while continuing to probe the limits of the enduring white cube in myriad ways.[11]

Although video art-music was once located at the radical edges of audiovisual culture and shunned from the mainstream gallery space, it now occupies an important position within the contemporary art world. But despite this acceptance, some major works still lurk beyond traditional spaces: think of *Doug Aiken: Sleepwalkers* that enjoyed evening rambles across the outside walls of MoMA (16 January to 12 February 2007 [see video 6.1▶]), or Bill Viola's audiovisual triptych *Ocean Without a Shore* created for a sixteenth-century Venetian chapel (Venice Biennale, 2007).

Those multiscreen works that do reside within gallery walls not only demonstrate how commonplace sound has become within the traditional viewing space; they also indicate the longevity enjoyed by the immersive, mobile form of experiencing art envisaged by the earliest artist-composers. As we saw in chapter 5, contemporary multiscreen video art-music can create an environment that envelops visitors entirely while not requiring active participation in the unravelling audiovisual flow (although the flow can be randomly generated, as in Viola's *The Stopping Mind*, 1991). The result is a form of "mimetic engulfment" (Claire

Bishop) in which the materiality of the installation recedes into the background and the sounds and images appear to take on a palpable, living existence within the audience's space.[12] Yet although these works create immersive, communal areas in which visitors are free to view and listen from various angles and durations, their predetermined structures place less emphasis on the collective, process-driven, *creative* experience promoted by those artist-composers operating in the midst of Happenings and aleatoric performances of the 1960s. One implication of reduced communal creativity is the increased presence of the single authorial voice. Because video came to prominence as a gluelike medium able to draw together various disparate elements, it thrived as a tool for team creation in either small collaborative partnerships (Paik and Moorman and the Vasulkas), collectives (Ant Farm and the Videofreex), or multimedia teamwork (the Fluxus affiliation, Warhol's Exploding Plastic Inevitable, and so on). To return to Jud Yalkut's recollection of his time working with USCO, each contribution to a collective event was "anonymous": "You did not know who did any particular thing."[13] Although different forms of collaborative audiovisual work can still be found within collectives such as San Francisco's Artists' Television Access, which continues to promote the democratic potential of television, or the recently formed online video trio Unclassified Time, creative group efforts are no longer the norm. This is due in part to technological improvements that enable large-scale, high-definition displays more amenable to the current cinematic aesthetic; and in part to a shifting ideology in which the communal, participatory culture of the 1960s New York City art scene has fragmented into a more singular, individualist (and perhaps even financially driven) society.

Although the anonymity described by Yalkut has become rare, the rise of the single authorial voice hasn't hindered the evolution of reactive video environments. Several contemporary artists have continued to explore the possibilities for audiovisual interactivity in their gallery-based pieces. Camille Utterback's video work is characterised by visitor participation, for example, and many of her pieces only come to life in response to movement from the gallery floor: visitors to her reactive video sculpture, *Vicissitudes* (1998), are asked either to climb a ladder or to lie on the floor in order to determine the volume, and thus the narrative trajectory, of her soundtrack; *See/Saw* (2001, with Adam Chapman), on the other hand, gives control of an audio monologue to visitors physically participating in the eponymous children's game (see video 6.2⏵). Like Utterback, Christa Erickson asks visitors to perform a variety of activities from swinging (*Invertigo*, 1997), blowing (*Whirl*, 2007), to simply moving about (*Search*, 2005–2007 [see video 6.3⏵]) in order to set off motion-tracking devices, which either set an audiovisual video piece into motion, or changed the direction of already-flowing events. The type of interactivity encouraged by these works, however, belongs to an aesthetic very different from that of the 1960s intermedial revolution. In the spirit of the aleatoric, open-ended gesture, earlier works, such as Les Levine's *Iris* and Paik's *TV Cello* used the visitor as compositional material without asking them to perform in a certain way: in fact, audience members were given the freedom to contribute as much or as little as possible; and in whichever way they pleased. Thus dematerialised, the event was sure to progress differently in every performance. More recent interactive work, such as *See/Saw* and *Whirl* also require the visitor to participate in the course of the work; but they are asked to react according to predetermined, preprogrammed criteria that can limit their creative contribution. And yet, by handing over even small elements of the audiovisual flow to visitors, contemporary interactive video invites them into an intermedial space between artist, composer, and audience first realised by the earliest video artist-composers.

While the influence of the early video art-music aesthetic can be traced through various schools of more recent work, one of the most exciting spheres of influence can be found beyond the art world entirely. The early video aesthetic has spread beyond the circumstances in which it was first envisioned to form the creative and physical basis of numerous audiovisual genres. To break the barriers between art and life—to destroy the commodification and objectification of artworks, to attack the sanctified art space, to bring the audience and the popular media into the discussion—was a key objective of early video work, and the move into popular culture is therefore of key significance. The increasingly expansive musical gestures and nonlinear narratives of mainstream film can clearly be linked to the convergence of music and art histories, while the real-time visual processing by VJs can be read as a contemporary form of visual music. Music video, while always audiovisual, is also morphing into ever more interactive, participatory realms. Arcade Fire's video "The Wilderness Downtown" (2010) for their song "We Used to Wait" asks the viewer to submit her childhood address before launching into a blizzard of Google Chrome windows that show various images, including pictures of the user's early home from Google's Street View and Maps; at one stage the user is asked to communicate with her younger self. On a larger scale, the reconfiguration of our everyday environment by urban projection mapping artists and composers such those working under the banner Nuformer, or audiovisual firework displays (such as London New Year's Eve 2011, designed by Kimbolton Fireworks or the London Olympic opening ceremony show accompanied by Pink Floyd's "Eclipse") offer an expansive palette that video practitioners in the 1960s could only have dreamed of (see video 6.4▶).

To visualise music or sound images in real time has also become increasingly achievable. The immersive experiences of gaming are predicated on both interactivity and audiovisuality, with games such as *The Legend of Zelda: Ocarina of Time* (1998) allowing the player to progress at will according to various musical ditties. Interactive hypermediality is most clearly articulated via the Internet, a "global groove" that would seem to the early artist-composers like a mass-communication utopia. The interactive displays of computers, tablets, and mobile phones enable continual audiovisual engagement, while the increasing prevalence of live, interactive reality television and amateur digital film archives such as YouTube suggests that our current audiovisual topography is beginning to fulfill the desires of early video practitioners. Björk's recent *Biophilia* project takes us one step closer. While her live show featured audiovisual instruments created especially for the project that could be manipulated live, Björk's interactive app album invites listeners across the threshold and into her creative hub. Each track comes with an accompanying app that provides the user with musical analyses and information about the song. But there is also an interactive component: "each app isn't just a music video or even an instrument: it's something inbetween," explains interactive media artist and *Biophilia* designer Scott Snibbe.[14] Part of the app for "Crystalline," for instance, allows the user to make her "own song structure" (Björk) by tilting the iPad to direct moving crystals around a system of tunnels (fig. 6.1). The choice of tunnel leads the user into different musical passages, enabling a recombination of "the song into tens of thousands of different versions" (Snibbe), each determined by a different musico-visual transformation (see video 6.5(▶)).[15]

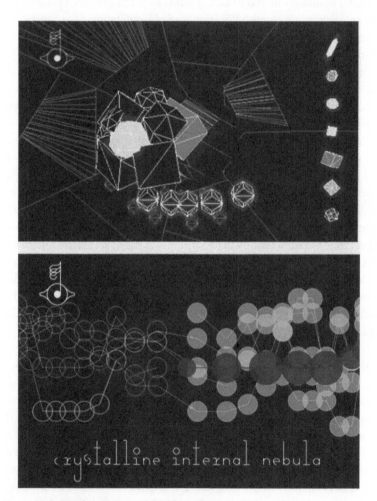

Figure 6.1 Björk and Scott Snibbe, stills from "Crystalline": *Biophilia* Project (2011).

To return to Paik's retrospective at Tate Liverpool, the exhibition was undoubt-edly a fabulous opportunity to experience the bones of the early video artist-composer's work: but at the same time, it was a rather forlorn recollection of a silenced radical voice. None of the *TV Robots* met the same sticky end as Paik's earlier creature and the *TV Cello* stood quietened and alone. And yet the gestures of Paik and his contemporaries have certainly not been forgotten. During the late 1960s, video artist-composers were coming to grips with a rapidly changing environment in which the rise of television, electronic music, a burgeoning film industry, and shifting social structures created a culture ripe for change. Video technology was considered a vehicle by which to understand and articulate these changes as it could fuse together, intermedially and spatially, two distinct creative disciplines. As the material remains of early video art-music become fascinating historical objects, the conversation is being carried forward in myriad ways by new and expanded participatory media: the gestures of early video art-music, in other words, can be found everywhere within our current audiovisual culture.

Notes

Introduction

1. Cage quoted in RoseLee Goldberg, *Performance Art,* 124.
2. See, for example, Nicholas De Oliveira, Nicola Oxley, and Michael Petry, *Installation Art,* 13.
3. Anna Bakalis, "It's Unreel: DVD Rentals Overtake Videocassettes."
4. See: http://sabrinapenayoung.blogspot.com/; and http://www.kathyhinde.co.uk/ (accessed 20 February 2012).
5. The Hugo Boss moving image artist winners were: 1996 (Matthew Barney), 1998 (Douglas Gordon), 2002 (Pierre Huyghe), 2004 (Rirkrit Tiravanija), and 2006 (Tacita Dean). Marjetica Potrč, an architect and artist, won in 2000.
6. The manifesto states further that it aims: "[t]o provide new spaces for art forms new to Tate—including photography, film, video and performance": http://www.tate.org.uk/about/projects/tate-modern-project (accessed 20 February 2012).
7. See http://www.eno.org/see-whats-on/productions/production-page.php?itemid=26; and http://www.roh.org.uk/whatson/production.aspx?pid=13699 (accessed 20 February 2012).
8. See Jess Hamlin, "Grand Opera Gets Grander with State-of-the-art-Screens," E-1. Of the Royal Opera House's purchase of Opus Arte, Marc A. Scorca, president of Opera America, said: "[i]t again demonstrates the close link between opera and today's multimedia world. Opera is the traditional art form that translates most effectively to multimedia representation"; quoted in Daniel J. Wakin, "Royal Opera Steps into New Act."
9. Charles Esche, for instance, explains that while the presence of Bill Viola's *Nantes Triptych* in London's Tate Gallery underlines both the achievement of video in being accepted into the art world, it also signals the loss of its early extremist sensibilities; "Video Installation," 196.
10. Oliveira, Oxley, and Petry define video installation art in this way, continuing that "it is a multi-media, multi-dimensional art form that exists only as long as it is installed"; *Installation Art,* 1–2.
11. Giedion, *Space, Time and Architecture.*
12. Bolter and Grusin, *Remediation,* 15.
13. Spielmann, *Video,* 14.
14. Statement from Hall to Spielmann, quoted in Ibid., 76–77.
15. Vasulka, "Sony CV Portapak," 150.
16. Jonas, "Transmission," 126.
17. Paik quoted in Dieter Daniels, "John Cage and Nam June Paik," 118. See also Susan Rennert, "'We Have Time'," 55–68.

Chapter One

1. Vasulka speaking of her work in the late 1960s, quoted in Judy Malloy, *Woman, Art and Technology,* xxiv.

2. This exhibition, which ran from 20 September to 10 December 2006, was intended to recount "the history of this very contemporary field, punctuating the main phases of contemporary art from 1965 to 2005": the exhibition notes can be found at http://www.miamiartcentral. org (accessed 20 February 2012).

3. Paik's journey is charted in Douglas Davis, *Art and the Future,* 149. Spielmann points out that Warhol used the Norelco video system and that, as a result, the "hour of video's birth as a medium . . . does not arrive with the introduction of the Sony Portapak camera and not with Paik"; *Video,* 78.

4. Ross quoted in Marita Sturken, "Paradox in the Evolution of an Art Form," 107.

5. Paik, "Versatile Color TV Synthesizer," 55.

6. Paik quoted in Davis, *Art and the Future,* 148.

7. Marinetti, *"The Variety Theatre"* (1913); quoted in Goldberg, *Performance Art,* 17.

8. Youngblood, *Expanded Cinema,* 134.

9. Lovejoy, *Postmodern Currents,* 195.

10. Sturken, for instance, claims that it is "no surprise to discover [video] as the medium of many feminist-minded artists"; "Review: *Revising Romance*", 273.

11. For a more in-depth discussion of feminism and the art world, see Rizsika Parker and Griselda Pollock, eds., *Framing Feminism*; Norma Broude and Mary D. Garrard, eds., *Feminism and Art History*; Broude and Garrard, eds., *The Expanding Discourse*; and Lucy Lippard, *The Pink Glass Swan.*

12. Sturken, "Feminist Video: Reiterating the Difference," 9.

13. Liner notes cited in Maria Troy, "I Say I Am: Women's Performance Video from the 1970s."

14. *Revising Romance: New Feminist Video* was curated by Linda Podheiser and Bob Riley.

15. William Furlong discusses this free space in *Audio Arts,* 128.

16. Bartlett quoted in Youngblood, *Expanded Cinema,* 264.

17. Belton, "Looking Through Video," 65. This is no new idea, however: as early as 1975, Raymond Williams pointed out that, "[u]nlike all previous communications technologies, radio and television were systems primarily devised for transmission and reception as abstract processes, with little or no definition of preceding content"; *Television: Technology and Cultural Form,* 25.

18. "Television can't be used as an art medium," claims Levine, "because it already *is* art. CBS, NBC, and ABC are among the greatest art producers in the world." Levine quoted in Youngblood, *Expanded Cinema,* 366.

19. McLuhan, "The Medium Is the Message," 23–35.

20. Daniels, "Television—Art or Anti-Art? Conflict and Cooperation Between the Avant-Garde and the Mass Media in the 1960s and 1970s."

21. This information comes from a behind-the-scenes documentary called *A Passage to Middle-Earth: Making of Lord of the Rings (The Sci-Fi Channel,* USA: 9 December 2001).

22. Michael O'Pray discusses Warhol's methods of filming in *Andy Warhol: Film Factory.*

23. For more information, see Fred Camper, "Brakhage Wants to Make you See," 16.

24. The passage continues: "An art for the eye that distinguishes itself from painting in that it takes paces temporally (like music) and the artistic emphasis does not (as in the image) consist in the reduction of a (real or formal) process to a single moment, but precisely in the temporal development of formal aspects. That this art develops temporally is one of its most important elements of the temporal rhythm of optic events. It will therefore produce an entirely new type of artist, up until now only latently present, positioed somewhere half-way between painting and music"; Ruttmann, "Malerei mit Zeit" (1919), quoted in Heike Helfert, "Technological Constructions of Space-Time."

25. Belton has pointed out that "[n]o technology develops autonomously. It is always a direct or indirect product (or by-product) of other technologies, which leave their imprint upon it. Video is no exception"; "Looking Through Video," 61.

26. Viola quoted in Viola and Robert Violette, eds., *Reasons for Knocking at an Empty House,* 159.

27. Belton, "Looking Through Video," 63.

28. Ibid.

29. Sherman argues that: "the myth of Paik's first work of video art appears to pre-date its own possibility"; "The Premature Birth of Video Art."

30. Spielmann, *Video*, 77.

31. Viola, *Reasons for Knocking at an Empty House*, 63.

32. Viola explains, "The divisions into lines and frames are solely divisions in time, the opening and closing of temporal windows that demarcate periods of activity within the flowing stream of electrons. Thus, the video image is a living dynamic energy field, a vibration appearing solid only because it exceeds our ability to discern such fine slices of time"; Ibid., 158.

33. Schneider, *Jump-Cut*, 52.

34. Arns quoted in Viola and Violette, *Reasons for Knocking at an Empty House*, 63. This notion was already prevalent in 1916: Hugo Münsterberg, for instance, explained that in cinema, "apparent movement is in no way the mere result of an afterimage...but is superadded, by the action of the mind, to motionless pictures"; *The Film: A Psychological Study*, 29.

35. Belton, "Looking Through Video," 67.

36. Godard quoted in Youngblood, *Expanded Cinema*, 264.

37. Barthes, "Rhetoric of the Image," 44.

38. Metz, *Film Language*, 11.

39. Altman, "Inventing the Cinema Soundtrack," 341. Elsewhere, Altman stresses that every sound event includes multiple sounds, "each with its particular fundamental array of partials, each with its characteristic sound envelope, each possessing its own rhythm within the sound event's overall temporal range"; "The Material Heterogeneity of Recorded Sound," 19.

40. Vasulka, "Sony CV Portapak: Industrial, 1969," 150.

41. Paik uses these terms when he explains that: "[v]ideo art imitates nature, not in its appearance or mass, but in its intimate 'time-structure'...which is the process of AGING (a certain kind of *irreversibility*)" (italics his); Paik, "Input-Time and Output Time," 98.

42. Stravinsky, "The Phenomenon of Music," 30.

43. Donnelly, "*Performance* and the Composite Film Score," 152–66.

44. Although the soundtrack includes pre-existent work by Nina Simone and Penderecki, amongst others, Lynch wrote and performed the tracks *Walkin on the Sky* and *Ghost of Love*, and cowrote *Polish Night Music No.1* with Merek Zebrowski and *Polish Poem* with Chrysta Bell.

45. Ruttman quoted in Daniels, "Sound & Vision in Avantgarde & Mainstream [1]."

46. Ruttmann quoted in Standish D. Lawder, "Der Abstrakte Film: Richter und Eggeling", 30.

47. Several scholars, including Jean Paul Goergen, have suggested that Richter back-dated his films. There is evidence to suggest, for instance, that *Rhythmus 21* was not finished or shown in 1921, but possibly only in 1925 or later (although this is uncertain): see Ulrich Gregor, Goergen, and Angelika Hoch, eds, *Hans Richter. Film ist Rhythmus*.

48. Fischinger, "Sounding Ornaments"; quoted in William Moritz, *Optical Poetry*, 179.

49. Nesthus, "The Influence of Olivier Messiaen on the Visual Art of Stan Brakhage," 234.

50. Brakhage's films offer as direct as possible experience of what vision is, what the act of seeing actually consists of; see Robert A. Haller, ed., *Brakhage Scrapbook*.

51. Brakhage quoted in Inez Hedges, "Stan Brakhage's Film Testamount: The Four Faust Films," 179.

52. Hanhardt, *The Worlds of Nam June Paik*, 20.

53. *Hommage à John Cage* was recently included on the soundtrack to Martin Scorsese's *Shutter Island* (2008).

54. Koenig quoted in Hanhardt, "Foreword," 9.

55. This performance formed part of a series of events called *12 Evenings of Manipulations: Deconstructionist Art Happenings* (Judson Gallery, Oct. 5–22, 1967). However, as Yalkut's interview with Sabrina Gschwandtner continues, the artist points out that he may have misremembered events and that "There are a lot of different accounts of that": Gschwandtner, "Between Film and Video—The Intermedia Art of Jud Yalkut."

56. Hanhardt speaks about this incident in *The Worlds of Nam June Paik*, 30.

57. Ibid., 24.

58. Vasulka, "Orka."

59. 59. Spielmann describes the instrument in *Video*, 113; quote, 202.

60. Vasulka discussing *"Violin Power*: The Performance."

61. Vasulka, "Description and Technical Specifications of the Performance of *Violin Power*" (1992), quoted in Spielmann, *Video*, 334 (footnote 110).

62. The artist discusses his work in "Robert Cahen: *Passage* at Preston Harris Museum & Art Gallery."

63. Cahen quoted in Chris Meigh-Andrews, "Robert Cahen: Passage," 39.

64. Lischi, *The Sight of Time: Films and Videos by Robert Cahen,* 8.

65. Conrad, "LYssophobia: On Four Violins," 316.

66. Conrad later wrote several essays on musical topics, including an exploration of non-Western scales and Schenker. See "Preparing for the Propaganda War in the Time of Global Culture: Trance, Form, and Persuasion in the Renovation of Western Music."

67. Conrad continues: "The experience of 'flicker'—its peculiar entrapment of the central nervous system, by ocular driving—occurs over a frequency range of about 4 to 40 flashes per second (fps). I used film (at 24 fps) as a sort of 'tonic,' and devised patterns of frames which would represent combinations of frequencies—heterodyned, or rather multiplexed together. I was interested to see whether there might be combination-frequency effects that would occur with flicker, analogous to the combination-tone effects that are responsible for consonance in musical sound." Brian Duguid, "Tony Conrad Interview."

68. Viola, *Reasons for Knocking at an Empty House,* 151–52.

69. Vasulka speaking in *Six Programs for Television,"Matrix"*; quoted in Spielmann, *Video,* 99.

70. Spielmann, *Video,* 198.

71. Nauman quoted in *Please Pay Attention Please,* 147.

72. Spielmann, *Video,* 8.

73. Ibid., 60–61.

74. Attali, *Noise,* 4.

75. Hegarty, *Noise/Music,* 3.

76. Unnamed critic (1826) quoted in Margaret Notley, "'With A Beethoven-Like Sublimity'," 325; Stravinsky, quoted in Lucy Miller, *Adams to Zemlinsky,* 44.

77. Perloff, *The Futurist Moment.*

78. Russolo, "The Art of Noises," 208.

79. Varèse quoted in *Perspectives on American Composers,* 36.

80. Kerse, *The Law Relating to Noise,* 8.

81. Schaeffer, *À la recherche d'une musique concréte,* 22; quoted and translated by Hegarty, *Noise/Music,* 32.

82. Cage, "The Future of Music Credo," 55.

83. Ibid., 54.

84. Hegarty, *Noise/Music,* 4.

85. Fontana, "Sound as Virtual Image."

86. Licht, *Sound Art,* 13.

87. Ibid, 14. Interestingly, the term "Sound/Art" was first documented in America by The Sculpture Center in New York City in 1983. The exhibition, curated by William Hellerman, included the work of Acconci, Levine, and Carolee Schneemann, artists also involved in video work. Such inclusion highlights the multidisciplinarity of many of those working with video.

88. One recent exception is the winning piece for the 2010 Turner Prize: for her sound installation *Lowlands Away,* Susan Philipsz sang a sixteenth-century Scottish song; in its original setting, recorded versions of the song could be heard from speakers situated underneath three bridges over the river Clyde in Glasgow; http://www.tate.org.uk/britain/turnerprize/ (accessed 20 February 2012).

89. Licht, *Sound Art,* 35.

90. Ibid., 13.

91. Gaudreault and Marion, "The Cinema as a Model for the Genealogy of Media," 12.

92. Ibid.

93. Ibid., 14.

94. Spielmann, *Video*, 87, 117.

95. Kaprow, "Video Art: Old Wine, New Bottle," 148.

96. Baudrillard, "In the Shadow of the Millennium" (1998), quoted in Zeitlin, *Bill Viola*, 57.

97. Cubitt, *Timeshift*, 1.

98. Higgins, *Horizons*, 9, 27–28.

99. Spielmann, "Intermedia in Electronic Images," 60.

100. Ibid., 59.

101. Spielmann, *Video*, 9.

102. Vasulka, "Sony CV Portapak: Industrial, 1969," 150.

103. Meigh-Andrews continues: "[t]echnological developments in the related fields of broadcast television, consumer electronics, computer hardware and software, video surveillance and emerging imaging technologies such as thermal imaging, magnetic resonance imaging (MRI), and so forth, have all had an influence on the developing aesthetics of video art. Changes in technology, reliability, miniaturization and advances in electronic imaging systems, synchronization and computer control devices have also influenced the potential for video installation and image display"; *A History of Video Art*, 5–6.

104. Hall, "Video Art," 47.

105. Paik quoted in Youngblood, *Expanded Cinema*, 302.

106. Wittgenstein, *Philosophical Investigations*.

107. Wyver, "The Necessity of Doing Away with 'Video Art'" (1991), 318.

108. Daniels, "Television—Art or Anti-Art?"

109. Sontag concluded that the two positions are essentially "irreconcilable" except that "both are invoked to support a perennial modern quest—the quest for the definitive art form": "Film and Theatre," 35.

110. Davis, "Art and Technology," 29.

111. For example, two that are relevant to this chapter: Hanhardt, *The Worlds of Nam June Paik*; and David A. Ross, *Bill Viola*.

112. Reiss, *From Margin to Center*, xv.

113. Hanhardt, *The Worlds of Nam June Paik*, 31.

114. Paik quoted in Davis, "Nam June Paik," 148.

Chapter Two

1. Severini, "The Plastic Analogies of Dynamism—Futurist Manifesto," 110.

2. Gaudreault and Marion, "The Cinema as a Model for the Genealogy of Media," 14; Spielmann, *Video*, 87, 117.

3. Randall Packer and Ken Jordan, "Overture," xviii.

4. Wagner, "Outlines of the Artwork of the Future," 5.

5. Heilig quoted in Packer and Jordan, "Overture," xxii.

6. "Installation (Environment)," in *Grove Art Encyclopaedia*.

7. Albright refers to this as the "Laocoön problem"; *Untwisting the Serpent*, 7.

8. Virgil, *The Aeneid*, Lines 220–240.

9. Lessing is just one example used by Albright.

10. Lessing quoted in Albright, *Untwisting the Serpent*, 9.

11. Lessing quoted in Albright, *Beckett and Aesthetics*, 6–7.

12. The quote continues: "But if painting, by virtue of its signs or its means of imitation, which it can combine in space alone, must completely renounce time, then progressive acts, because progressive, do not belong among its subjects—painting must content itself with acts next to one another, or with mere bodies": Lessing quoted in Albright, *Untwisting the Serpent*, 9.

13. Babbitt calls Wagner an "eleutheromaniac" (freedom-crazed); *The New Laokoon*, 199.

14. Greenberg quoted in Albright, *Untwisting the Serpent*, 11.

15. Ibid., 12.

16. Apollinaire, *Oeuvres en prose complètes*, 864–65.

17. Spielmann, "Intermedia in Electronic Images," 60.
18. Leppert, *The Sight of Sound*, xxi.
19. Lachenmann quoted in David Ryan and Lachenmann, *Composer in Interview*, 21.
20. *Unsung Voices* is the title of Carolyn Abbate's book.
21. Stockhausen quoted in Richard Toop, "Stockhausen and the Sine-Wave, 375.
22. Kyle Gann, *The Music of Conlon Nancarrow*, 2.
23. Kramer quoted in Ibid., 9: Nancarrow quoted on page 10.
24. Abbate, "Drastic or Gnostic," 506 ("domesticating"); 508 ("wild").
25. You can listen to these works here: http://www.auralaura.com/contents.html (accessed 20 February 2012).
26. Harold Rosenberg, *The Tradition of the New*, 25.
27. Cretien van Campen, "Artistic and Psychological Experiments with Synaesthetisia," 10.
28. Leppert, *The Sight of Sound*, xxi.
29. Ibid., xxii.
30. Ibid.
31. Albright, *Untwisting the Serpent*, 6 (italics his).
32. Gauguin (1895), quoted in Pierre Schneider, *Matisse*, 308 (footnote 73).
33. Examples include Jean Theodore Fantin-Latour, *Rhinegold—First Scene* (*L'Or du Rhin—Première Scène*) (1888), Max Klinger's etching sequence, *Brahms Fantasies* (1894), Marsden Hartley's *Musical Theme No.2—Bach Préludes et fugues* (1912), or, more recently, Robert Strübin's *Music Picture—Stravinsky, A Few Bars from the "Firebird Suite"* (*Musikbild—Strawinsky, Einige Takte aus "Feurvogel"*), ca. 1960.
34. Klimt quoted in Jean-Paul Bouillon, *Klimt—Beethoven*, 24–25.
35. Lessing cited in Albright, *Untwisting the Serpent*, 17.
36. Adorno quoted in Ibid.
37. Kandinsky quoted in Jelena Hahl-Koch, *Arnold Schönberg / Wassily Kandinsky*, 21.
38. Kandinsky quoted in Karin V. Maur, *The Sound of Painting*, 35.
39. Pound quoted in Albright, *Untwisting the Serpent*, 69.
40. Albright, *Untwisting the Serpent*, 69 (Italics his).
41. Ibid., 33.
42. Runge quoted in Jörg Träger, *Philipp Otto Runge und seine Werke*, 82.
43. Kupka quoted in Maur, *The Sound of Painting*, 46.
44. Futurists cited in Ibid., 69.
45. Klee quoted in Hajo Düchting, *Paul Klee*, 65, 28.
46. See Amy Ione and Christopher Tyler, "Neuroscience, History and the Arts," 58–65.
47. Messiaen quoted in Paul Griffiths, "Catalogue de Couleurs," 1035.
48. *Quatuor pour la fin du temps* reference comes from John Harrison and Simon Baron-Cohen, "Synaesthesia," 343; Messiaen quoted in Robert Sherlaw-Johnson, *Messiaen*, 119.
49. Jonathan Bernard, "Messiaen's Synaesthesia," 41–42.
50. Messiaen quoted and translated by Johnson, *Messiaen*," 166–67.
51. Cook, *Analysing Musical Multimedia*, 30.
52. Ibid., 32.
53. Ibid.
54. Ibid., 35.
55. Sabaneev also notes that Scriabin doesn't associate colour with minor keys; Sabaneev and S.W. Pring, "Relation Between Sound and Colour," 273.
56. Scriabin quoted in Golo Föllmer and Julia Gerlach, "Audiovisions: Music as an Intermedia Art Form."
57. See for example Bulat Makhmudovich Galeyev and Irena Leonidovna Vanechkina, "Was Skryabin a Synesthete?," 357–61.
58. Clarence Lucas writing in the *Musical Courier*, quoted in Hugh MacDonald, "Lighting the Fire: Skryabin and Colour," 600.
59. Reviewer quoted in Campen, "Artistic and Psychological Experiments with Synaesthetisia," 10.
60. Cook, *Analysing Musical Multimedia*, 37.
61. Ibid., 38.

62. See, for instance, Jörg Jewanski and Natalia Sidler, eds., *Farbe-Licht–Musik*; and Kevin Dann, *Bright Colors Falsely Seen*.
63. Kandinsky discussed in Campen, "Artistic and Psychological Experiments with Synaesthetisia," 10.
64. Kandinsky, *Rückblicke*, 14.
65. Kandinsky quoted in Maur, *The Sound of Painting*, 30–31.
66. Kandinsky quoted in Christopher Butler, *Early Modernism*, 37.
67. Kandinsky, *Concerning the Spiritual in Art*, 25.
68. Albright, *Untwisting the Serpent*, 6.
69. Cook, *Analysing Musical Multimedia*, 73.
70. Ibid., 23.
71. Huxley, *Brave New World* and *Brave New World Revisited*, 78.
72. Castel quoted in Thomas L. Hankins, "The Ocular Harpsichord of Louis-Bertrand Castel," 143.
73. Quotes from Maur, *The Sound of Painting*, 86.
74. Rimington quoted in Michael Betancourt, A. Wallace Rimington's *Colour-Music*, 64–65.
75. Peacock, "Instruments to Perform Color-Music," 402.
76. *Prometheus* qroup quoted in Galeyev, "Music-Kinetic Art Medium," 177.
77. Blanc-Gatti quoted in *Retrospective*, 23 (footnote 54). See also MacDonald-Wright's 1960 *Synchromous Kineidoscope*, which enabled the translation of "the forms and colours of any modern painting into a formal arrangement of movements and pure, saturated colours of the light spectrum"; Maur, *The Sound of Painting*, 88–89.
78. Moritz, "Non-Objective Film," 59.
79. Critics cited in Moritz, *Optical Poetry*, 12.
80. Marinetti, Bruno Corra, Emilio Settimelli, Arnaldo Ginna, Giacomo Balla, and Remo Chiti, "The Futurist Cinema," 12.
81. Richter quoted in Barbara John, "The Sounding Image: About the Relationship Between Art and Music—An Art-Historical Retrospective View."
82. As mentioned in chapter 1, Jean Paul Goergen is among those who believe that Richter back-dated his films: he even speculates that the Rhythm Films may not have been fully edited and released until 1951. See Ulrich Gregor, Goergen, and Angelika Hoch, eds., *Hans Richter*; and "Research: Errata: Common Errors, and Errata in Recent Publications and Websites Regarding Visual Music."
83. Richter quoted in Jennifer Valcke, *Static Films and Moving Pictures*, 170.
84. MacDonald, "Introduction to 'Avant-Garde Film'," 3.
85. Moritz, *Optical Poetry*, 4.
86. Ibid.
87. Ibid., 4–5.
88. Not all of his adverts were charcoal drawings.
89. See Moritz, "Fischinger at Disney, or Oskar in the Mousetrap,"
90. Fischinger quote taken from Fischinger's writings, found on eight narrow strips of paper.
91. Fischinger, "Excerpts from Unpublished Typescript."
92. Moritz points out that "Fischinger never intended to illustrate music, but rather hoped that the viewer, reminded that music is really abstract 'noise' with a 1000-year artistic tradition behind it, would more easily be able to relate to his graphics. Unfortunately the plan back-fired, and his films became widely misinterpreted as illustrations of music"; "Non-Objective Film: The Second Generation."
93. Moritz, *Optical Poetry*, 12.
94. See Keefer, "Raumlichtmusik: Early Twentieth Century Abstract Cinema Immersive Environments."
95. Fischinger speaking to Hilla Rebay, 28 June, 1942: quoted in Keefer, "Raumlichtmusik".
96. Fischinger quoted in Keefer, "'Space Light Art'."
97. Fischinger cited in Moritz, *Optical Poetry*, 12.
98. Magazine quoted in Keefer, "'Space Light Art'," 25. Despite his devotion to the film format, Fischinger later returned to the idea of audiovisual synchronicity and, some twenty-five

years later, developed the Lumigraph (1950), a type of silent colour organ that he used to respond to various pieces of art music.

99. Fischinger, "Ornaments are Music."
100. Ibid.
101. Ibid.
102. This information was provided by an email correspondence with Dr. Dobson. For more information on the collaboration between McLaren and Lambart, see Dobson, *The Film Work of Norman McLaren*, 201–03.
103. McLaren quoted in William E. Jordan, "McLaren: His Career and Techniques," 5.
104. Ibid., 6.
105. Dobson, *The Film Work of Norman McLaren*, 208.
106. Moritz, "Jordan Belson: Last of the Great Masters," 1.
107. Belson quoted in Youngblood, *Expanded Cinema*, 160, 162.
108. Moritz, "Musique de la Couleur," 9.
109. Moritz, "Non-Objective Film," 59–71.
110. Whitney, "To Paint on Water," 46.
111. Whitney, *Digital Harmony*, 41.
112. Ibid., 14.
113. Ibid., 38.
114. Youngblood, *Expanded Cinema*, 69.
115. Ross quoted in Sturken, "Paradox in the Evolution of an Art Form," 107.
116. Viola quoted in Jörg Zutter, "Interview with Bill Viola," 101.
117. Oliveira, Oxley, and Petry define *détournement* as "the appropriation of previously existing aesthetic artefacts in order to divert their meaning or intent"; *Installation Art*, 27.
118. Bolter and Grusin, *Remediation*.
119. Turim, "The Image of Art in Video," 29–30.
120. Ibid., 35, 48.
121. Stravinsky quoted in Craig Ayrey, "Stravinsky in Analysis," 208.
122. "Each figure from the original canvas is removed, one by one" she writes: and "each evacuation is punctuated by a single tone of music"; Turim, "The Image of Art in Video," 34.
123. One of Paik's most famous video-wall works is *Family of Robots* (1986): the seven members of his family were made from old television monitors and radio parts.
124. Kaprow, "Video Art," 148.

Chapter Three

1. Lissitzky (1967); quoted in Salter, *Entangled*, 83.
2. McLaren quoted in Jordan, "McLaren," 5; Whitney, *Digital Harmony*.
3. Gaudreault and Marion, "The Cinema as a Model for the Genealogy of Media," 14.
4. Maciunas, "240.XXII George Maciunas," 166.
5. Iles, "Video and Film Space," 252.
6. Spielmann, *Video*, 117.
7. Viola quoted in Zutter, "Interview with Bill Viola," 100.
8. Viola, *Reasons for Knocking at an Empty House*, 151–52.
9. Oliveira, Oxley, and Petry, *Installation Art*, 8.
10. Princenthal, "Rooms With a View," 26–31.
11. Lefèbvre, *The Production of Space*, 1.
12. Giedion, *Space, Time and Architecture*, 496–97.
13. Moholy-Nagy, *The New Vision*, 62.
14. Ibid., 61.
15. Giedion, *Space, Time and Architecture*, 356.
16. Moholy-Nagy, "Theatre, Circus, Variety," 116–17.
17. Albers, "The Origin of Art" (1952), quoted in Goldberg, *Performance Art*, 121. The early theoretical and practical relocations from objects to the spaces in which they collide continue to inform architectural practice: according to architect Branko Kolarevic performative

architecture can "respond to changing social, cultural, and technological conditions": "culture, technology, and space form a complex active web of connections, a network of interrelated constructs that affect each other simultaneously and continually"; Kolarevic and Malkawi, *Performative Architecture*, 205.

18. Fenlon, "Venice: Theatre of the World", 114.
19. Howard and Moretti, *Sound and Space in Renaissance Venice*.
20. Stage direction quoted in Adlington, *The Music of Harrison Birtwistle*, 48.
21. Ibid.
22. The move towards the "Teatricalization of the concert hall" (Salzman), for instance, can be seen in Kagel's *Sur Scène* (1960) and *Antithèse* (1962), a "play for one actor with electronic and public sounds"; operating in a different way, Maxwell Davis transformed musicians into actors or props and integrated slides, film, and projected images into the musical score: Salzman quoted in Salter, *Entangled*, 199.
23. Ibid., 198.
24. Blesser and Salter, *Spaces Speak, Are you Listening?*, 130.
25. Schechner, "6 Axioms for Environmental Theatre," 44.
26. Schafer, "Music, Non-Music and the Soundscape," 35.
27. Kevorkian, "The Reception of the Cantata During Leipzig Church Services, 1700–1750," 34.
28. Kevorkian continues: "Seating was mapped socially among these burghers, with status hierarchies reflected in the type of pew held and the location of that pew": ibid., 27, 28.
29. Small, *Musicking*, 29
30. Johnson, *Listening in Paris*, 53.
31. Ibid., 1.
32. Ibid., 9–10.
33. Architect quoted in ibid., 13.
34. Ibid., 59.
35. Ibid., 54.
36. Ibid., 55.
37. Barron, *Auditorium Acoustics and Architectural Design*, 314.
38. Wagner cited in Paul Kuritz, *The Making of Theatre History*, 263.
39. Barron, *Auditorium Acoustics and Architectural Design*, 314.
40. Small, *Musicking*, 23.
41. Small attempts to show that the traditional symphony concert "partakes of the nature of a ritual, a celebration, undertaken not fully aware, of the shared mythology and values of a certain group within our deeply fragmented society"; "Performance as Ritual," 11.
42. Small, *Musicking*, 27, 26.
43. Schechner, "6 Axioms for Environmental Theatre," 42.
44. Chion, *Audiovision*, 68.
45. Schechner, "6 Axioms for Environmental Theatre," 45.
46. Kantor, "Lesson 3," quoted in Wiles, *A Short History of Western Performance Space*, 13.
47. Blesser and Salter, *Spaces Speak, Are you Listening?*, 128.
48. Xenakis, *Formalized Music*, 237.
49. Ibid., 148.
50. While Xenakis, Kurtag, Ligeti, and others attempted to satirise and even sabotage the sacred conventions and traditions of the concert, Small suggests that their attempts did not "rise above the level of undergraduate pranks"; "Performance as Ritual," 28.
51. Peter Bürger distinguished this school conceptually from modernism through its rejection of the "institution of art" (which led him to conclude the movement was "the true avant-garde"); Bürger and Christa Bürger, *The Institutions of Art*.
52. Motto quoted in Wim Mertens, *American Minimal Music*, 21.
53. Feldman's *Intersections* pieces, written between 1950 and 1953, are a series of "graph" compositions in which time is represented by space, while the spaced boxes specify only instrument, register, number of simultaneous sounds, mode of production, and duration: the composer states that "the player is free to choose any dynamic at any entrance but must maintain sameness of volume"; quoted in *The Boulez-Cage Correspondence*, 104. Riley's *In C* is written in "open

score": it can be played by any combination of instruments. Several other members of the Fluxus group, including Takehisa Kosugi, George Brecht, and Yoko Ono, experimented with different notations: Dick Higgins, for instance, used graphic notation in works both for solo instruments (*Piano Album*, 1980) and in larger works (*Variations on a Natural Theme for Orchestra*, 1982).

54. The performer's role, according to Cage, was to animate the process he had set forth, producing results that, while having certain similarities, would differ in detail during each realisation; see Michael Nyman, *Experimental Music*.

55. Mertens, *American Minimal Music*, 22.

56. Critic cited in Goldberg, *Performance Art*, 138.

57. Nyman speaks about this in "Cage and Satie," 70.

58. Ross, "Stockhausen's *Gruppen* in Berlin: 'Supersonic'."

59. Stockhausen later mixed the work to just four.

60. LaBelle, *Background Noise*, ix.

61. Stockhausen, "Music and Space" (1958); quoted in Simon Emmerson, *Living Electronic Music*, 158.

62. Le Corbusier quoted in Giedion, *The Eternal Present*, 526.

63. Kalff quoted in Karin Schlte, *Temporary Buildings*, 37.

64. Le Corbusier quoted in ibid.

65. Schechner, "6 Axioms for Environmental Theatre," 165–66.

66. Xenakis, *Formalized Music*, 10.

67. For more information, see Karl H. Wörner, *Stockhausen*, 256.

68. Schechner, "6 Axioms for Environmental Theatre," 58.

69. Searing, *New American Art Museums*, 11.

70. Carrier, *Museum Skepticism*, 16.

71. Searing, *New American Art Museums*, 13.

72. Maroević, *Introduction to Museology*, 53.

73. Searing, *New American Art Museums*, 18.

74. Maroević, *Introduction to Museology*, 53.

75. Searing, *New American Art Museums*, 36.

76. O'Doherty, *Inside the White Cube*, 9, 15.

77. Ibid., 14.

78. McEvilley, "Introduction," 8.

79. Ibid.

80. Kwon, "One Place After Another," 40.

81. Crary, *Techniques of the Observer*, 4, 5.

82. Ibid., 5.

83. Whitehead, *The Public Art Museum in Nineteenth Century Britain*, xvi.

84. Ibid., 38.

85. Staff opinion recorded in Colin Emery, *A Celebration of Art and Architecture*, 47.

86. Jed Perl, "Welcome to the Funhouse," 31.

87. The authors continue: "However, it is also possible that viewers not conditioned to the antiseptic installations of modern museums may feel uncomfortable and self-conscious in such an environment. Paradoxically, the clean blank space could turn attention to the self rather than to the work of art, and itself become a distraction.... The same conflict is true for another important dimension of space, namely, its scale"; Csíkszentmihályi and Robinson, *The Art of Seeing*, 141–42.

88. Ibid., 163.

89. Ibid., 145.

90. For more information on eighteenth-century art criticism and theory, see Reed Benhamou, "Public and Private Art Education in France, 1648–1793," 1–183; Norman Bryson, *Word and Image*; Marian Hobson, *The Object of Art*; and Robert Rosenblum, *Transformations in Late Eighteenth-Century Art*.

91. For more information on the internal frame in painting, see Tarmo Pasto, *The Space-Frame Experience in Art*.

92. Giedion, *Space, Time and Architecture*, 31.
93. O'Doherty, *Inside the White Cube*, 79.
94. Calvocoressi, "Introduction," 10.
95. Searle continues that "it puts one in mind of exotic locations: a Venetian palace, the hall of a Mughal emperor, the decaying salon of a crumbling dynasty. Or gastro-pub, retro bar, modern Indian restaurant, palais de dance. Somewhere chic and louche, at any event. Primarily, one thinks gallery make-over." Searle, "Quick, Fetch a Mop," in *The Guardian* (Tuesday 13 June 2006).
96. Graham-Dixon, "Howard Hodgkin, at Tate Britain," in *Sunday Telegraph* (18 June 2006).
97. Giedion, *Space, Time and Architecture*, 357.
98. O'Doherty, *Inside the White Cube*, 14.
99. Denis quoted in ibid., 22.
100. O'Doherty, *Inside the White Cube*, 22.
101. Greenberg, "'American-Type' Painting", 93–104.
102. Giedion, *Space, Time and Architecture*, 357.
103. Youngblood, *Expanded Cinema*, 79.
104. Boccioni, "Technical Manifesto of Futurist Sculpture," 63.
105. Boccioni in "Preface" to *First Exhibition of Futurist Sculpture* (1913), quoted in *Modern Artists on Art*, 43 (italics his).
106. Ohana, *The Futurist Syndrome*, 34.
107. Marinetti, "The Pleasure of Being Booed", 113–15.
108. Marinetti, "Futurist Aesthetics of War" (1935), cited in Goldberg, *Performance Art*, 16.
109. O'Doherty, *Inside the White Cube*, 69.
110. Meyer, "The Functional Site," 25.
111. McShine, "The Museum as Muse," 515.
112. The artists were assisted by students from the School of the Chicago Art Institute of Design for the outside wrap.
113. O'Doherty describes *Wrapped Museum* as "art-like" in *Inside the White Cube*, 70.
114. Suderburg, "Introduction: On Installation and Site Specificity," 4.
115. Gopnik, "Empty Frames," 110.
116. Pierre Restany's invitation cited in Edward Strickland, *Minimalism*, 35.
117. Lineage and etymological change traced in Julie H. Reiss, *From Margin to Center*, xii.
118. Licht, *Spaces*, quoted in Ibid., 96.
119. Bishop, *Installation Art*, 11.
120. Reiss, *From Margin to Center*, xiii.
121. Kwon, "One Place After Another," 43.
122. Kaprow, "Notes on the Creation of a Total Art", 11.
123. Ibid., 12.
124. Abbate, "Music: Drastic or Gnostic?" 505–36.
125. Lippard quoted in Oliveira, Oxley, and Petry, *Installation Art*, 28.
126. Goldberg, *Performance Art*, 154.
127. Acconci quoted in Amelia Jones, "The 1970s 'Situation' and Recent Installation," 338.
128. Acconci quoted in McShine, "The Museum as Muse," 518.
129. Tamblyn, "Qualifying the Quotidian," 14.
130. Acconci quoted in McShine, "The Museum as Muse," 518.
131. Youngblood, *Expanded Cinema*, 41.
132. Jenkins, "The Machine in the Museum," 266.
133. Belson quoted Youngblood, *Expanded Cinema*, 391.
134. Cohen quoted in ibid., 371.
135. Ibid., 374.
136. VanDerBeek quoted in Salter, *Entangled,* 167.
137. Iles, "Video and Film Space," 253.
138. Salter, *Entangled*, 168.
139. Cage quoted in Youngblood, *Expanded Cinema*, 378.

140. Nameth quoted in ibid.

141. Iles, "Video and Film Space," 253.

142. Salter, *Entangled*, 169.

Chapter Four

1. McLuhan, *Understanding Media*, 63.

2. The first video installation collected by the Whitney was Paik's *V-Yramid* (1982): see Iles and Henriette Huldische, "Keeping Time," 69.

3. Schwarz, "Discourse 1: Media Museums," 11.

4. Sturken, "Set in Motion: The New York State Council on the Arts Celebrates 30 Years of Independents The Moving Image in Space: Public Funding and the Installation Form."

5. Kaprow, "Video Art," 152.

6. Ibid., 152, 150–51.

7. Gopnik, "Empty Frames," 120.

8. Smith, "In Installation Art," 31.

9. O'Doherty, *Inside the White Cube*, 15.

10. Suderburg, "Introduction," 4.

11. Tucker and Monte quoted in Monte, "Anti-Illusion," 5.

12. O'Doherty, *Inside the White Cube*, 79.

13. Leeson quoted in Pierre Restany, "San Francisco and the Grand Dame of Digital Art," 114.

14. Stravinsky, "The Phenomenon of Music," 30; Morse, "Video Installation Art," 166.

15. See Francis Frascina, *Art, Politics and Dissent*, 174.

16. Battcock quoted in Lippard, "The Art Workers' Coalition: Not a History," 173.

17. Aycock interviewed by Joan Simon, quoted in Mary Jane Jacob, *Gordon Matta-Clarke*, 33.

18. Art Workers' Coalition, *Documents 1*, 114.

19. Maciunas, "240.XXII George Maciunas," 166.

20. Jameson quoted in De Oliveira, Oxley, and Petry, *Installation Art*, 28.

21. Belton, "Looking Through Video," 67.

22. Kwon, "One Place After Another," 43.

23. Bartlett quoted in Youngblood, *Expanded Cinema*, 264.

24. Sturken, "Paradox in the Evolution of an Art Form," 104 (italics hers).

25. Ibid., 104.

26. Viola, "History, 10 Years, and the Dreamtime," 19.

27. Sturken, "Paradox in the Evolution of an Art Form," 102.

28. Ibid., 104.

29. Youngblood, *Expanded Cinema*.

30. Yalkut quoted from an email message to Spielmann (18 April 2004), cited in Spielmann, *Video*, 79.

31. Iles makes this point in "Inside Out: Expanded Cinema and its Relationship to the Gallery in the 1970s," spoken paper presented at the conference *Expanded Cinema: Activating the Space of Reception* (London: Tate Modern, 17 April 2009).

32. Daniels, "Television—Art or Anti-Art?"

33. Cage, "Nam June Paik: A Diary," 90.

34. Paik quoted in Youngblood, *Expanded Cinema*, 302.

35. Levine quoted in ibid., 366.

36. Belton, "Looking Through Video," 67.

37. Paik, *Nam June Paik*, 11.

38. Ibid.

39. Frieling, "No Rehearsal—Aspects of Media Art as Process."

40. Vostell quoted in Otto F. Walter and Helmut Heissenbüttel, eds., *Vostell*, 293.

41. Vostell quoted in Hanhardt, "Dé-collage/Collage," 74.

42. Cage quoted in David Revill, *The Roaring Silence*, 212.

43. Brockman, "Prologue."

44. Ibid.
45. Paik quoted in an interview with Ross: "A Conversation with Nam June Paik," 59.
46. The quote continues: "We did shows in museums and we did shows with Marshall McLuhan and Timothy Leary. We toured all over"; Yalkut interviewed by Keith Pandolfi (April 2000).
47. Kirby quoted in Davidson Gigliotti, "The Early Video Project," 49; Cage quoted in Goldberg, *Performance Art*, 123.
48. Cook, *Analysing Musical Multimedia*, 73.
49. Lippard and John Chandler, "Visible Art and the Invisible World," 27–30.
50. Klüver and Rauschenberg, *E.A.T. News*, 1.
51. *The Village Voice* quoted in Hanhardt, *The Worlds of Nam June Paik*, 61.
52. Henning, *Museums, Media and Cultural Theory*, 87.
53. Reichardt, "'Cybernetic Serendipity'," 176–77.
54. Catalogue quoted in Margot Lovejoy, *Digital Currents*, 174.
55. The review continues: "inviting visitors to touch, push buttons, talk or sing into microphones and television screens, or listen to speakers and earphones issuing sounds and information"; Mario Amaya, "Software in the Mall," quoted in Henning, *Museums, Media and Cultural Theory*, 87.
56. These figures, however, are contradictory: Reichardt reported "more than 60,000 visitors during the eleven weeks of the exhibition"; "'Cybernetic Serendipity'," 176–77.
57. Usselmann, "The Dilemma of Media Art," 389–96; Shepard, "Machine Mind," in *Sunday Telegraph* (11 August 1968), quoted by Usselmann, 391.
58. Shepard quoted in ibid.
59. Melville, "Signalling the End," quoted by Usselmann in ibid., 392.
60. Shepard quoted by Usselmann in ibid.
61. Youngblood, *Expanded Cinema*, 293.
62. The tour was funded by the New York State Council on the Arts.
63. Licht quoted in Reiss, *From Margin to Center*, 94–95.
64. LaBelle, *Background Noise*, 88.
65. Asher quoted in ibid.
66. Asher quoted in ibid., 89.
67. These figures are according to Leta E. Miller, "Cage's Collaborations," 167; Pritchett, *The Music of John Cage*, 158.
68. Nauman quoted in Coosje van Bruggen, *Bruce Nauman*, 18.
69. Daniels, "Television—Art or Anti-Art?"
70. Visitor quoted in David L. Shirey, "Art is Light," 101.
71. Sturken, "TV as a Creative Medium," 5.
72. The EAI now holds one of the largest collections of video art in America.
73. Sturken, "Paradox in the Evolution of an Art Form," 109.
74. Gigliotti, "Video Art in the Sixties," 43.
75. Schneider quoted in Roy Ascott, *Telematic Embrace*, 58.
76. Paik quoted in the Exhibition Flier, at http://eai.org/kinetic/ch1/creative/pdfs/exhibition-brochure.pdf (accessed 20 February 2012).
77. Anonymous reviewer, "The Medium: Taking the Waste Out of the Wasteland," 74.
78. John Gruen, "Art in New York," 57.
79. Yalkut, "TV as a Creative Medium at Howard Wise," 18.
80. Adorno discussed in Albright, *Untwisting the Serpent*, 17.
81. Paik quoted in Hanhardt, *The Worlds of Nam June Paik*, 62 (italics his).
82. Weintraub quoted in Exhibition Flier.
83. The first show, for example, was edited by David Cort, Parry Teasdale, and Mary Curtis Ratcliff and featured an interview with Black Panther leader Fred Hampton, who was later killed in his bed by the Chicago police, and a profile of one of the America's first alternative schools, the Pacific High School in Palo Alto.
84. Barzyk quoted in Youngblood, *Expanded Cinema*, 298.

85. The quote continues: "Compared with the book market, it is as if a successful writer could only keep in touch with his public through poetry readings, with his novels going through print-runs of millions. I am forced to the conclusion that in terms of possible communication between artwork and art public we are at about the same point as literature was before Gutenberg's invention of the letterpress.... I cannot see why modern art can only be publicised on a wider scale when it is no longer modern"; Schum quoted in Daniels, "Television—Art or Anti-Art?"

86. This quote is taken from a letter from Schum to Youngblood in 1969; letter cited in Wulf Herzogenrath, ed., *Nam June Paik*, 56.

87. Levine quoted in Youngblood, *Expanded Cinema*, 366; Belton, "Looking Through Video," 67.

88. The first issue of *Radical Software* proclaimed that "[o]ur species will survive neither by totally rejecting nor unconditionally embracing technology—but by humanizing it; by allowing people access to the information tools they need to shape and reassert control over their lives"; quoted in Sturken, "Paradox in the Evolution of an Art Form," 110.

89. Ross quoted in Sturken, "Paradox in the Evolution of an Art Form," 107.

90. Viola, "History, 10 Years, and the Dreamtime," 19.

Chapter Five

1. Borges, "Mirrors," 60.

2. Vostell quoted in Hanhardt, "Dé-collage/Collage," 74.

3. O'Doherty, *Inside the White Cube*; Small, *Musicking*, 26.

4. Whitney, *Digital Harmony*, 14.

5. Wagner cited in Kuritz, *The Making of Theatre History*, 263.

6. Dyson, *Sounding New Media*, 3.

7. David Bordwell applies the term fabula to film in *Narration in the Fiction Film*, 53.

8. Gorbman, *Unheard Melodies*, 145.

9. See Burch, *Theory of Film Practice*, 21.

10. Bazin, quoted in Pascal Bonitzer, "Off-Screen Space," 293.

11. Chion, *Audio-Vision*, 68.

12. Gorbman continues: "if we must summarise music-image and music-narrative relationships in two words or less, mutual implication is more accurate"; *Unheard Melodies*, 15, 13. See also Siegfried Kracauer, *Theory of Film*, 124–61.

13. The paradoxical silence of film music was noticed by Kurt London as early as 1936 and has been the starting point of many critical studies since, famously making the title of Gorbman's book (*Unheard Melodies*); London, *Film Music*.

14. Gorbman, *Unheard Melodies*, 12.

15. Ibid., 59.

16. Flinn, *Strains of Utopia*, 37.

17. Doane, "The Voice in the Cinema," 33–50.

18. Rosolato, "La Voix," 75–94; Anzieu, "L'envelope sonore du soi," 161–79.

19. On a more practical level, Flinn explains that music can also conceal editing that may jeopardise the illusion of wholeness: looking at flashbacks that are inaugurated by musical performance, for instance, she demonstrates how music can help to veil the jarring effects possible from such a break in linear narration; *Strains of Utopia*, 109. While many (with Silverman at the fore) scorn such psychoanalytical expositions, arguing that the sonorous envelope is but a fantasy constructed retroactively by the subject on the grounds that already socialised adults cannot regress, the notion is nevertheless an interesting one: Silverman, "The Female Authorial Voice," 191–224.

20. Anahid Kassabian argues this point in *Hearing Film*.

21. Bordwell, *Narration in the Fiction Film*. Because of this view, however, Bordwell has been criticised for ignoring emotion; see, for example, Robert Stam, *Film Theory*, 243.

22. Wittgenstein quoted in Youngblood, *Expanded Cinema*, 70.

23. Ibid., 381.

24. Whitman quoted in Goldberg, *Performance Art*, 137.

25. Schneemann quoted in Youngblood, *Expanded Cinema*, 367.

26. Iles has gone so far as to suggest that "[t]hese two very different sensibilities epitomized the differences between the media of film and video": "Video and Film Space," 253.

27. Kaprow, "Video Art," 149.

28. Small, *Musicking*, 27, 26.

29. Viola quoted in Zutter, "Interview with Bill Viola," 100.

30. Belton, "Looking Through Video," 67.

31. Paik quoted in Paik, *Nam June Paik*, 11.

32. Belton, "Looking Through Video," 67.

33. Dyson, *Sounding New Media*, 1.

34. Ibid., 2.

35. Gaudreault and Marion, "The Cinema as a Model for the Genealogy of Media," 14.

36. Meigh-Andrews, *A History of Video Art*, 5–6.

37. Elwes, *Video Art*, 153.

38. Ibid.

39. Bolter and Grusin, *Remediation*.

40. Bryson, *Vision and Painting*, 92; Bolter and Grusin, *Remediation*, 6.

41. Bolter and Grusin, *Remediation*, 6.

42. Bishop, *Installation Art*, chap. 3 (82–101).

43. Kotz, "Video Projection," 379.

44. Bolter and Grusin, *Remediation*, 19.

45. Speaking of the computer screen, Bolter and Grusin write: "The multiplicity of windows and the heterogeneity of their contents mean that the user is repeatedly brought back into contact with the interface, which she learns to read just as she would read any hypertext. She oscillates between manipulating the windows and examining their contents, just as she oscillates between looking at a hypertext as a texture of links and looking through the links to the textual units as language," Ibid., 33.

46. "Art is the manifesting of art"; Greenberg quoted in Albright, *Untwisting the Serpent*, 12.

47. Boccioni in "Preface" to *First Exhibition of Futurist Sculpture* (1913), 43 (italics his).

48. Levine quoted in Youngblood, *Expanded Cinema*, 339.

49. Salter, *Entangled*, xxvii.

50. Small, *Musicking*, 27, 26.

51. Ross, *No Respect*, 114.

52. Goldberg, *Performance Art*, 7.

53. Acconci, "Performance After the Fact" (1989), quoted in Nick Kaye, *Multi-Media: Video*, 74.

54. Kaprow speaking about his Environment Works: "About *Words*," quoted in Reiss, *From Margin to Center*, 14.

55. Kaprow, "Video Art," 150.

56. Wagner cited in Kuritz, *The Making of Theatre History*, 263.

57. Tambellini quoted in Youngblood, *Expanded Cinema*, 313.

58. Kaprow, "Video Art," 150.

59. Rosalind Krauss argues that Acconci's gesture highlights the self-involved nature of video and its users: Ann Wagner, on the other hand, reads the pointing finger as being directed at not only at the artist's reflection, but also at the viewer. Krauss, "Video," 50–64; Wagner, "Performance, Video, and the Rhetoric of Presence," 59–80.

60. Krauss, "Video," 57.

61. Grabes points out that the magical appearance of distant places revealed in mirrors can be traced back to Middle English literature in the Romance *The Seven Sages*, "which recounts the tale of Virgil's mirror, placed on a high column in Rome to herald the approach of the enemy"; *The Mutable Glass*, 126.

62. This legend was recounted by painter John Varley, amongst others: see Horace Welby, *Predictions Realized in Modern Times*, 103.

63. Kassinger, *Glass*, 25.

64. Borges, "The Library of Babel," 112.
65. Carroll, *Alice in Wonderland / Through the Looking Glass*, 139.
66. Iles, "Video and Film Space," 146, 259.
67. Jonas, "Transmission," 117–18.
68. Iles, "Reflective Spaces," 146.
69. David Hook, "Lacan's Mirror Stage," 266.
70. Lacan, *Écrits*, 20.
71. Evans, *An Introductory Dictionary to Lacanian Psychoanalysis*, 20.
72. Spielmann, *Video*, 146.
73. Jonas, "Transmission," 119.
74. Crimp, *Joan Jonas*, 8.
75. Iles, "Reflective Spaces," 146.
76. Jonas, "Transmission," 117.
77. Iles, "Reflective Spaces," 146–47.
78. Jonas, "interview," at http://www.moma.org/explore/multimedia/audios/47/959 (Accessed 20 February 2012).
79. Crimp, *Joan Jonas*, 8.
80. Jonas, "Transmission," 125.
81. Acconci quoted in Acconci and Moure, *Writings, Works, Projects*, 272.
82. Jonas, "Transmission," 127.
83. Krauss, "Video," 55.
84. Spielmann, *Video*, 151.
85. van Bruggen, *Bruce Nauman*, 14.
86. Krauss, "Video," 53.
87. Licht, *Spaces*, 96.
88. Cage quoted in Goldberg, *Performance Art*, 124.
89. Morse, "The Poetics of Interactivity," 18, 22.
90. Steina and Woody Vasulka quoted in Salter, *Entangled*, 120.
91. Schneider quoted in Youngblood, *Expanded Cinema*, 342.
92. Youngblood, *Expanded Cinema*, 339
93. Schimmel, "Pay Attention," 77.
94. Morse, "The Poetics of Interactivity," 153.
95. Nauman quoted in Salter, *Entangled*, 125.
96. Grabes, *The Mutable Glass*, 132.
97. Campus, "The Question," 15.
98. Campus quoted in Iles, "Video and Film Space," 255.
99. Graham quoted in Goldberg, *Performance Art*, 162.
100. Albright, *Untwisting the Serpent*, 6 (italics his).
101. DeWitt, "The Video Synthesizer," 165.
102. Ruttmann, "Malerei mit Zeit" (1919), quoted in Helfert, "Technological Constructions of Space-Time: Aspects of Perception."
103. Paik quoted in Salter, *Entangled*, 119.
104. Paik quoted in Davis, *Art and the Future*, 152.
105. Moorman speaking to Edith Decker in 1983; quoted in Rothfuss, "The Ballad of Nam June and Charlotte," 145.
106. Moorman speaking to Gisela Gronemeyer in 1980, quoted in ibid., 145–46.
107. When *TV Cello* was bought by the Walker Art Center in 1992, Paik created new video images for the piece, combining existing footage of Moorman with excerpts from his video work *Global Groove* (1973).
108. Viola quoted in Zutter, "Interview with Bill Viola," 100.
109. Dyson, *Sounding New Media*, 2.

Epilogue

1. Blesser and Salter, *Spaces Speak, Are you Listening?*, 130.
2. Hanhardt, *The Worlds of Nam June Paik*, 15.
3. Spielmann, *Video*, 22.
4. McShine, *The Museum as Muse*, 502.
5. Coulter-Smith, "Introduction: The Museum Problem."
6. Hanhardt, *The Worlds of Nam June Paik*, 14.
7. Sook-Kyung Lee and Susanne Rennert, eds., "Introduction," 9.
8. Lee speaking at the symposium *The Future is Now: Media Arts, Performance and Identity after Nam June Paik* (18 February 2011, at FACT, Liverpool).
9. Albright, *Untwisting the Serpent*, 6.
10. Spielmann, "Intermedia in Electronic Images," 59.
11. Elwes, *Video Art*, 153.
12. Bishop, *Installation Art*, 82–101.
13. The quote continues: "We did shows in museums and we did shows with Marshall McLuhan and Timothy Leary. We toured all over"; Yalkut interviewed by Pandolfi.
14. Snibbe, "Björk: *Biophilia*: Tour App Tutorial," at http://www.youtube.com/watch?v=n8cOx6dO2bg (accessed 20 February 2012).
15. Snibbe, "Björk: *Biophilia*: Crystalline App Tutorial," http://www.youtube.com/watch?v=Ezfz XNssNns&feature=relmfu (accessed 20 February 2012).

Bibliography

Abbate, Carolyn. "Drastic or Gnostic?" In *Critical Inquiry* 30:3 (Spring 2004): 505–536.

Abbate, Carolyn. *Unsung Voices: Opera and Musical Narrative in the Nineteenth Century*. Princeton: Princeton University Press, 1996.

Acconci, Vito and Gloria Moure. *Writings, Works, Projects*. Barcelona: Ediciones Poligrafa, 2001.

Adlington, Robert. *The Music of Harrison Birtwistle*. Cambridge: Cambridge University Press, 2000.

Albright, Daniel. *Beckett and Aesthetics*. Cambridge: Cambridge University Press, 2003.

Albright, Daniel. *Untwisting the Serpent: Modernism in Music, Literature and Other Arts*. Chicago and London: University of Chicago Press, 2000.

Altman, Rick. "Inventing the Cinema Soundtrack: Hollywood's Multiplane Sound System." In *Music and Cinema*. Edited by David Neumeyer, James Buhler, and Caryl Flinn, 339–359. New England: Wesleyan University Press, 2000.

Altman, Rick. "The Material Heterogeneity of Recorded Sound." In *Sound Theory, Sound Practice*. Edited by Rick Altman, 15–34. New York, London: Routledge, 1992.

Anonymous reviewer. "The Medium: Taking the Waste Out of the Wasteland." In *Time* (May 30, 1969), 74.

Anzieu, Didier. "L'envelope sonore du soi." In *Nouvelle revue de psychoanalyse* 13 (1976): 161–179.

Apollinaire, Guillaume. *Oeuvres en prose completes*. Paris: Éditions Gallimard, 1991.

Art Workers' Coalition. *Documents 1*. New York: Art Workers' Coalition, 1969.

Ascott, Roy. *Telematic Embrace: Visionary Theories of Art, Technology, and Consciousness*. Berkeley: University of California Press, 2007.

Attali, Jacques. *Noise: The Political Economy of Music*. Minneapolis: University of Minnesota Press, 1985.

Axelrod, Alan and Charles Phillips, eds. *What Every American Should Know About American History: 200 Events That Shaped the Nation*. Avon, MA: Adams Media, 2003.

Ayrey, Craig. "Stravinsky in Analysis: The Anglophone Traditions." In *The Cambridge Companion to Stravinsky*. Edited by Jonathan Cross, 203–229. Cambridge: Cambridge University Press, 2003.

Babbitt, Irving. *The New Laokoon: An Essay on the Confusion of the Arts*. Boston, New York: Houghton Mifflin Company, 1924.

Bakalis, Anna. "It's Unreel: DVD Rentals Overtake Videocassettes." *Washington Times* (21 June, 2003). Online. Available: http://nl.newsbank.com/nl-search/we/Archives?p_action=list&p_topdoc=11. 20 February 2012.

Barron, Michael. *Auditorium Acoustics and Architectural Design*. New York: Routledge, 1993.

Barthes, Roland. "Rhetoric of the Image." In *Image, Music, Text*. Edited and translated by Stephen Heath, 32–51. New York: Hill and Wang, 1977.

Belton, John. "Looking Through Video: The Psychology of Video and Film." In *Resolutions: Contemporary Video Practices*. Edited by Michael Renov and Erika Suderburg, 61–72. Minneapolis, London: University of Minnesota Press, 1996.

Benhamou, Reed. "Public and Private Art Education in France, 1648–1793." In *Studies on Voltaire and the Eighteenth Century* 308 (1993): 1–183.

Bernard, Jonathan. "Messiaen's Synaesthesia: The Correspondence Between Colour and Sound Structure in his Music." In *Music Perception* 4:1 (1986): 41–68.

Bishop, Claire. *Installation Art: A Critical History*. London: Tate Publishing, 2005.

Blesser, Barry and Lindy-Ruth Salter. *Spaces Speak, Are you Listening? Experiencing Aural Architecture*. Cambridge MA: MIT Press, 2007.

Boccioni, Umberto. "Technical Manifesto of Futurist Sculpture." In *Futurist Manifestos*. Edited by Umbro Apollonio, 51–65. London: Thames & Hudson, 1973.

Bolter, Jay and Richard Grusin. *Remediation: Understanding New Media*. Cambridge MA: The MIT Press, 1999.

Bonitzer, Pascal. "Off-Screen Space." In *Cahiers du Cinéma, Volume 3, 1969–1972: The Politics of Representation*. Edited by Nick Browne, 291–305. London: Routledge, 1990.

Bordwell, David. *Narration in the Fiction Film*. Madison: University of Wisconsin Press, 1985.

Borges, Jorge Luis. "The Library of Babel" (1944). In *Jorge Luis Borges: Collected Fictions*. Translated by Andrew Hurley, 112–118. London: Penguin Books, 1998.

Borges, Jorge Luis. "Mirrors." In *Dreamtigers*. Translated by Mildred Boyer and Harold Morland, 60–61. 1964; reprint, Texas: Texas University Press, 2004.

Bouillon, Jean-Paul. *Klimt—Beethoven: The Frieze for the Ninth Symphony*. Translated by Michael Heron. New York: Skira, 1987.

Brockman, John. "Prologue." In *Digerati: Encounters with the Cyber Elite*. San Francisco: HardWired Books, 1996. Online. Available: http://www.edge.org/documents/digerati/Prologue.html. 20 February 2012.

Broude, Norma and Mary D. Garrard, eds. *Feminism and Art History: Questioning the Litany*. New York: Harper & Row, 1982.

Broude, Norma and Mary D. Garrard, eds. *The Expanding Discourse: Feminism and Art History*. New York: Harper Collins, 1992.

Bruggen, Coosje van. *Bruce Nauman*. New York: Rizzoli, 1988.

Bryson, Norman. *Vision and Painting: The Logic of the Gaze*. New Haven, CT: Yale University Press, 1983.

Bryson, Norman. *Word and Image: French Painting of the Ancien Régime*. Cambridge: Cambridge University Press, 1983.

Burch, Noël. *Theory of Film Practice*. Translated by Helen R. Lane. Princeton: Princeton University Press, 1981.

Bürger, Peter, and Christa Bürger. *The Institutions of Art*. Translated by Loren Kruger. Introduction by Russell A. Berman. Lincoln, Nebraska: University of Nebraska Press, 1992.

Butler, Christopher. *Early Modernism: Literature, Music and Painting in Europe, 1900–1916*. Oxford: Clarendon Press, 1994.

Cage, John. *A Year From Monday: New Lectures and Writings*. 1967. Reprint, London: Marion Boyars, 1975.

Cage, John. "The Future of Music Credo." 1937. Reprint. In *Audio Culture: Readings in Modern Music*. Edited by Christopher Cox and Daniel Warner, 25–28. London: Continuum, 2004.

Cahen, Robert. "Robert Cahen: *Passage* at Preston Harris Museum & Art Gallery." Online. Available: http://www.culture24.org.uk/art/art64388. 20 February 2012.

Calvocoressi, Richard. "Introduction." In Howard Hodgkin, *Howard Hodgkin: Large Paintings, 1984–2002*, 9–11. Edinburgh: National Galleries of Scotland, 2002.

Campen, Cretien van. "Artistic and Psychological Experiments with Synaesthetisia." In *Leonardo* 32.1 (1999): 9–14.

Camper, Fred. "Brakhage Wants to Make you See." In *By Brakhage: An Anthology*. New York: The Criterion Collection DVD liner notes, 2003.

Campus, Peter. "The Question." In *Art-Rite* 7 (Autumn 1974): 15.

Carrier, David. *Museum Skepticism: A History of the Display of Art in Public Galleries*. North Carolina: Duke Press, 2006.

Carroll, Lewis. *Alice in Wonderland / Through the Looking Glass*. 1865. Reprint, London: Bibliolis Books, 2010.

Chion, Michel. *Audiovision: Sound on Screen*. Translated by Claudia Gorbman. New York: Columbia University Press, 1994.

Cone, Edward T. and Benjamin Boretz, eds. *Perspectives on American Composers*. London: W.W. Norton and Company, 1971.

Conrad, Tony. "LYssophobia: On Four Violins." In *Audio Culture: Readings in Modern Music*. Edited by Christopher Cox and Daniel Warner, 313–318. London: Continuum, 2004.

Conrad, Tony. "Preparing for the Propaganda War in the Time of Global Culture: Trance, Form, and Persuasion in the Renovation of Western Music." Online. Available: http://tonyconrad.net/bard.htm. 20 February 2012.

Cook, Nicholas. *Analysing Musical Multimedia*. Oxford: Oxford University Press, 1998.

Coulter-Smith, Graham. *Deconstructing Installation Art: The End of the Old Avant-Garde and the Beginning of the New*. Online. Available: http://www.installationart.net/MenuItems/contents.html. 20 February 2012.

Crary, Jonathan. *Techniques of the Observer: On Vision and Modernity in the Nineteenth Century*. Cambridge MA: MIT Press, 1992.

Crimp, Douglas. *Joan Jonas, Scripts and Descriptions, 1968–1982*. California: University Art Museum, University of California Press, 1983.

Crow, Thomas. *Painters and Public Life in Eighteenth-Century Paris*. Yale: Yale University Press, 1987.

Csíkszentmihályi, Mihály and Rick Emery Robinson. *The Art of Seeing: An Interpretation of the Aesthetic Encounter*. Los Angeles: Getty Publications, 1990.

Cubitt, Sean. *Timeshift: On Video Culture*. London, New York: Routledge, 1991.

Daniels, Dieter. "John Cage and Nam June Paik: 'Change Your Mind or Change Your Receiver (Your Receiver is Your Mind)'." In *Nam June Paik*. Edited by Sook-Kyung Lee and Susanne Rennert, 107–125. London: Tate Publishing, 2010.

Daniels, Dieter. "Sound & Vision in Avantgarde & Mainstream [1]." Translated by Michael Robinson. In *Media Art Net*. Online. Available: http://www.medienkunstnetz.de/themes/image-sound_relations/sound_vision/. 20 February 2012.

Daniels, Dieter. "Television—Art or Anti-Art? Conflict and Cooperation Between the Avant-Garde and the Mass Media in the 1960s and 1970s." Translated by Michael Robinson. In *Media Art Net*. Online. Available: http://www.medienkunstnetz.de/themes/overview_of_media_art/massmedia/1/. 20 February 2012.

Dann, Kevin. *Bright Colors Falsely Seen: Synaesthesia and the Search for Transcendent Knowledge*. Yale: Yale University Press, 1998.

Davis, Douglas. "Art and Technology: The New Combine." In *Art in America* 56 (1968): 28–47.

Davis, Douglas. *Art and the Future: A History/Prophecy of the Collaboration Between Science, Technology and Art*. London: Thames and Hudson, 1973.

De Oliveira, Nicholas, Nicola Oxley, and Michael Petry. *Installation Art*. London: Thames and Hudson Ltd, 1994.

DeWitt, Tom. "The Video Synthesizer." In *Eigenwelt der Apparate-Welt. Pioneers of Electronic Art*. Edited by David Dunn, Woody Vasulka and Steina Vasulka, 165–167. Santa Fe, NM: The Vasulkas and Linz: Ars Electronica, 1992.

Doane, Mary Ann. "The Voice in the Cinema: The Articulation of Body and Space." In *Yale French Studies* 60 (1980): 33–50.

Dobson, Terence. *The Film Work of Norman McLaren*. Hertfordshire: John Libbey Publishing, 2007.

Donnelly, Kevin. "*Performance* and the Composite Film Score." In *Film Music: Critical Approaches*. Edited by Kevin Donnelly, 152–166. Edinburgh: Edinburgh University Press, 2001.

Düchting, Hajo. *Paul Klee: Painting Music*. Munich, London, New York: Prestel Verlag, 1997.

Duguid, Brian. "Tony Conrad Interview." In *EST Magazine* (June 1996). Online. Available: http://media.hyperreal.org/zines/est/intervs/conrad.html. 20 February 2012.

Dyson, Frances. *Sounding New Media: Immersion and Embodiment in the Arts and Culture.* Berkeley, Los Angeles, and London: University of California Press, 2009.

Elwes, Catherine. *Video Art: A Guided Tour.* 2005. Reprint, London: University of the Arts, 2006.

Emery, Colin. *A Celebration of Art and Architecture: the National Gallery Sainsbury Wing.* London, Washington: University of Washington Press, 1991.

Emmerson, Simon. *Living Electronic Music.* Aldershot: Ashgate, 2007.

Esche, Charles. "Video Installation: Conceptual Practice and New Media in the 1990s." In *Diverse Practices: A Critical Reader on British Video Art.* Edited by Julia Knight, 195–206. Luton: Luton University Press, 1996.

Evans, Dylan. *An Introductory Dictionary to Lacanian Psychoanalysis.* London: Routledge, 1996.

Fenlon, Iain. "Venice: Theatre of the World." *In The Renaissance: From the 1470s to the End of the 16th Century.* Edited by Iain Fenlon, 102–132. Englewood Cliffs, New Jersey: Prentice Hallm 1989. Filippo Marinetti. *Marinetti: Selected Writings*, ed. R. W. Flint, trans. Flint and Arthur A. Coppotelli. London: Secker and Warburg, 1972.

Fischinger, Oskar. "Excerpts from Unpublished Typescript." 1947. Online. Available: http://www.centerforvisualmusic.org/Fischinger/OFCorresp.htm. 20 February 2012.

Fischinger, Oskar. "Sounding Ornaments." In *Deutsche Allgemeine Zeitung* (July 8, 1932). Online. Available: http://www.oskarfischinger.org/Sounding.htm. 20 February 2012.

Flinn, Caryl. *Strains of Utopia: Gender, Nostalgia and Hollywood Film Music.* Princeton: Princeton University Press, 1992.

Föllmer, Golo and Julia Gerlach. "Audiovisions: Music as an Intermedia Art Form." In *Media Art Net.* Online. Available: http://www.medienkunstnetz.de/themes/image-sound_relations/audiovisions/. 20 February 2012.

Fontana, Bill. "Sound as Virtual Image." Online. Available: http://www.resoundings.org/Pages/sound%20As%20Virtual%20Image.html. 20 February 2012.

Frascina, Francis. *Art, Politics and Dissent: Aspects of the Art Left in Sixties America.* Manchester: Manchester University Press, 1999.

Frieling, Rudolf. "No Rehearsal—Aspects of Media Art as Process." In *Media Kunst Interaktion-die 60er und 70er Jahre in Deutschland.* Edited by Rudolf Frieling and Dieter Daniels, 163–169. Vienna, New York: Springer, 1997.

Furlong, William. *Audio Arts: Discourse and Practice in Contemporary Art.* London: Academy Editions, 1994.

Galeyev, Bulat Makhmudovich. "Music-Kinetic Art Medium: On the Work of the Group Prometei (SKB) Kazan, USSR." In *Leonardo* 9:3 (1976): 177–82.

Galeyev, Bulat Makhmudovich and Irena Leonidovna Vanechkina. "Was Skryabin a Synesthete?" In *Leonardo* 34:4 (2001): 357–61.

Gann, Kyle. *The Music of Conlon Nancarrow.* Cambridge: Cambridge University Press, 2006.

Gaudreault, André, and Philippe Marion. "The Cinema as a Model for the Genealogy of Media." In *Convergence* 8:4 (2002): 12–18.

Giedion, Sigfried. *The Eternal Present: The Beginning of Art 1957.* London, Oxford: Oxford University Press, 1962.

Giedion, Sigfried. *Time and Architecture: The Growth of a New Tradition.* Cambridge, MA: Harvard University Press, 1941.

Gigliotti, Davidson. "The Early Video Project." Online. Available: http://207.56.97.90/Exhibitions.html. 20 February 2012.

Gigliotti, Davidson. "Video Art in the Sixties." In *Abstract Painting 1960–69.* Long Island City, NY: Institute for Art and Urban Resources, Inc., 1983.

Goldberg, RoseLee. *Performance Art: From Futurism to the Present.* 1979. Reprint, London: Thames and Hudson, 2001.

Gopnik, Adam. "Empty Frames." In *The New Yorker* (25 November, 1991): 110.

Gorbman, Claudia. *Unheard Melodies: Narrative Film Music.* London, Indiana: Indiana University Press/BFI, 1987.

Grabes, Herbert. *The Mutable Glass: Mirror-Imagery in the Titles and Texts of the Middle Ages and the English Renaissance.* Translated by Gordon Collier. Cambridge: Cambridge University Press, 1982.

Graham-Dixon, Andrew. "Howard Hodgkin at Tate Britain." In *Sunday Telegraph* (18 June 2006). Online. Available: http://www.andrewgrahamdixon.com/archive/readArticle/419. 20 February 2012.

Greenberg, Clement. "'American-Type' Painting" (1955). Reprint, *Modern Art and Modernism: A Critical Anthology*. Edited by Francis Frascina, Charles Harrison, and Deirdre Paul, 93–104. Los Angeles: Sage Publications Ltd, 1982.

Gregor, Ulrich, Jeanpaul Goergen and Angelika Hoch, eds. *Hans Richter. Film ist Rhythmus.* Berlin: Freunde der Deutschen Kinemathek, 2003.

Griffiths, Paul. "Catalogue de Couleurs: Notes on Messiaen's Tone Colours on His 70th Birthday." In *The Musical Times* 119:1630 (December 1978): 1035–1037.

Gruen, John. "Art in New York: This is Where We Came In." In *New York* 2:23 (June 9, 1969): 57.

Gschwandtner, Sabrina. "Between Film and Video—The Intermedia Art of Jud Yalkut; An Interview with Jud Yalkut." In *Millennium Film Journal* 42 (Fall 2004). Online. Available: http://mfj-online.org/journalPages/mfj42/gschwanpage.html. 20 February 2012.

Hahl-Koch, Jelena. *Arnold Schönberg/Wassily Kandinsky: Letters, Pictures and Documents.* Translated by J. C. Crawford. London: Faber & Faber, 1984.

Hall, David. "Video Art: The Significance of an Educational Environment." In *Video Positive 1989.* Edited by Lisa Haskel. Liverpool: Merseyside Moviola Exhibition Catalogue, 1989.

Haller, Robert A., ed. *Brakhage Scrapbook: Collected Writings 1964–1980.* New Paltz: Documentext, 1982.

Hamlin, Jess. "Grand Opera Gets Grander with State-of-the-Art-Screens." In *San Francisco Chronicle* (June 2, 2007): 1.

Hanhardt, John. *The Worlds of Nam June Paik.* New York: Guggenheim, 2000.

Hanhardt, John. "Dé-collage/Collage: Notes Toward a Re-Examination of the Origins of Video Art." In *Illuminating Video: An Essential Guide to Video Art.* Edited by Doug Hall and Sally Jo Fifer, 71–80. San Francisco: Apature/Bay Area Video Coalition, 2005.

Hankins, Thomas L. "The Ocular Harpsichord of Louis-Bertrand Castel; Or, The Instrument That Wasn't." In *Osiris* 9 (1994): 141–156.

Harrison, John and Simon Baron-Cohen. "Synaesthesia: An Account of Coloured Hearing." In *Leonardo* 27:4 (1994): 343–346.

Hedges, Inez. "Stan Brakhage's Film Testament: The Four Faust Films." In *Avant-Garde Film.* Edited by Alexander Graf and Dietrich Scheunemann, 165–182. New York: Rodopi, 2007.

Hegarty, Paul. *Noise/Music: A History.* New York: Continuum, 2009.

Henning, Michelle. *Museums, Media and Cultural Theory.* Maidenhead, New York: Open University Press, 2006.

Herbert, Robert L., ed. *Modern Artists on Art.* 1964. Reprint, New York: Dover Publications, 1999.

Herzogenrath, Wulf, ed. *Nam June Paik: Fluxus, Video.* Munich: Schreiber, 1983.

Higgins, Dick. *Horizons.* New York: Roof Books, 1998.

Hobson, Marian. *The Object of Art: The Theory of Illusion in Eighteenth-Century France.* Cambridge: Cambridge University Press, 1982.

Hook, David. "Lacan's Mirror Stage." In *Developmental Psychology.* Edited by Jacki Watts, Norman Duncan and Kate Cockcroft, 261–282. 2002. Reprint, Cape Town: UCT Press, 2009.

Howard, Deborah and Laura Moretti. *Sound and Space in Renaissance Venice: Architecture, Music, Acoustics.* New Haven: Yale University Press, 2009.

Huxley, Aldous. *Brave New World* and *Brave New World Revisited.* 1931 and 1958. Reprint, New York: Harper Collins, 2004.

Iles, Chrissie and Henriette Huldische. "Keeping Time: On Collecting Film and Video Art in the Museum." In *Collecting the New: Museums and Contemporary Art.* Edited by Bruce Altshuler, 65–84. Princeton: Princeton University Press, 2005.

Iles, Chrissie. "Reflective Spaces: Film and Video in the Work of Joan Jonas." In *Joan Jonas: Performance Video Installation 1968–2000.* Edited by Johann-Karl Schmidt, 144–54. Stuttgart: Galerie der Stadt Sttutgart and Hatje Cantz Verlag, 2000.

Iles, Chrissie. "Video and Film Space." In *Space, Site, Intervention: Situating Installation Art.* Edited by Erika Suderburg, 252–62. London, Minneapolis: University of Minnesota Press, 2000.

Ione, Amy and Christopher Tyler. "Neuroscience, History and the Arts: Synesthesia, Is F-sharp Colored Violet?" In *Journal of the History of the Neurosciences* 13 (2004): 58–65.

Jacob, Mary Jane. *Gordon Matta-Clarke: A Retrospective*. Chicago: Museum of Contemporary Art, 1985.

Jenkins, Bruce. "The Machine in the Museum: or, The Seventh Art in Search of Authorisation." In *Space, Site, Intervention: Situating Installation Art*. Edited by Erika Suderburg, 263–274. London, Minneapolis: University of Minnesota Press, 2000.

Jewanski, Jörg and Natalia Sidler, eds. *Farbe-Licht–Musik: Synaesthesie und Farblichtmusik*. Bern: Peter Lang, 2006.

Johnson, James. *Listening in Paris: A Cultural History*. Berkeley: University of California Press, 1995.

Jonas, Joan. "Transmission." In *Woman, Art and Technology*. Edited by Judy Malloy, 114–133. Cambridge MA: MIT Press, 2003.

Jones, Amelia. "The 1970s 'Situation' and Recent Installation: Joseph Santarromana's Intersubjective Engagements." In *Space, Site, Intervention: Situating Installation Art*. Edited by Erika Suderburg, 332–246. London, Minneapolis: University of Minnesota Press, 2000.

Jordan, William E. "McLaren: His Career and Techniques." In *The Quarterly of Film, Radio and Television* 8:1 (Autumn 1953): 1–14.

Kandinsky, Wassily. *Concerning the Spiritual in Art*. Translated by Michael Sadler. 1914. Reprint, New York: Dover Publications, 1977.

Kandinsky, Wassily. *Rückblicke*. 1913. Reprint, Bern: Benteli, 1977.

Kaprow, Allan. *Essays on the Blurring of Art and Life*. Edited by Jeff Kelley. California: University of California Press, 1993.

Kassabian, Anahid. *Hearing Film: Tracking Identifications in Contemporary Hollywood Film Music*. London: Routledge, 2001.

Kassinger, Ruth. *Glass: From Cinderella's Slippers to Fiber Optics*. Connecticut: Twenty-First Century Books, 2003.

Kaye, Nick. *Multi-Media: Video, Installation, Performance*. Oxford: Routledge, 2007.

Kotz, Liz. "Video Projection: The Space Between Screens." In *Art and the Moving Image: A Critical Reader*. Edited by Tanya Leighton, 371–387. London: Tate Publishing, 2008.

Keefer, Cindy. "'Space Light Art': Early Abstract Cinema and Multimedia, 1900–1959." In *White Noise*. Melbourne: Australian Centre for the Moving Image, 2005.

Kerse, C. S. *The Law Relating to Noise*. London: Oyez, 1975.

Kevorkian, Tanya. "The Reception of the Cantata During Leipzig Church Services, 1700–1750." In *Early Music* 30:1 (2002): 27–46.

Klüver, Billy and Robert Rauschenberg. *E.A.T. News* 1:2 (June 1967).

Kolarevic, Branco and Ali Malkawi. *Performative Architecture: Beyond Instrumentality*. New York, London: Spon Press, 2005.

Kracauer, Siegfried. *Theory of Film: The Redemption of Physical Reality*. New York: Oxford University Press, 1960.

Krauss, Rosalind. "Video: The Aesthetics of Narcissism." In *October* 1 (Spring 1976): 50–64.

Kuritz, Paul. *The Making of Theatre History*. New Jersey: Prentice Hall College Division, 1988.

Kwon, Miwon. "One Place After Another: Notes on Site Specificity." In *Space, Site, Intervention: Situating Installation Art*. Edited by Erika Suderburg, 38–63. London, Minneapolis: University of Minnesota Press, 2000.

LaBelle, Brandon. *Background Noise: Perspectives on Sound Art*. London, New York: Continuum, 2006.

Lacan, Jacques. *Écrits*. Translated by Alan Sheridan. London: Routledge, 1977.

Lachenmann, Helmut and David Ryan. "Composer in Interview: Helmut Lachenmann." In *Tempo* 210 (Oct., 1999): 20–25.

Lack, Russell. *Twenty Four Frames Under: A Buried History of Film Music*. London: Quartet Books, 1997.

Lawder, Standish D. "Der Abstrakte Film: Richter und Eggeling." In *Hans Richter 1888–1976: Dadaist, Filmpionier, Maler, Theoretiker*, 27–35. Berlin: Akademie der Künst, 1982.

Lefèbvre, Henri. *The Production of Space.* Translated by Donald Nicholson-Smith. 1974. Reprint, Oxford: Blackwell, 1991.

Leppert, Richard. *The Sight of Sound: Music, Representation, and the History of the Body.* Berkeley, Los Angeles, London: University of California Press, 1993.

Lessing, Gotthold. *Laocoön: An Essay on the Limits of Painting and Poetry.* Translated by Edward Allen McCormick. Baltimore, Maryland: Johns Hopkins University Press, 1984.

Licht, Alan. *Sound Art: Beyond Music, Between Categories.* New York: Rizzoli, 2007.

Lippard, Lucy and John Chandler. "Visible Art and the Invisible World." In *Art International* 11:5 (May 1967): 27–30.

Lippard, Lucy. "The Art Workers' Coalition: Not a History." In *Studio International* 180: 927 (November 1970): 171–174.

Lippard, Lucy. *The Pink Glass Swan: Selected Essays on Feminist Art.* New York: New Press, 1995.

Lischi, Sandra. *The Sight of Time: Films and Videos by Robert Cahen.* Pisa: Edizioni ETS, 1997.

London, Barbara. *Bill Viola: Installations and Videotapes.* London; New York: MOMA, 1987.

London, Kurt. *Film Music.* Translated by Eric S. Bensinger. London: Faber and Faber, 1936.

Lovejoy, Margot. *Digital Currents: Art in the Electronic Age.* New York: Routledge, 2004.

Lovejoy, Margot. *Postmodern Currents: Art and Artists in the Age of Electronic Media.* London: UMI Research Press, 1989.

MacDonald, Hugh. "Lighting the Fire: Skryabin and Colour." In *The Musical Times* 124:1688 (1983): 600–602.

MacDonald, Scott. *Avant-Garde Film: Motion Studies.* Cambridge: Cambridge University Press, 1993.

Maciunas, George. "240.XXII George Maciunas (Fluxus objectives & Ideology) 1964." In *Fluxus etc. Addemda II: The Gilbert and Lila Silverman Collection.* Edited by Jon Hendricks, 166. Pasadena: Baxter Art Gallery at the California Institute of Technology, 1983.

Malloy, Judy, ed. *Woman, Art and Technology.* Cambridge MA: MIT Press, 2003.

Marinetti, Fillipo, Bruno Corra, Emilio Settimelli, Arnaldo Ginna, Giacomo Balla, and Remo Chiti. "The Futurist Cinema" (1916). Translated by R. W. Flint. In *Multimedia: From Wagner to Virtual Reality.* Edited by Randall Packer and Ken Jordan, 10–15. New York: W. W. Norton and Co., 2001.

Marinetti, Filippo. *Marinetti: Selected Writings.* Edited by R. W. Flint. Translated by R. W. Flint and Arthur A. Coppotelli. London: Secker and Warburg, 1972.

Maroević, Ivo. *Introduction to Museology: The European Approach.* München: C. Müller-Straten, 1998.

Mathews, Timothy. *Reading Apollinaire: Theories of Poetic Language.* Manchester: Manchester University Press, 1987.

Maur, Karin V. *The Sound of Painting: Music in Modern Art.* Munich, London, New York: Prestel Verlag, 1999.

McLuhan, Marshall. "The Medium Is the Message." In *Understanding Media: The Extensions of Man,* 23–35. New York: Signet Books, 1964.

McShine, Kynaston. *The Museum as Muse: Artists Reflect:* "Introduction." 1999. Reprint, *Museum Studies: An Anthology of Contexts.* Edited by Bettina Carbonell, 491–502. 2004. Reprint, Oxford: Blackwell, 2012.

Meigh-Andrews, Chris. "Robert Cahen: Passage." In *Art Monthly* 326 (May 2009): 40.

Meigh-Andrews, Chris. *A History of Video Art: The Development of Form and Function.* Oxford; New York: Berg, 2006.

Mertens, Wim. *American Minimal Music.* Translated by J. Hautekiet. New York: Alexander Broude, 1983.

Metz, Christian. *Film Language: A Semiotics of the Cinema.* Translated by Michael Taylor. New York, Oxford: Oxford University Press, 1974.

Meyer, James. "The Functional Site; or, The Transformation of Site Specificity." In *Space, Site, Intervention: Situating Installation Art.* Edited by Erika Suderburg, 23–37. London, Minneapolis: University of Minnesota Press, 2000.

Miller, Lucy. *Adams to Zemlinsky.* New York: Concert Artists Guild, 2006.

Moholy-Nagy, László. *The New Vision: From Material to Architecture*. Translated by Daphne M. Hoffmann. New York: Brewer, Warren & Putnam Inc, 1932.

Monte, James and Marcia Tucker, eds. *Anti-Illusion: Procedures / Materials*. Edited by James Monte and Marcia Tucker. New York: Whitney Museum of American Art, 1969.

Moritz, William. "Jordan Belson: Last of the Great Masters." In *Animation Journal* 7:2 (Spring, 1999): 4–17.

Moritz, William. "Musique de la Couleur: Cinéma Intégral" ("Color Music: Integral Cinema"). In *Poétique de la Couleur*, 9–13. Paris: Musée du Louvre, 1995.

Moritz, William. "Non-Objective Film: The Second Generation." In *Film as Film: Formal Experiment in Film, 1910–1975*, 59–71. London: Hayward Gallery, 1979.

Moritz, William. *Optical Poetry: The Life and Work of Oskar Fischinger*. Bloomington: Indiana University Press, 2004.

Morse, Margaret. "Video Installation Art: The Body, The Image, and the Space-in-Between." In *Illuminating Video: An Essential Guide to Video Art*. Edited by Doug Hall and Sally Jo Fifer, 153–167. New York: Aperture, 1990.

Münsterberg, Hugo. *The Film: A Psychological Study*. 1916. Reprint, New York: Dover, 1970.

Nattiez, Jean-Jacques and Robert Samuels, eds. *The Boulez-Cage Correspondence*. Translated by Robert Samuels. Cambridge: Cambridge University Press, 1993.

Nauman, Bruce and Janet Kraynak, eds. *Please Pay Attention Please: Bruce Nauman's Words: Writings and Interviews*. Cambridge, MA: MIT Press, 2002.

Nesthus, Marie. "The Influence of Olivier Messiaen on the Visual Art of Stan Brakhage in *Scenes from under Childhood Part One*." In *Film Culture* 63 (1977): 39–50.

Nicholls, David. *The Cambridge Companion to Cage*. Cambridge: Cambridge University Press, 2002.

Notley, Margaret. "'With A Beethoven-Like Sublimity': Beethoven in the Works of Other Composers." In *The Cambridge Companion to Beethoven*. Edited by Glenn Stanley, 219–239. Cambridge: Cambridge University Press, 2000.

Nyman, Michael. "Cage and Satie." In *Writings about John Cage*. Edited by Richard Kostelanetz, 66–72. Ann Arbor: University of Michigan Press, 1993.

Nyman, Michael. *Experimental Music: Cage and Beyond*. London, New York: Studio Vista, 1974.

O'Doherty, Brian. *Inside the White Cube: The Ideology of the Gallery Space*. 1976. Reprint and expanded, Berkeley, Los Angeles, London: University of California Press, 1986.

O'Pray, Michael. *Andy Warhol: Film Factory*. London: BFI, 1989.

Ohana, David. *The Futurist Syndrome*. Sussex: Sussex Academic Press, 2010.

Paik, Nam June. "Input-Time and Output Time." In *Video Art: An Anthology*. Edited by Beryl Korot and Ira Schneider, 98–124. New York: The Raindance Foundation, 1976.

Paik, Nam June. "Versatile Color TV Synthesizer." 1969. Reprint, *Nam June Paik, Videa 'n' Videology: 1959–1973*. Edited by Judson Rosebush, 55. New York: Everson Museum of Art, 1974.

Parker, Rozsika and Griselda Pollock, eds. *Framing Feminism: Art and the Women's Movement*. New York: Pandora, 1987.

Pasto, Tarmo. *The Space-Frame Experience in Art*. New York: A.S. Barnes, 1964.

Peacock, Kenneth. "Instruments to Perform Color-Music: Two Centuries of Technological Experimentation." In *Leonardo* 21:4 (1988): 397–406.

Perl, Jed. "Welcome to the Funhouse: Tate Modern and the Crisis of the Museum." In *The New Republic* 222:25 (19 June 2000): 30–36.

Perloff, Marjorie. *The Futurist Moment: Avant-Garde, Avant Guerre, and the Language of Rupture*. Chicago: Chicago University Press, 2003.

Princenthal, Nancy. "Rooms With a View." In *Sculpture* 9:2 (March/April 1990): 26–31.

Pritchett, James. *The Music of John Cage*. Cambridge: Cambridge University Press, 1996.

Reichardt, Jasia. "'Cybernetic Serendipity': Getting Rid of Preconceptions." In *Studio International* 176: 905 (November 1968): 176–177.

Reiss, Julie. *From Margin to Center: The Spaces of Installation Art*. Cambridge, MA, London: MIT Press, 2001.

Rennert, Susan. "'We Have Time'. Music, Fluxus, Video: Paik's Time in Düsseldorf, in the Rhineland." In *Nam June Paik*. Edited by Sook-Kyung Lee and Susanne Rennert, 55–68. London: Tate Publishing, 2010.

Restany, Pierre. "San Francisco and the Grand Dame of Digital Art." In *Domus* (June 1999): 114.

Revill, David. *The Roaring Silence: John Cage, A Life*. New York: Arcade Publishing, 1993.

Rosenberg, Harold. *The Tradition of the New*. Chicago: University of Chicago Press, 1982.

Rosenblum, Robert. *Transformations in Late Eighteenth-Century Art*. Princeton: Princeton University Press, 1967.

Rosolato, Guy. "La Voix: Entre corps et langage." In *Revue française de psychoanalyse* 38 (1974): 75–94.

Ross, Andrew. *No Respect: Intellectuals and Popular Culture*. New York: Routledge, 1989.

Ross, David. "A Conversation with Nam June Paik." In *Nam June Paik: Video Time-Video Space*. Edited by Thomas Kellein and Toni Stooss, 56–65. New York: Harry N. Abrams, 1993.

Ross, David. *Bill Viola*. New York: Whitney Museum of Art / Flammarion, 1997.

Rothfuss, Joan. "The Ballad of Nam June and Charlotte: A Revisionist History." In *Nam June Paik*. Edited by Sook-Kyung Lee and Susanne Rennert, 145–155. London: Tate Publishing, 2010.

Russolo, Luigi. "The Art of Noises." 1913. Reprint, *Manifesto: A Century of Isms*. Edited by Mary Ann Caws, 205–211. Nebraska: University of Nebraska Press, 2001.

Sabaneev, Leonid and S.W. Pring, "Relation Between Sound and Colour." In *Music & Letters* 10:3 (1929): 266–277.

Salter, Chris. *Entangled: Technology and the Transformation of Performance*. Cambridge MA: MIT Press, 2010.

Schaeffer, Pierre. *À la recherche d'une musique concréte*. Paris: La Seuil, 1952.

Schafer, R. Murray. "Music, Non-Music and the Soundscape." In *A Companion to Contemporary Musical Thought*. Edited by John Paynter, Tim Howell, Richard Orton and Peter Seymour, 34–45 (Vol 1). London and New York: Routledge, 1992.

Schechner, Richard. "6 Axioms for Environmental Theatre." In *The Drama Review* 12:3 (1968): 41–64.

Schlte, Karin. *Temporary Buildings: The Trade-Fair Stand as a Conceptual Challenge*. Stuttgart: AVEdition, 1999.

Schneider, Arthur. *Jump-Cut: Memoires of a Pioneer Editor*. Jefferson: McFarland, 1997.

Schneider, Pierre. *Matisse*. Munich: Rizzoli, 1984.

Schwarz, Hans-Peter. "Discourse 1: Media Museums." In *Media Art History*. Edited by Rebecca Picht and Birgit Stöckmann, 11–42. New York: Prestel, 1997.

Searing, Helen. *New American Art Museums*. Berkley, Los Angeles: University of California Press, 1982.

Sherlaw-Johnson, Robert. *Messiaen*. London: Dent, 1975.

Sherman, Tom. "The Premature Birth of Video Art." *Experimental Television Centre, 2007*. Online. Available: http://www.experimentaltvcenter.org/premature-birth-video-art. 20 February 2012.

Shirey, David L. "Art is Light." In *Newsweek* (February 20, 1967): 101.

Silverman, Kaja. *The Acoustic Mirror: The Female Voice in Psychoanalysis and Cinema*. Bloomington: Indiana University Press, 1988.

Small, Christopher. *Musicking: The Meanings of Performing and Listening*. Middletown, Connecticut: Wesleyan University Press, 1998.

Small, Christopher. "Performance as Ritual: Sketch for Enquiry into the True Nature of a Symphony Concert." In *Lost in Music: Culture, Style and the Musical Event*. Edited by Avron Levine White, 6–32. London, New York: Routledge, 1987.

Smith, Roberta. "In Installation Art: A Bit of the Spoiled Brat." In *New York Times* (3 January 1993): 31.

Sontag, Susan. "Film and Theatre." In *Tulane Drama Review* II.i (1966): 24–37.

Spielmann, Yvonne. "Intermedia in Electronic Images." In *Leonardo* 34:1 (2001): 55–61.

Spielmann, Yvonne. *Video: The Reflexive Medium*. Cambridge, MA; London: The MIT Press, 2008.

Stam, Robert. *Film Theory: An Introduction*. Oxford: Blackwell, 2000.

Stravinsky, Igor. "The Phenomenon of Music." In *Poetics of Music in the Form of Six Lessons*. 1942. Reprint, Harvard: Harvard University Press, 2003.

Strickland, Edward. *Minimalism: Origins*. Bloomington: Indiana University Press, 1993.

Sturken, Marita. "Feminist Video: Reiterating the Difference." In *Afterimage* 12:9 (April, 1985): 9–11.

Sturken, Martia. "Paradox in the Evolution of an Art Form: Great Expectations and the Making of a History." In *Illuminating Video: An Essential Guide to Video Art*. Edited by Doug Hall and Sally Jo Fifer, 101–24. New Jersey: Aperture Foundation, 1990.

Sturken, Marita. "Review: *Revising Romance: New Feminist Video*." In *Art Journal* 45:3 (Autumn, 1985): 273–277.

Sturken, Marita. "TV as a Creative Medium: Howard Wise and Video Art." In *Afterimage* 11:10 (May 1984): 5–9.

Suderburg, Erika. "Introduction: On Installation and Site Specificity." In *Space, Site, Intervention: Situating Installation Art*. Edited by Erika Suderburg, 1–22. Minneapolis, London: University of Minnesota Press, 1996.

Tamblyn, Christine. "Qualifying the Quotidian: Artist's Video and the Production of Social Space." In *Resolutions: Contemporary Video Practices*. Edited by Michael Renov and Erika Suderburg, 13–28. London, Minneapolis: University of Minnesota Press, 1996.

Toop, Richard. "Stockhausen and the Sine-Wave: The Story of an Ambiguous Relationship." In *The Musical Quarterly* 65:3 (1979): 379–391.

Träger, Jörg. *Philipp Otto Runge und seine Werke*. Munich: Prestel, 1975.

Turim, Maureen. "The Image of Art in Video." In *Resolutions: Contemporary Video Practices*. Edited by Michael Renov and Erika Suderburg, 29–50. Minneapolis, London: University of Minnesota Press, 1996.

Usselmann, Rainer. "The Dilemma of Media Art: *Cybernetic Serendipity* at the ICA London." In *Leonardo* 36:5 (2003): 389–396.

Valcke, Jennifer. Static Films and Moving Pictures: Montage in Avant-Garde Photography and Film. Norderstedt, Germany: GRIN Verlag, 2008.

Vasulka, Steina. "Sony CV Portapak: Industrial, 1969." In *Eigenwelt der Apparate-Welt: Pioneers of Electronic Art*. Edited by David Dunn, Steina Vasulka, and Woody Vasulka, 150–152. Santa Fe, NM: The Vasulkas and Linz: Ars Electronica, 1992.

Viola, Bill. "History, 10 Years, and the Dreamtime." In *Video: A Retrospective*. Edited by Kathy Rae Huffman, 18–23. Long Beach, CA: Long Beach Museum of Art, 1984.

Viola, Bill and Robert Violette, eds. *Reasons for Knocking at an Empty House: Writings 1973–1994*. London: Thames and Hudson, 1995.

Virgil. *The Aeneid*, Book II. 19B.C. Reprint and translated by Robert Fitzgerald. New York: Everyman's Library, 1992.

Wagner, Ann. "Performance, Video, and the Rhetoric of Presence." In *October* 91 (Winter 2000): 59–80.

Wagner, Richard. "Outlines of the Artwork of the Future," 1849. Reprint, translated by William Ashton Ellis. In *Multimedia: From Wagner to Virtual Reality*. Edited by Randall Packer and Ken Jordan, 3–9. New York, London: W. W, Norton and Company, 2001.

Walter, Otto F. and Helmut Heissenbüttel, eds. *Vostell: Happening & Leben*. Berlin: Neuwied, 1970.

Welby, Horace. *Predictions Realized in Modern Times*. London, Kent and Co Paternoster Row, 1862.

Whitehead, Christopher. *The Public Art Museum in Nineteenth Century Britain: The Development of the National Gallery*. Aldershot: Ashgate, 2005.

Whitney, John. "To Paint on Water: The Audiovisual Duet of Complementarity." In *Computer Music Journal* 18:3 (Autumn 1994): 45–52.

Whitney, John. *Digital Harmony: On the Complementarity of Music and Visual Art*. New York: McGraw-Hill, 1980.

Wiles, David. *A Short History of Western Performance Space.* Cambridge: Cambridge University Press, 2003.

Williams, Raymond. *Television: Technology and Cultural Form.* New York: Schocken Books, 1975.

Wittgenstein, Ludwig. *Philosophical Investigations.* Oxford: Blackwell Press, 1963.

Wörner, Karl H. *Stockhausen: Life and Work.* Translated by Bill Hopkins. Berkley and Los Angeles: University of California Press, 1973.

Wyver, John. "The Necessity of Doing Away with 'Video Art'" (1991). In *Diverse Practices: A Critical Reader on British Video Art.* Edited by Julia Knight, 315–320. Luton: Luton University Press, 1996.

Xenakis, Iannis. *Formalized Music: Thought and Mathematics in Composition.* New York: Pendragon Press, 1992.

Yalkut, Jud. "TV as a Creative Medium at Howard Wise." In *Arts Magazine* 44:1 (September-October 1969): 18–22.

Youngblood, Gene. *Expanded Cinema.* Boston: E P Dutton, 1970.

Zeitlin, Marilyn A. *Bill Viola: Buried Secrets.* Arizona: Arizona State University Art Museum, 1995.

Zutter, Jörg. "Interview with Bill Viola." In *Bill Viola: Unseen Images.* Edited by Marie Luise Syring, 99–104. Düsseldorf: Städtische Kunsthalle, 1992.

Index

Note: Page numbers in italics indicate illustrations. Numbers preceded by 'n' indicate a note number (e.g., 187n5 indicates note 5 on page 187).

Abbate, Carolyn, 51–52, 111
Abe, Shuya, 173, 178
Absolute filmmakers, 24, 66–67, 73
Acconci, Vito, 40
  Air Time, 162
  Centers, 162, *163*
  on close-ups, 167
  on "performance," 161
  Proximity Piece, 112, *113*
  Running Tape, 37
  Service Area, 112
  and solitary spaces, 171
  Stages, 32
  Theme Song, 32
  on video, 156
"Accumulation," 39
"Action music," 27
Activated spectatorship, 161
AC/TV (Audio-Controlled Television)
  (Weintraub), 146
Adlington, Robert, 87
Administering Eternity (Rist), 158–59, *159*
Adorno, Theodor, 55–57
AFA. *See* American Federation of Arts (AFA)
After Degas (Hodgkin), 77
A.I.R. (Levine), 150
Air Time (Acconci), 162
Albers, Josef, 85
Albright, Daniel, 9
  on artistic media, 172
  on the concord between artistic media, 172, 180
  Figures of Consonance, 54
  on gestures, 62
  on Japanese Noh theatre, 56–57
  Untwisting the Serpent: Modernism in Music,
    Literature and Other Arts, 47–48
Allures (Belson), 73
The Alternative Media Conference, 150
Altman, Rick, 21, 23–24
Altschuler, Modest, 61

American Broadcasting Company (ABC), 18
American Federation of Arts (AFA), 13
Amorpha: Fugue in Two Colours (Kupka), 57
Ampex Corporation, 18–19
  Quadruplex system, 20
Analogue video, first availability of, 1
Anastasi, William, 107, 178
Anderson, P.T., 155
André, Carl, 122
"Animated sound," 72, 82
Annual National Video Festival (Minneapolis
    College of Art and Design), 151
Ant Farm community, 140, 182
Anti-art gestures, 82, 108, 123, 148–49
Anti-Illusion: Procedures/Materials (Whitney
    Museum of American Art), 122–23,
    142–43
Anzieu, Didier, 154
Arabesque (Whitney), 74
Arcade Fire, 183
Architecture, 83
Arman, 109–10
Arns, Robert, 20
Art in America, 143
"Art is Life and Life is Art," 94
Artist-composer, 2–4, 8, 9, 11, 18, 22–26
"Artistic dishonesty," 49, 50, 58, 80
The Art of Noises (Russolo), 34
The Art of Time (Kirby), 134
Arts Magazine, 146
Art Workers' coalition, 124
Asher, Michael, 142
Ashley, Robert, 115
Assche, Christine, 11, 14
Atelier, Mary Baumeister, 28
Atwood, David, 173
Audio-image, 26–32
Audio Recordings of Great Works of Art: The Aural
    Aura of Masterworks (Osborn), 52–53
Audio Video Piece for London, Ontario (Nauman), 32

Audiovisual interaction, 6, 46–47, 129, 154, 173
Avant-garde painting, 49
Aviary, 136
Aviation Institute (Kazan), 65
Awakening Conscience (Hunt), 54
Awakening of a City (Russolo), 34
Aycock, Alice, 124

Babbitt, Irving, 49, 63
Bach, Johann Sebastian, 25, 65, 67, 77, 89
    Brandenburg Concerto No. 1, 25
    Brandenburg Concerto No. 3, 68
    cantatas, 98
Baldessari, John, 40
Balla, Giacomo, 57
Ballets Russes, 49
Baranoff-Rossine, Vladimir, 65
Barron, Michael, 90–91
Barthes, Roland, 21, 22
Bartlett, Scott, 14, 126–27
Barzyk, Fred, 148
Battcock, Gregory, 124
Baudrillard, Jean, 39
Bauhaus, 61, 84, 119
Bayreuth *Festspielhaus*, 90–91, *91*, 119
Bazin, André, 153, 176
The Beach Boys, 53
The Beatles, 173
Beethoven Frieze (Klimt), 55, 56, *55*, 60
Beethoven, Ludwig van
    Fifth Symphony, 57
    Ninth Symphony, 69
Begone Dull Care (McLaren), 71–72
Behrman, David, 137
Belson, Jordan, 73–74, 114, 119
Belton, John, 15, 20–21, 23, 44, 125, 149, 156
Berkeley University Art Museum, 123
Berio, Luciano, 87, 114
Bernard, Jonathan, 59
Beuys, Joseph, 27, 37, 129, 174
Bing Crosby Enterprises, 19
The Bing Crosby Show (radio), 18
Biophilia (Björk), 184, *184*
"Birth" of a new medium, pinpointing, 38
Bishop, Claire, 110, 157, 161, 182
Björk, 184, *184*
Blackburn, Maurice, 72
Black Gate Cologne (Tambellini), 140
Black Gate Electromedia Theatre, 115, 140
Black Mountain College (North Carolina),
    85, 119
Black Video 2 (Tambellini), 136
Black Zero (Tambellini), 115, 141
Blair Witch Project (Myrick and Sánchez), 16
Blake, Peter, 53
Blesser, Barry, 88, 92–93, 95, 103, 178
Blind Song (Cahen), 30
Blue and orange chords, 59

Blue Calzone (Videofreex), 150
Bluish-Green Sound (Itten), 55
Boccioni, Umberto, 53, *53*, 106, 160
Body Works (Sharp), 150
Bolter, Jay David, 6, 157, 159–60
Book Bargain (McLaren), 72
Boomerang (Serra), 169, *169*, 172
Bordwell, David, 154
Borges, Jorge Luis, 152, 164
Borkin, Harold, 115
Bornemann Fritz, 97
Bosch, Hieronymus, 78
Botschuijver, Theo, 116
Boulez, Pierre, 87, 88, 195–96n53
Boutourline, Serge, 144
Brahms-Fantasies (Klinger), 69
Brahms, Johannes, 25
    Hungarian Dance No. 5, 25, 67
Brakhage, Stan, 16, *17*, 25–26, 78, 137
Brandenburg Concerto No. 1 (Bach), 25
Brandenburg Concerto No. 3 (Bach), 68
Brave New World (Huxley), 63
Brecht, Bertolt, 62
British video art, 8, 40
Britten, Benjamin, 51, 87
Brockman, John, 132, 141
Brooklyn Academy of Music, 141
Brooklyn Museum, 136
Brown, Earle, 94, 137
Bryson, Norman, 157
Burch, Noël, 153
Burden, Chris, 179
Burnham, Jack, 150
Burton, Tim, 21
Butting, Max, 67
The Byrds, 133

Café-au-Go-Go, 11, 119
Cage, John, 1, 107, 116, 121
    aleatoric procedures, 7, 35
    and audio-image, 28
    The Boulez-Cage Correspondence, 195–96n53
    on broadcast television, 128
    chance-determined performances, 125
    collaborations, 115, 119, 174
    *Cybernetic Serendipity: The Computer and the
        Arts* (Galeria Bonino), 138
    4'33," 94, 135
    HPSCHD, 115, 142
    Imaginary Landscape #4, 35, 94
    In Between, 25
    Indeterminacy, 94
    interactive work of, 87, 111, 136
    on live music, 106
    "messy" potential of performance, 161
    New York Annual Avant-Garde Festival, 137
    and Paik, Nam June, 8, 26–28, 132
    and solitary interactivity, 170

sound, 35, 157
theories of, 148
Tribute to John Cage (Paik), 94
26'1.1499" for a String Player, 174
Variations IV, 94
Variations V, 131–33
Variations VII, 35, *36*, 135
and venue for concerts, 121
Cahen, Robert, 1, 8, 30, 34, 35
Cale, John, 31
Californian Visual Music Artists, 73, 82
Calvocoressi, Richard, 103
Camino, Luis F., 78, 79
Campus, Peter, 32, 122, 151, 171, 172
Canaletto, 86, 89
Caravaggio (Jarman), 53
Caravaggio, Michelangelo Merisi da, 78
Cardew, Cornelius, 26, 34, 87
Carrier, David, 98
Carroll, Lewis, 164
Cassen, Jackie, 116
Castelli, Leo, 150
Castel, Louis-Bertrand, 63
Catalogue des oiseaux (Messiaen), 59
Cathode Ray Tube, 12, 132, 146–47
The Cave (Reich and Korot), 4
Centers (Acconci), 162, *163*
Centre Pompidou (Paris), 11, 41, 101, 179
Cezanne, Paul, 77
Chaucer, Geoffrey, 163
Chicago World's Fair, 16
Chion, Michel, 30, 92, 153, 176
Christo and Jeanne-Claude, 108
Chromatic Fantasy (Giacometti), 55
Chromophonic Orchestra, 65
"Cinema of the future," 47
Circles (Berio), 87
"Circus approach" to performance, 142
Čiurlionis, Mikalojus Konstantinas, 57
Closed-circuit video feed, 2, 13, 18, 29, 122, 125,
    134–35, 137, 140, 144, 147–48, 160–62,
    164, 167, 170–71, 175, 181
Cloverfield (Reeves), 16
Coen Brothers, 172
Cohen, Milton, 115
Coker, Cecil, 135
Coleridge, Samuel Taylor, 39
Cologne School, 51
Colour and sound, 59–63
    blue and orange chords, 59
Colour-Music: The Art of Mobile Colour
    (Rimington), 64
Colour organ, 22, 63–66, *64*, 69, 76–77, 173
Commediation (collective), 140
Communal consciousness, 172–77
"Communal dream space," 115
The Company of Us (USCO), 133, 141, 144, 150, 182
Composer. *See* Artist-composer

Composers Inside Electronics, 31
Composing with technology. *See* Technology,
    composing with
"Composite score," 23
Concerto for Double String Orchestra (Tippett), 87
Concerto for TV Cello (Moorman and Paik), 174,
    175, 177, 180–81
Concret PH, 96
Condensation Cube (Haacke), 107
Coney, John, 141
Connor, Russell, 150
Conrad, Tony, 1, 31, 32, 190n67
Consonant spaces, intermedial merging, 9
Constitution period, 39–40, 46, 76, 82, 84, 125,
    157, 162
Contextual audiovisual engagement, 6
Cook, Nicholas, 9, 60–63, 136
Cook, Thomas, 9
Cori spezzati method of composing, 86, 90
Cort, David, 140, 147
Couleurs de la cité céleste (Messiaen), 60
Courtyard (Kaprow), 112
Crary, Jonathan, 100–104
Crimp, Douglas, 166–67
Crosby, Bing, 18, 19
Crow, Thomas, 99
"Crystalline" (Björk), 184, *184*
Csíkszenmihályi, Mihály, 102
Cuba, Larry, 74
Cubist artists, 17, 55–56, 85, 105–6, 116
Cubitt, Sean, 39
Cunningham, Merce, 119, 132, 134–36, 174
CV-2000 Portapak, 19
CV-2400 Portapak, 19
Cybernetic Serendipity: The Computer and the Arts
    (Galeria Bonino), 138, 139
Cybernetics (Paik), 133

Daniels, Dieter, 15, 42, 127, 143
Davis, Douglas M., 42–43, 162
Debussy, Claude, 22, 56
Dee, John, 163
Delacroix and Mengs, 53
Delay, Delay (Jonas), 165–66
Delford-Brown, Robert and Rhett, 131
Deliberation, film, 15–16, 20, 22, 26
De Maria, Walter, 113
The dematerialisation of the art object, 85, 108, 111
Denis, Maurice, 105
"Desire and the Home," 13
Desynchronized delay, 166
Dewey, Ken, 141
DeWitt, Tom, 127, 173
Diaghilev, 49
*Digital Harmony: On the Complementarity of Music
    and Visual Art* (Whitney), 74
Digital visual media, 6
"Direct animation," 16, 71

Direct sound, 21
Disney, Walt, 67
Doane, Mary Ann, 154
Dobson, Terence, 71, 72
Dogme 95 movement, 16
Domaines (Boulez), 87, 88
Donnelly, Kevin, 23
Don Quixote (Borges), 77
The Doors, 32
Double lineage, 41–45
Double Negative (Heizer), 112
Downey, Juan, 162
Dragset, Ingar, 179
Dream Reel (Yalkut), 116
The Dream Syndicate, 31
Dub Side of the Moon (Easy Stars All-Stars), 77
Duchamp, Marcel, 11, 35
    conceptual work of, 7
    Erratum Musicale, 37
    fusion of art and life, 131
    International Exhibition of Surrealism, 107
    kinetic solutions, 17
    metaphorical urination, 126
    noise art, 35
    Sonata, 57
Dulwich Picture Gallery, 98, 99
Duomo (Florence), 83
Durand, Jean-Nicolas-Louis, 98
DVD, 3
Dwan Gallery, 107
Dylan, Bob, 32
Dynamic Polyphonic Group (Klee), 58
Dyson, Frances, 152–53, 156–57, 160, 177

Early video, influence, 10
Eastwood, Clint, 23
Easy Stars All-Stars, 77
"Eclipse" (Pink Floyd), 183
Edison, Thomas, 16
Ed Sullivan Show, 52
Eggeling, Viking, 24, 66, 73
Eine Kleine Nachtmusik (Mozart), 67
Eisenstein, Sergei, 136
The Electric Eye performance group, 140
Electronic Arts Intermix (EAI), 144
Electronic Opera No. 1 (Paik), 148
Elfman, Danny, 21
Elmgreen, Michael, 179
"Elvis the Pelvis," 52
Empire (Warhol), 16
Emshwiller, Ed, 127, 151
English National Opera, 4
Entrance of the Gladiators (Fucik), 65
"Environment," 109–110
Epitome Café, 119
Erased de Kooning Drawing (Rauschenberg), 77
Erickson, Christa, 182–83
Erratum Musicale (Duchamp), 37

Etude aux chemins de fer (Schaeffer), 34
Etude for Pianoforte (Paik), 28
Evans, Dylan, 165
Everson Museum of Art, 118, 151
Expanded Cinema, 12, 114–17, 119, 127, 132, 156
Expanded Cinema Festival, 132, 133
Expanded Cinema (Youngblood), 12, 132
Experiments in Art and Technology (E.A.T.), 136
Exploding Plastic Inevitable (Warhol), 116, 133, 182
Expo '58 (Brussels), 95
EXPORT, VALIE, 8, 115, 161
Exposition, 44
Exposition of Music—Electronic Television (Paik),
    15, 127–29, *128*, *130*, 131

Family Guy, 181
Fan, George, 141
Fantasia (Disney), 67
Farblichtmusik (László), 65–66, 69
"Fast forward" function, 38
Faust, 31
Feldman, Morton, 37, 94, 137, 195–96n53
The Feminist Studio Workshop (Los Angeles), 13
Fenlon, Iain, 86
Fernandez, Armand Pierre, 109
Festival of Lights (Tambellini and Boutourline), 144
Fieber I, II, III (Fischinger), 69
Fifty Nine Productions, 4
Film. *See also specific film*
    "deliberation," 15–16, 22
    process, 14–19
Film Exercises (Whitney Brothers), 73
Filmmakers' Cinematheque, 132, 137, 174
Film music discourse, 10, 152–155
Film No. 7: Color Study (Smith), 73
"Filmstage," 155–56
Flinn, Caryl, 176
Fire of Waters (Brakhage), 25
Fischinger, Oskar, 24–26, 67–73, *68*, 74–78
    display card, *70*
    Sounding Ornaments, 24, *70*, 70–72
    evolution of, 73–74
Fish Flies on Sky (Paik), 80
Five Angels for the Millennium (Viola), 157–59, *158*
Flavin, Dan, 111, 122
The Flicker (Conrad), 31, 190n67
Flinn, Caryl, 154, 200n19
Fluxus, 6, 11, 39, 42, 44, 49, 82–83, 94, 119, 124,
    131, 182
Foley artists and editors, 21
Fontana, Bill, 36
Forest, E., *99*
Fortner, Wolfgang, 26
4'33" (Cage), 94, 135
Fragmentation, 165–66, 168–69
Frank, Joseph, 6
Frieling, Rudolf, 129
Fučik, Julius, 65

Fugue (Hölzel), 57
Fugue in Blue and Red (Javlensky), 57
Fugue in Red (Klee), *58,* 58–60, 66
Fugue (Kandinsky), 57
Fuller, Buckminster, 150
Furniture Music (Satie), 94
"The Futurist Cinema" (Marinetti), 66
Futurist movement, 12, 34, 106, 112

Gabrieli, Andrea and Giovanni, 86
Galeria Bonino, 133, 138, 143, 173, 174
Galerie Beaux-Arts, 107, 124
Galerie Parnass (Germany), 15, 127–29, *128,*
    130, 131
Gallagher, Liam and Noel, 52
Gatti, Charles Blanc, 65, 67, 78
Gaudreault, André
    and birth of new medium, 38–40
    constitution period, 46, 82, 157
    theoretical work of, 9
Gauguin, Paul, 54–55
Gehry, Frank, 101
Genealogy of media, 38
Georgiades, Thrasybulus, 26
Gershuny, Phyllis, 150
Gesamtkunstwerk, 47, 49, 84–85
Gesang der Jünglinge, 35, 95
Giacometti, Augusto, 55
Giedion, Siegfried
    on architecture, 84, 97, 116
    on consonant spaces, 9
    on modern art, 102–105
    on perspective, 102–3
    Space, Time and Architecture: The Growth of a
        New Tradition, 85
    theories of, 6
Gielen, Michael, 61
Gigliotti, Davidson, 144, 147
Gilbert and George, 145
Gillette, Frank, 140, 143–45, *145,* 147, 162, 170
Ginger Spice, 52
The Girl with the Pearl Earring (Webber), 53
Glass, Elliot, 149
Glass, Philip, 32, 168–69
Global Groove, 149–51, 183
Global Groove and the Video Common Market (Paik),
    149
Global Village, 13, 14
Goldberg, RoseLee, 112, 161
Golden Globes (2005), 23
Golden Voyage (Vasulkas), 78
Good Morning, Mr. Orwell (Paik), 41
Gorbman, Claudia, 153–54, 176
Gordon, Douglas, 3
Goya, Francisco de, 78
Grabes, Herbert, 163, 171
Graham, Dan, 10, 171–72
Graham-Dixon, Andrew, 104

Grateful Dead, 116
Greenaway, Peter, 21
Greenberg, Clement
    art and music, 9
    and "artistic dishonesty," 49–50, 55, 58, 80
    and Klee, Paul, 58–59
    opacity, 160
    on Pollock, Jackson, 105
    theories of, 6
    "Towards a Newer Laocoon," 49
The Greeting (Viola), 78
Grimm's fairy tales, 164
Gropius, Walter, 84–85
Gropnik, Adam, 121
Grove Dictionary of Art, 47
The Growth of a New Tradition (Moholy-Nagy), 85
Gruppen (Stockhausen), 95
Grusin, Richard, 6, 157, 159–60
Gschwandtner, Sabrina, 189n55
Guggenheim Museum, 101, 107, 143, 179–80
Gun Powder Plot conspiracy, 164
Gustafson, Julie, 13
Gutstadt, Howard, 140

Haacke, Hans, 107
Hall, David
    Land Truth Circus, 140
    memories regarding video, 8
    multiscreen installation show, 80
    and video, 40–41
        television and video, use of, 127
Hall, Diane, 140
Hamilton, Richard, 107
Handel, George Frideric, 95
The Hand of the Violinist (Balla), 57
Hanhardt, John, 26, 28, 44, 178–80
Hansa Gallery, 111
Happening 1962, *120*
Harithas, James, 138
Harmonic Choir, 95
Harris, Ed, 53
Harry Potter and the Philosopher's Stone
    (Columbus), 164
Hayward Gallery (London), 158–59, *159*
Hegarty, Paul, 34, 35
Heilig, Morton, 47
Heizer, Michael, 112, 113, 124
Hello (Kaprow), 148–49
Henning, Michelle, 138
Henry Art Gallery (Washington), 179
Herrmann, Bernard, 21
Herton, Calvin C., 115
Higgins, Dick, 39
Hiller, Lejaren, 115, 142
Hinde, Katherine, 3, 4
Hirsh, Hy, 73
Hitchcock, Alfred, 21
Hobbs, John, 95

Hodgkin, Howard, 77, 103–4
Holst, Gustav, 87
Holt, Nancy, 169
Hölzel, Adolf, 57
Hommage à John Cage (Paik), 26–27
House (Wooster), 13
Howard, Deborah, 86
Howard Wise Gallery, 142–46, 170, 174
HPSCHD, 115, 142
Hugo Boss Prize, 3, 187n5
Hultén, Pontus, 139
Human Cello (Moorman), 174
Hungarian Dances (Brahms), 25, 67
Hunt, William Holman, 54
Huxley, Aldous, 63
Hykes, David, 95
Hypermediacy, 157–61, 174–75, 177, 183

Identification, reflection and, 163–65
Ideograms, 62
Idomeneo (Mozart), 4
Ihnatowicz, Edward, 138
Iles, Chrissie, 83, 155, 164–66
Image and music interaction. *See* Visual music
Imaginary Landscape #4 (Cage), 35, 94
Immateriality, 158
Immediacy, 41, 129, 144, 150, 157–59, 162, 177
Immersion, 47, 106, 115, 151–52, 156–59
Impermanence, 109
Impression III (Concert) (Kandinsky), 56
Interactivity, 136, 169–72, 182–83
"Inaudibility," 154
Inclusion, 159–62
In C (Riley), 94
Indeterminacy, 94
Industrial Revolution, 34
"The Inextinguishable," 87
Infiltration Homogen für Cello (Beuys), 174
Ingerland (Pook), 4, *4*
In Between (Brakhage), 25
Inland Empire (Lynch), 23, 155
Installation, 107–11
Instruments for Zen Exercises (Paik), 129
Interaction of music and image. *See* Visual music
Interim (Brakhage), 25
Intermedia '68 tour, 141
Intermedial expansion, 9, 15, 39–40
International Exhibition of Surrealism, 107, 124
Interpenetration of the planes, 106, 116, 160
Intersections (Feldman), 94
Iris (Levine), 140, 144, 160, 170–71, 182
I Say I Am (video compilation), 13
It's Gonna Rain (Reich), 168
Itten, Johannes, 55

Jackson, Peter, 16
Jacobs, Henry, 73, 114
Ja Ja Ja Ne Ne Ne (Beuys), 37

James I (king of England), 164
Jameson, Fredric, 125
Japanese culture, mirror in, 166
Japanese Kabuki theatre, 166
Japanese Noh theatre, 56–57, 166
Järling, Rolf, 127, 129
Jarman, Derek, 53, 78
Javlensky, Alexei von, 57
Jenkins, Bruce, 114
Jewish Museum, 113, 150
John F. Kennedy Staten Island Ferry Boat, 137
Johns, Jasper, 12, 111, 134
Johnson, James, 89–90, 99–100
Johnson, Lyndon B., 137
Jonas, Joan
    and audio-image, 32
    Delay, Delay, 165–66
    events of, 79
    Jones Beach Piece, 165–66
    and male predecessors, 12–13
    memories regarding video, 8
    Mirror Piece I and *Mirror Piece II,* 165
    Organic Honey, 13, 167, 169
    Organic Honey's Vertical Roll, 13, 167, *168*
    Organic Honey's Visual Telepathy, 167
    interactivity, 172
    performances of, 77
    performance videos of, 10,156
    reflection, nature of, 164–65
    use of video in work, 127
Jones Beach Piece (Jonas), 165–66
Joplin, Janis, 176
Judd, Donald, 111
Judson Hall, 137
Juncosa, Enrique, 103
Juste le Temps (Cahen), 30–31

Kabuki theatre, 166
Kalff, Louis, 96
Kaminski, Bill, 135
Kanarek, Mimi, 134
Kandinsky, Wassily, 56–57, 61–62, 65, 70–71, 148
Kantor, Tadeusz, 92, 103
Kaprow, Allan, 39, 80, 116
    and audio-image, 27
    condemnation of video art, 42, 80–81, 121
    Courtyard, 112
    early video art, 39
    "Environment," term, 109
    on format of video, 161–62
    fusion of art and life, 131
    Happening 1962, *120*
    Hello, 148–49
    installation, 111
    performance-based practices of, 7
    on performance videos, 156
    venue for events, 119–21
Karajan, Herbert von, 57

Kassinger, Ruth, 164
Kelley, Edward, 164
Kennedy, John F., 133, 178, 180
Kennedy, Robert, 123
Kevorkian, Tanya, 89
Kimbolton Fireworks, 183
Kinetoscope, 16
King, Martin Luther, 123
Kirby, Michael, 134
The Kitchen (New York City), 13, 28, 95, 147, 170
Kiva (Campus), 171
Klavier Intégral (Paik), *27*, 129
Klee, Paul, *58*, 58–60, 62, 66–67, 76
Klein, Yves, 27, 109, 111
Klenze, Leo von, 98
Klimt, Gustav, 55–56, *55*, 60, 65, 69
Klinger, Max, 69
Klüver, Billy, 134, 136, 169
Koenig, Gottfried Michael, 27
Kolarevic, Branko, 194–95n17
Korot, Beryl, 4, 150
KQED, 141
Kramer, Jonathan D., 51
Krauss, Rosalind, 162, 168
Krautrock group, 31
Kuba TV (Paik), 14, 129
Kubota, Shigeko, 12
Kubrick, Stanley, 23, 25–26
Kupka, František, 57–58
Kurtág, György, 93
Kwon, Miwon, 100, 125, 137

Labart, Evelyn. *See* National Film Board (NFB)
LaBelle, Brandon, 95, 142
Lacan, 165
Lacey, Bruce, 138
Lachenmann, Helmut, 34, 50, 76
Lady Gaga, 52
La légende dorée (Magritte), 78
Land Truth Circus (Hall, Hall, and Proctor), 140
Lanesville TV (TV station), 147
Laocoön: An Essay on the Limits of Painting and Poetry of 1766 (Lessing), 48–49, 55–56, 63
Las Meninas series (Picasso), 77–79
Last Night of the Proms, 92
La Strada entra nella casa (Boccioni), 53, *53*
László, Alexander, 65–66, 69
"Lateralisation," 105–6
Lautgedicht (Sound Poem) (Man Ray), 37
Le Corbusier, 95–96, *96*
Leeson, Lynn Hershman, 123
Lee, Sook-Kyung, 180
Lefèbvre, Henri, 84
The Legend of Zelda: Ocarina of Time, 183
Le Grand Macabre (Ligeti), 93
Le Grice, Malcolm, 127
Le Guitariste (Picasso), 105–6
Leo Castelli Gallery, 150

Le Plein (Arman), 109–10
Leppert, Richard, 9, 50, 54, 76
   promotion of separation of arts, 47–49, 85
Leroy, Louis, 105
Lessing, Gotthold, 9
   Lacoön: An Essay on the Limits of Painting and Poetry of 1766, 48–49, 56
   on *Nacheinander*, 48, 54, 57, 76, 81, 147
   on *Nebeneinander*, 48–50, 54, 57, 60, 76, 81, 147
   poetry, criticism of, 56
   separation of arts, promotion of, 47
Lesson of the Nightingale (Runge), 57
Le Thoronet Abbey, 95
Le Vide (Klein), 109, 111
Levine, Les, 135, 140, 149
   on aesthetic medium, 15
   A.I.R., 150
   Intermedia 88 tour, 141
   Iris, 140, 144, 160, 170–71, 182
   television, comments on, 128
Lewis Gluckman Gallery (Ireland), 101
"The Library of Babel" (Borges), 164
Licht, Alan, 36–37
Licht, Jennifer, 110–11, 142, 169
Life magazine, 132
Ligeti, György, 103–4
   and audio-image, 26
   colour and sound, 59
   coloured scores, 63
   Le Grand Macabre, 93
   pre-existent music, 23
   single events, 125
Light/Motion/Space (Walker Art Center, Minneapolis), 144
The Lightning Field (De Maria), 113–14
Lights in Orbit (Walker Art Center, Minneapolis), 144
Lindsay Tape (Paik), 139
Lindsay, John, 137
Lippard, Lucy, 111, 136
Lip Sync (Nauman), 168, 172
"Liquid architecture" (Whitney), 74–75, *75*, 152
Lissitzky, El, 82
Listening in Paris (Johnson), 89–90
Live-Taped Video Corridor (Nauman), 142–43, *143*, 171
Living sculpture, 141–49
Lloyd, Barbara, 132
Lockwood, Annea, 36
Lo Giudice Gallery (New York), 167
Lohengrin (Wagner), 61–62
London: Interior of the Rotunda in Ranelagh (Canaletto), 89
Long, Richard, 124
Lord, Chip, 140
The Lord of the Rings (Jackson), 16
Louvre, 95, 98
Lovejoy, Margaret, 12
Lowlands Away (Philipsz), 190n88

Luce diagram, 63

Lye, Len, 16, 71

Lynch, David, 23, 155

The Machine: As Seen at the End of the Mechanical Age (Hultén), 139

Maciunas, George, 83, 124

Magnetic tape recordings, 18–19

Magnet TV (Paik), 132–33, 179–80

Magnolia (Anderson), 155

Magritte, René, 78

Mahler, Gustav, 51, 87

Manet, Edouard, 77, 101

Mann, Aimee, 155

Marc, Franz, 57

Marinetti, Filippo, 12, 66, 106

Marion, Philippe

    and birth of new medium, 38–40

    constitution period, 46, 82, 157

    theoretical work of, 9

Maroević, Ivo, 98

Marsh, Ken, 140, 149

Matrix 1, Black Sunrise (Vasulka), 32

Matrix III (Whitney), 75

Matt's Gallery (London), 179

Mauceri, John, 61

McEvilley, Thomas, 100

McLaren, Norman, 71–73, 82

McLuhan Caged (Paik), 139

McLuhan, Marshall, 15, 118, 150

McQueen, Steve, 3

McShine, Kynaston, 107, 150, 179

McWilliams, Jim, 137

McWilliams, Joseph, 174

The Medium is the Medium (tv show), 148

Meigh-Andrews, Chris, 40, 157

Melville, Robert, 139

Mem (Campus), 171

Menard, Pierre, 77

Mercer Arts Center, 170

Merzbau (Schwitters), 112

Messiaen, Olivier, 25, 59–60

Metz, Christian, 21, 23

Michels, Doug, 140

Mile of String (Duchamp), 107

Million Dollar Baby (Eastwood), 23

"Mimetic engulfment," 157

Minneapolis College of Art and Design, 151

Mirrored images, 162–69

Mirror Piece I and *Mirror Piece II* (Jonas), 165

Mitchell, Katie, 4

Mixed media performance, 10

A Modern Olympia (Cezanne), 77

Moholy-Nagy, Laszló, 6, 9

    on audiovisual space, 116

    on creator and receiver, 92

    The New Vision; From Material to Architecture, 85

    MoMA. *See* Museum of Modern Art (MoMA)

Monet, Claude, 105, 106

Monte, James, 122

Moog, Robert, 132

Moorman, Charlotte, 27–28, 112, 132

    Concerto for TV Cello (with Paik), 174, *175*, 177, 180–81

    Human Cello, 174

    Opera Sextronique, 137, 174

    Paik, Nam June, collaboration with, 137, 145–47, 161, 174–77, 182

    striptease, 137, 174

    TV Bra for Living Sculpture, 145–47

Moretti, Laura, 86

Moritz, William, 65, 73

Morris, Franklin, 31

Morrison, Van, 32

Morris, Robert, 131, 142

Morse, Margaret, 123, 170, 171

Mothlight (Brakhage), 16, *17*

Motion Painting No. 1 (Fischinger), 68

Movie Drome (VanDerBeek), 115, 131, 132

Movie Movie (Shaw and Botschuijver), 116

Mozart, Wolfgang Amadeus, 4

    Eine Kleine Nachtmusik, 67

    Piano Concerto No. 18, 178

Multimedia environments, 133–37

Mumma, Gordon, 115, 132

Museum genre, 83

Museum Kunst Palast, 180

Museum of Contemporary Art (San Diego), 142

Museum of Modern Art (MoMA), 110, 112, 118, 123–24, 139, 142, 150–51

Music and image, 2. *See also* Visual music

"'Music' for the eyes" (Brakhage), 25–26

"Music in Space" (Stockhausen), 95

Music is Like Painting (Picabia), 54

Music with Balls (Riley), 141

Muybridge, Eadweard, 17, 131

Myrick, Daniel, 16

Mystic gulf or mystic chasm (Wagner), 90–91, 93, 155, 162

Mythologisation of space, 93

Nacheinander, 48, 54, 57, 76, 81, 147

Nameth, Ronald, 115

Nam June Paik: Cybernetics, Art and Music, 132

Nam June Paik: Electronic Art II, 138

"Nam June Paik: Video Artist, Performance Artist, Composer and Visionary," 180

Narration in the Fiction Film (Bordwell), 154

National Film Board (NFB), 81

National Gallery (London), 101

Nauman, Bruce

    on closed-circuit feed, 162

    early works, 122

    Lip Sync, 168, 172

    Live-Taped Video Corridor, 171

    Performance Corridor, 142–43, *143*

Record, 37
  solitary interactivity, 172
  sound, early interest in, 32
  video and television, use of, 127
Nebeneinander, 48–50, 54, 57, 60, 76, 81, 147
Neighbours (McLaren), 72
Nesbitt, Lowell, 138
Nesthus, Marie, 25
Neubauer, Bärbel, 75
Neuhaus, Max, 36
Neun Nein Décoll/agen (Vostell), 131
The New Laokoon: An Essay on the Confusion of the Arts (Babbitt), 49
The New Project: Subject to Change (tv show), 147
New Statesman, 139
Newton, Isaac, 59, 105
The New Vision; From Material to Architecture (Moholy-Nagy), 85
New York Annual Avant-Garde Festival, 137
The New Yorker, 121
New York Metropolitan Opera, 4
"New York School," 94
New York State Council on the Arts (NYSCA), 118
The New York Times, 121
New York Times Magazine, 132
NFB. *See* National Film Board (NFB)
Nicholas Wilder Gallery, 142
Night Crawlers (Schneemann), 116
9/23/69 Experiment with David Atwood (Paik), 173
Nine Evenings (Klüver), 134, 138, 169
Nixon Tape (Paik), 139
No. 25 (Vasulka), 33
No Country for Old Men (Coen brothers), 172
Noh theatre, 56–57, 166
Noise, 2, 136
  "noise objects," 33
  and technology, 33–38
Nondiegetic image, 10
Nondiegetic music, 153
North, Alex, 23
Now is the Time (McLaren), 72
Nyman, Michael, 21
NYSCA. *See* New York State Council on the Arts (NYSCA)

Oasis, 52
"Obesity of information" (Baudrillard), 39
Object to process, 104–14
Objet mathematique, 96
Objets Sonores (Paik), 129, 132
Ocean Without a Shore (Viola), 181
O'Doherty, Brian
  on consonant spaces, 9
  on Duchamp, Marcel, 107
  on galleries, 100
  gallery space, 122, 138
  the spatial, 103–5
  on the white cube, 122–23, 152

O'Donnell, Sheila, 101
Ohana, David, 106
Oldenburg, Claes, 132, 155
"Older media," 6
Oliveira, Nicholas, 83
Olsen, Charles, 119
Olympia (Manet), 77
One Point TV (Paik), 129
Ono, Yoko, 27, 37, 119, 174
Opacity, 49, 54, 59, 160
Open Circuits: The Future of Television (MoMA), 151
Open Score (Rauschenberg) *134,* 134–135*Opera Sextronique* (Paik and Moorman), 137, 174
OperaShots, 4
OperaVision, 4
Oppenheim, Dennis, 40, 108, 124, 150, 162, 171
Optiks (Newton), 59
Optophonic piano (Baranoff-Rossiné), 65–66
Opus Arte, 4
Orchestration of Colour (Richter), 55
Organic Honey (Jonas, Joan), 13, 167, 169
Organic Honey's Vertical Roll (Jonas), 167, *168*
Organic Honey's Visual Telepathy (Jonas), 167
"Organized sound" (Cage), 35, 157
Osborn, Ed, 52–53
Ospedale degli Incurabili, 86
Oxley, Nicola, 83

Paik-Abe Video Synthesizer, 173, 176
Paik, Nam June, 1, *129*
  Cage, John, influence of, 35
  Commediation, collaboration with, 140
  Concerto for TV Cello (with Moorman), 174, *175,* 177, 180–81
  Cybernetics, 133
  death, 180
  early compositional work, 26–28, 82–83, 125
  Electronic Opera No. 1, 148
  Etude for Pianoforte, 28
  Exposition of Music--Electronic Television, 15, 127–29, *128, 130*
  as "father of video art," 3
  Galerie Parnass exhibit, 15, 127–29, *128, 130*
  on gesture, 51
  Global Groove and the Video Common Market (Paik, 149
  Good Morning Mr. Orwell, 41
  "history criticism in performance," 80
  immediacy, interest in, 41
  Instruments for Zen Exercises, 129
  intermedial expansion, 40
  and Järling, Rolf, 127, 129
  Klavier intégral, 27, 129
  Kuba TV, 129
  Lindsay Tape, 139
  Magnet TV, 132–33, 180
  McLuhan Caged, 139

Paik, Nam June (*cont.*)
    Moorman, Charlotte, collaboration with, 137, 145–47, 161, 174–77, 182
    Nam June Paik: Cybernetics, Art and Music, 132
    Nam June Paik: Electronic Art II, 138
    "Nam June Paik: Video Artist, Performance Artist, Composer and Visionary," 180
    and New York creative scenes, 8–9
    9/23/69 Experiment with David Atwood, 173
    Nixon Tape, 139
    Objets Sonores, 129, 132
    One Point TV, 129
    Opera Sextronique, 137, 174
    Paik-Abe Video Synthesizer, 173, 176
    Participation TV, 129, 179
    Participation TV 2, 145
    and Portapak, 11–12, 19
    Random Access, 129, *130*
    Rembrandt Automatic, 128
    Robot K-456, 133, 138, 178, 180
    running time for works, 123
    "strategic position," 44
    Symphony for 20 Rooms, 28
    television, view of, 80
    on "TIME" art, 156
    Tribute to John Cage, 94
    TV Bed, 157
    TV Bra for Living Sculpture, 145–47
    TV Buddha, 162
    TV Burying, 130
    TV Cello, 10, 51, 76–77, 79, 83, 137, 174–77, *175,* 180–85
    TV Chair, 157
    TV Clock, 118
    TV Garden, 80, 118
    TV Robots, 180
    venues for concerts, 122–23
    video equipment, emphasis on, 157
    videotape, manipulation of, 19–20
    Videotape Study No. 3, 137
    WGBH-TV, 148
    Whitney Museum of American Art, retrospective, 118, 178, 180, 185
    The Worlds of Nam June Paik (Hanhardt), 179–80
    Zen for TV, 128
Paikpieces (Yalkut), 133
Parade (ballet), 49
Paris Opéra, 89–90
Participation TV (Paik), 129, 179
Participation TV 2 (Paik), 145
The Passions (Viola), 78
Paul VI (Pope), 11
Peacock, Kenneth, 64
Pena, Sabrina, 3
People's Video Theater (PVT), 149–50
Performance as one-way communication, 161
Performance Corridor (Nauman), 142–43, *143*

Perloff, Margorie, 34
Petry, Michael, 83
Pfleumer, Fritz, 18
Philips Pavilion, 95, *96,* 97
Philipsz, Susan, 190n88
Philosophie der neuen Musik (Adorno), 55–56
Piano Phase (Reich), 168
Piano Piece for David Tudor (Young), 37
Piano, Renzo, 101
Piatti, Urgo, 34
Picabia, Francis, 54
Picasso, Pablo, 49, 77, 105–7
Piene, Otto, 138, 140, 148, 174
Pilgrim (Rauschenberg), 107
Pink Floyd, 183
Pissarro, Camille, 105
The Planets (Holst), 87
"Playback" function, 38
"Pleasure of Being Booed" (Marinetti), 106
Poème électronique (Le Corbusier), 96
Poem for Tables, Chairs and Benches (Young), 37
Poetry and music, 56–57
Pollock (film), 53
Pollock, Jackson, 53, 105
Polyexpressiveness, 66
Pontormo, Jacopo, 78
Pook, Jocelyn, 4, *4*
Poons, Larry, 119
Poppy Nogood and the Phantom Band: All Night Flight (Coney), 141
Portapak, 3, 7–8, 11, 22, 28, 41, 165
    CV-2000, 19
    CV-2400, 19
    as revolutionary tool, 22
Portikus Gallery (France), 179
Postmodernism, 12
Pound, Ezra, 56, 62
Prelude and Fugue (Čiurlionis), 57
"Presentational," 114–15
Present Continuous Past (Graham), 172
Presley, Elvis, 52, 77
Pression (Lachenmann), 50
The Primitives, 113
Princenthal, Nancy, 83
Pritchett, James, 142
Process
    image as, 14–19
    from object to, 104–14
Proctor, Judy, 140
Prométhée (Scriabin), 60, 64, 66
Prometheus group, 65
Proximity Piece (Acconci), 112, *113*
Prune Flat (Whitman), 155
Psychoanalytical structures, "inaudible" sounds and, 154
"Psychological dimension," 23, 79, 123
Pulcinella (Stravinsky), 77
Pulsa, 142, 162

Quasi una Fantasia (Kurtág), 93
Quatuor pour la fin du temps (Messiaen), 59

Race riots (1964–1968), 123
Radical Software (Gershuny, Korot and Phyllis), 150
Raindance, 150
Rainforest project, 31
Random Access (Paik), 129, *130*
Ratcliff, Mary Curtis, 147
Raumlichtmusik (Fischinger), 69
Rauschenberg, Robert
  black and white canvases, 111
  collaborations, 119
  Erased de Kooning Drawing, 77
  expanded cinema, 132
  Experiments in Art and Technology (E.A.T.), 136
  Open Score, *134*, 134–135
  Pilgrim, 107
Raw Material (Nauman), 32
Ray, Man, 17, 37
Record (Nauman), 37
Reed, Jerry, 75
Reeves, Matt, 16
Reeves, Richard, 75
Reflection (mirrors), 162–69
Regression, 154, 165
Reichardt, Jasia, 138
Reich, Steve, 4, 32, 37, 168
Reilly, John, 147
Reiss, Julie H., 43, 110–11
Rembrandt Automatic (Paik), 128
Remediation, 6–7, 78, 157
Retour à la raison (Man Ray), 17
Revising Romance: New Feminist Video, 13
"Rewind" function, 38
Rhythmus 21 (Richter), 24, *24*, 66–67
Rhythmus 23 (Richter), 66–67
Richter, Hans, 24, *24*, 26, 55, 66–67, 172
Riley, Terry, 75, 94, 125, 135, 141, 165
Rimington, Alexander, 22, 63–64, *64*
Rimsky-Korsakov, Nikolai, 59
Rist, Pipilotti, 158–59, *159*
Robinson, Emery, 102
Robinson, Robby, 135
Robot K-456 (Paik), 133, 138, 178, 180
Rockefeller family, 123
Rockefeller Foundation, 118
Rogers, Richard, 101
"Roll with It" (Oasis), 52
Rose Art Museum, 144, 150
Rosenbach, Ulrike, 8, 161
Rosler, Martha, *14*, 77, 162
Rosolato, Guy, 154
Ross, Andrew, 161
Ross, David A., 11–12, 78, 118
Rosler, Martha, 13
Rowling, J. K., 164
Royal Academy of the Arts (London), 99

Royal Albert Hall, 92
Royal Opera House, 4, *4*
Rückblicke (Kandinsky), 61
Runge, Philippe Otto, 57, 67
Running Tape (Acconci), 37
Russell, Bertrand, 136
Russian Symphony Orchestra, 60
Russolo, Luigi, 34
Rutt/Etra Scan Processor, 29
Ruttmann, Walther, 17, 24, 26, 67, 73, 172–73

Sabaneev, Leonid, 60
Sacred art, 98
Sadeghi, Manoochelher, 74–75
Sakamoto, Ryuichi, 173–74
Salon Carré (Square Room), 98, *99*
Salter, Chris, 87–88, 92–93, 95, 116, 160–61
Salter, Linda-Ruth, 88, 92–93
Salzman, Eric, 87
Samson (Burden), 179
Sánchez, Eduardo, 16
San Francisco Opera, 4
San Francisco's Artists' Television Access, 182
Sansovino, Jacopo, 86
Satie, Erik, 49, 94
Scenes from Under Childhood (Brakhage), 25
Schaeffer, Pierre, 30, 34–35
Schafer, R. Murray, 88–89
Schechner, Richard, 88, 92, 97
Scherzo (McLaren), 72
Scheveningen Kurzall, 61
Schimmel, Paul, 171
Schinkel, Karl, 98
Schmit, Tomas, *128*
Schneemann, Carolee, 32, 116, 137, 141, 155
Schneider, Ira, 20, 144–45, *145*, 147, 150, 162, 170
Schönberg, Arnold, 56, 62
Schum, Gerry, 149
Schwarz, Hans Peter, 119
Schwitters, Kurt, 37, 112
Scriabin, Alexander, 59–61, 63–64, 66
Sculpture, 83
Sculpture, living, 141–49
The Sea (Debussy), 22, 56
Search (Erickson), 182–83
Searing, Helen, 98, 100
Searle, Adrian, 103–4
Seawright, James, 148
Sectionalisation, 91–92
Sedgwick, Edie, 11
See/Saw (Utterback and Chapman), 182–83
Segalove, Ilene, 12
Self Portrait as Another Person (Leeson), 123
Sellars, Peter, 4
Semiotics of the Kitchen (Rosler), 13, *14*
Semitic cultures, mirror in, 166
Semper, Gottfried, 84, 90, 98
Seoul Olympic Games, 173

Serota, Nicholas, 103
Serra, Richard, 127, 168–69, *169*
Sharp, Willoughby, 150
Shaw, Jeffrey, 116
Shelley, Percy Bysshe, 49, 58
Shepard, Michael, 139
Sherman, Tom, 19
Shore, Howard, 16
Silent music, static motion and, 46–81
    colour and sound, 59–63
    sounding image, 63–76
    static music, 52–59
    video art-music, 76–81
Simon, Harvey, 140
Sisley, Alfred, 105
69th Regiment Armory (New York City), 134–35
Slapping Pythagoras (Conrad), 31
Sleepwalkers (Aiken), 181
Small, Christopher
    on Canaletto painting, 89
    concert hall, 99–100, 152
    on consonant spaces, 9
    performance as one-way communication, 161
    sectionalisation identified by, 91–92
    on venues for concerts, 121–22
Smith-Editor, 20
Smith, Harry, 73
Smith, Roberta, 121
Smithson, Robert, 112, 113
Smolin Gallery, 15, 130
Snibbe, Scott, 184, *184*
Snow, Michael, 137
Soane, John, 98
Software (Burnham), 150
Solitary interactivity, 169–72
Solomon R. Guggenheim Foundation, 3. *See also*
    Guggenheim Museum
The Solomon R. Guggenheim (Hamilton), 107
Some More Beginnings (Brooklyn Museum), 136
Sonata (Duchamp), 57
Sonatina for Violin and Piano (Marc), 57
Sonic space, 86–92
Sonnier, Keith, 150, 162
Sontag, Susan, 42
Sony
    early machines, 22
    Portapak. *See* Portapak
Sound
    and colour, 59–63
    direct sound, 21
Sound Designer II, 71
Sound ("immediate"), 19–23, 37
Sounding image, 63–76
Sounding Ornaments (Fischinger), 24–25, *70*, 70–72
    evolution of, 74
Space, 82–117
    audiovisual space, 116–17
    "communal dream space," 115

decorative object, transformation of
    architectural space, 107–8
"environment," 109–110
expanded cinema. *See* Expanded Cinema
impermanence, 109
"installation," 109–110
and music, 92–97
mystic gulf or mystic chasm, 90–91, 93, 155
mythologisation of, 93
performing and listening space, 92
    segregation, 178–85
process, from object to, 104–14
role in modernist culture, 84
sanctity of art space, 97–100
sonic space, 86–92
spatial reconfiguration, 109
"special space," 92–94
timelessness concept, 102–3
viewing strategies, 100–104
Spaces [Museum of Modern Art (MoMA)], 110, 142
Space Theatre (Cohen), 115
Space, Time and Architecture: The Growth of a New
    Medium (Giedion), 85
The Spaghetti City Video Manual: A Guide to Use,
    Repair and Maintenance, 147
Spielberg, Steven, 21
Spielmann, Yvonne
    on accumulation, 39, 49
    and audio-image, 29, 32
    on contradictory elements, 49
    on integrating birth of video, 6, 39, 46, 73
    on intermedia, 39–40
    on new medium, 157, 178–79
    and noise, art of, 33
    on *Organic Honey's Vertical Roll*, 168
    on Portapak, 19
    and technology, 11
    theoretical work of, 9
    on *Violin Power*, 29
Spiral Jetty (Smithson), 112
"Squire's Tale" (Chaucer), 163
Stasis (Campus), 171
Static motion, silent music and, 46–81
    colour and sound, 59–63
    sounding image, 63–76
    static music, 52–59
    video art-music, 76–81
Static music, 52–59
Stella, Frank, 134
Stern, Gerd, 133
Stern, Rudi, 116, 147
Still Life With Chair Caning (Picasso), 106–7
Stockhausen, Karlheinz, 7
    Gesang der Jünglinge, 35, 135
    "Music in Space," 95, 97, 108, 114, 135
    and Paik, 26
    Studie 1, 51
Stoerchle, Wolfgang, 156

Stonewall Bar raid, 123
The Stopping Mind (Viola), 181
Strauss, Johann, 23
Strauss, Richard, 23, 49
Stravinsky, Igor, 23, 34, 55, 57, 65, 77, 79, 123
String Quartet II (Feldman), 37
Striptease
    Moorman, Charlotte, 137, 174
Studie 1 (Stockhausen), 51
Sturken, Marita, 12–13, 119, 126, 144–45, 151
Suderburg, Erika, 109, 122
Sullivan, Ed, 52
Sunday Telegraph, 104, 139
Sun in Your Head (Vostell), 131
SUNY Buffalo, 141
Surrealism, 107, 124
A Survey of the Avant Garde in Britain (Gallery
    House), 80
Swinging, Polyphonic (And a Complimentary Repeat)
    (Klee), 58
Symphony for 20 Rooms (Paik), 28
Symphony No. 2 (Mahler), 51, 87
"Synaesthetic alloy" (Youngblood), 141

The Tabernacle (USCO), 133
Table + Bottle + Block of Houses (Boccioni), 106
Tadlock, Thomas, 148
Tambellini, Aldo
    Black Gate Cologne, 140
    Black Gate Electromedia Theatre, 115, 140
    Black Video 2, 136
    Black Zero, 115, 141
    Festival of Lights, 144
    The Medium in the Medium, 148
    production, approaches to, 148
    TV as a Creative Medium, 143
    video collective, 147
    on video construction, 162
Tamblyn, Christine, 112
Tate Liverpool, 180–81
Tate Modern (London), 3–4, 32, 157
Teasdale, Parry, 147
"Technical Manifesto of Futurist Sculpture"
    (Boccioni), 106
Technology, composing with, 9, 11–45
    artist-composer, 22–26
    audio-image, 26–32
    double lineage, 41–45
    multiple histories, 38–41
    noise, art of, 33–38
    process, image as, 14–19
    sound ("immediate"), 19–22
"Television Gallery" (Schum), 149
Television, image as process, 14–19
Tenney, James, 25
Terretektorh (Xenakis), 93
Theatre of Eternal Music, 1, 31
Three Piano Pieces (Schönberg), 56, 62

"TIME" art, 127–33, 139, 151, 156
Timelessness concept, 102–3
Time Magazine, 139
Tinguely, Jean, 138
Tippett, Michael, 87
Tipton, Jennifer, 135
Tönende Ornamente (Fischinger), 24–25
Tone, Yasunao, 71
Top of the Pops (tv show), 52
"Towards a Newer Laocoon" (Greenberg), 49
Transformational environments, 171
Tribute to John Cage (Paik), 94
Tristan and Isolde (Wagner), 4
Tsai, Wen Ying, 138
Tucker, Marcia, 122
Tudor, David, 28, 31, 94, 119, 132, 135
Tuomey, John, 101
Turim, Maureen, 78–79
Turner Prize, 3, 190n88
Turn, Turn, Turn (Yalkut), 133
Turtle tank, 135
TV as a Creative Medium, 142–44, 174
TV Bed (Paik), 157
TV Bra for Living Sculpture (Paik and Moorman),
    145–47
TV Buddha (Paik), 162
TV Burying (Paik), 130
TV Cello (Paik), 10, 51, 76–77, 79, 83, 137, 174–77,
    175, 180–85
TV Chair (Paik), 157
TV Clock (Paik), 118
TV Dé-coll/age (Vostell), 15, 129–31
TV Garden (Paik), 80, 118
TV Robots (Paik), 180
*12 Evenings of Manipulations: Deconstructionist Art
    Happenings* (Yalkut), 189n55
26'1.1499" for a String Player (Cage), 174
2001: A Space Odyssey (Kubrick), 23
Two Holes of Water-3 (Whitman), 135–36, 160

Underneath the Arches (Gilbert and George), 145
Understanding Media: The Extensions of Man
    (McLuhan), 15
*Untwisting the Serpent: Modernism in Music,
    Literature and Other Arts* (Albright),
    47–48
Ursonate (Schwitters), 37
USCO. See *The Company of Us* (USCO)
Usselmann, Rainer, 139
Utterback, Camille, 182–83

VanDerBeek, Stan, 115, 127, 131–32
Varèse, Edgard, 34, 96, 137
Variations IV (Cage), 94
Variations V (Cage), 131–33
Variations VII (Cage), 35, *36*, 135
Vasulka, Steina
    career, beginning of, 1, 28–29

Vasulka, Steina (*cont.*)
  and computer interfaces, 181
  La légende dorée, reworking of, 78
  and male predecessors, 12
  Violin Power, 29–30, *29*, 33, 41, 174
Vasulka, Woody
  and audio-image, 32
  and The Kitchen (New York City), 28, 170
  La légende dorée, reworking of, 78
  No. 25 (film), 33
  on Portapak, 22
  on video, 8
  on video cassettes, 40
Velázquez, Diego, 77, 78
Velázquez Digital (Camino), 78–79
The Velvet Underground, 113, 116, 133–34
Venetian Polychoral School, 86, 92–93
  Vermeer, Jan, 78
Vicissitudes (Utterback), 182
Video. *See also* Video art-music
  defined, 15
  "invention" of, 126–27
  multiplicity, 43–44
  performance, combination with video, 161
  phases, evolution of, 83
  physical makeup of, 23
  process, image as, 14–19
Video: An Art, a History (Centre Pompidou), 11
Video and the Museum (Everson Museum), 151
Video art-music, 7, 10, 76–81, 118–51
  alternative spaces, 5, 124–26
  anti-art gestures, 148
  global groove, 149–51
  living sculpture, 141–49
  multimedia environments, 133–37
  nature of, conflict over, 137–41
  pre-video "TIME" art, 127–33, 139
  reactions against by galleries, 124–25
  single events, 125
  terminology, 29, 42
  venues for concerts, 119–23
    "Video Art: Old Wine, New Bottle"
      (Kaprow), 81
"Video art," use of term, 3, 40–43
Video cassettes, introduction of, 40
Video Collectives, 140–41, 147–50
Video Commune: The Beatles from Beginning to End
  (Paik), 173
Videofreex, 147, 149, 150, 182
Video noise. *See* Noise
Videotape
  editing, issues, 20–21
  manipulation of, 19–20
Videotape Study No. 3 (Paik), 137
Vietnam War protests, 142
Viewing strategies, 100–104
The Village Voice, 137
Vinterberg, Thomas, 16

Viola, Bill
  background of, 31–32
  and editing, 20
  Five Angels for the Millennium, 157–59, *158*
  The Greeting, 78
  "history criticism in performance," 80, 126, 151
  on invention of video, 151
  Museum of Modern Art (MoMA)
    retrospective, 118
  and noise objects, 33–34
  Ocean Without a Shore, 181
  on spatialisation, 83, 92, 156
  The Stopping Mind, 181
  on technology, 3, 18
  Tristan and Isolde, 4
  on "video artist" term, 79
Violin Power (Vasulka), 29, *29*, 33, 41, 174
Virtual Abbey (Hobbs and Hykes), 95
Vision and Television (Rose Art Museum), 143, 150
The Visitation (Pontormo), 78
"Visual container" of film, 155
Visual music, 9, 24–26, 46–81
  colour and sound, 59–63
Voice Piece for Soprano (Ono), 37
Von Trier, Lars, 16
Vortex Concerts, 114, 119–20
Vostell, Wolf
  interactive work of, 136, 152
  Neun Nein Décoll/agen, 131
  and noise art, 35
  and painting, 32
  Smolin Gallery show, 15
  Sun in Your Head, 131
  and television, 80
  total event, 141
  TV Dé-coll/age, 15, 129–31
  video equipment, emphasis on, 157
  YAM Festival, 130
  You, 131
VR-1000, 19

Wagner, Richard, 4, 61–62, 102
  Festspielhaus, 47, 90–91, *91*, 119
  Gesamtkunstwerk, 47, 49
  Lohengrin, 61–62
  mystic gulf or mystic chasm, 162
  "world of dreams," 152
Waldhauer, Fred, 136
Walker, Jerry, 141
Warehouse Show (Sonnier), 150
Warhol, Andy
  as "dabbler" in video, 127
  editing, lack of, 16
  expanded cinema events, 119
  Exploding Plastic Inevitable, 116, 133, 182
  and technology, 11
  and The Velvet Underground, 133–34
Warner, Kenneth, 137

War Requiem (Britten), 51, 87
Waterman Switch (Morris), 131
Water Music (Handel), 95
WDR-TV, 140
Wearing, Gillian, 3
Webber, Peter, 53
Weibel, Peter, 115–16
Weill, Kurt, 62
Weintraub, Joe, 146–47
West, Don, 147
"We Used to Wait" (Arcade Fire), 183
WGBH-TV, 148
Whirl (Erickson), 182–83
White cube, 100, 103–4, 106, 122–23, 127, 138, 141, 152, 181
Whitehead, Christopher, 101–2, 108
Whitman, Robert, 134–36, 140, 155, 160
Whitney, James, 73–74, 76
Whitney, John, 73–76, 75, 152
Whitney, John Jr., 116
Whitney, Michael, 116
Whitney Museum of American Art
    Anti-Illusion: Procedures/Materials, 122–23, 142–43
    and Nauman, 171
    Paik, Nam June retrospective, 118, 178
    The Worlds of Nam June Paik (Hanhardt), 179–80
"The Wilderness Downtown" (Arcade Fire), 183
Wilke, Hannah, 162
Willaert, Adrian, 86
Williams, John, 21
Wipe Cycle (Schneider and Gillette), 144–45, 145, 170
"Wise Up" (Mann), 155
Wittgenstein, Ludwig, 154
Wolff, Christian, 94
Woodstock Music Festival, 147
Wooster, Ann-Sargent, 13
Word Location (Serra), 168–69
World Fair (1970), 97
The Worlds of Nam June Paik (Hanhardt), 179–80

World War II, magnetic tape recordings, 18
Wounded Man'yo 2/2000 (Tone), 71
Wrap Around the World (Paik), 173–74
Wrapped Floor and Stairway (Christo and Jeanne-Claude), 108
Wrapped Museum of Contemporary Art (Christo and Jeanne-Claude), *108*
Wright, Frank Lloyd, 107

Xenakis, Iannis, 34, 93, 95–97, 103–4, 106

Yale Symphony Orchestra, 61
Yalkut, Jud
    Arts Magazine review of Paik, 146
    and *The Company of Us (USCO)*, 133, 141, 182
    as "dabbler in video," 127
    intermedia performances, 116
    on Paik's action music, 27
    Paik, Nam June, collaboration with, 133, 137
    tour, 141
    12 Evenings of Manipulations: Deconstructionist Art Happenings, 189n55
    and USCO, 133, 141, 182
    Vision and Television, 150
YAM Festival, 130
Youngblood, Gene
on artistic influence, 77
    contextualizing of medium, 126–27
    on cubism, 106
    Expanded Cinema, 12, 132
    on expanded cinema, 114, 132
    on intermedia, 155
    on Levine's *Iris*, 170–71
    on "synaesthetic alloy," 141
    theoretical work of, 9, 151
Young, La Monte, 31, 37, 132, 165
YouTube, 183
You (Vostell), 131

Zen for TV (Paik), 128
Zinovieff, Peter, 138